Communications in Computer and Information Science 1671

More information about this series at https://link.springer.com/bookseries/7899

Tong Xiao · Juan Pino (Eds.)

Machine Translation

18th China Conference, CCMT 2022
Lhasa, China, August 6–10, 2022
Revised Selected Papers

Springer

Editors
Tong Xiao
Northeastern University
Shenyang, China

Juan Pino
Meta AI
San Francisco, CA, USA

ISSN 1865-0929   ISSN 1865-0937 (electronic)
Communications in Computer and Information Science
ISBN 978-981-19-7959-0   ISBN 978-981-19-7960-6 (eBook)
https://doi.org/10.1007/978-981-19-7960-6

This Springer imprint is published by the registered company Springer Nature Singapore Pte Ltd.
The registered company address is: 152 Beach Road, #21-01/04 Gateway East, Singapore 189721, Singapore

Preface

The China Conference on Machine Translation (CCMT) is a national annual academic conference held by the Machine Translation Committee of the Chinese Information Processing Society of China (CIPSC), which brings together researchers and practitioners in the area of machine translation, providing a forum for those in academia and industry to exchange and promote the latest developments in methodologies, resources, projects, and products, with a special emphasis on the languages in China. Since the first session of CCMT in 2005, 17 sessions have been successfully organized (the first 14 sessions were called CWMT), and a total of 11 machine translation evaluations (2007, 2008, 2009, 2011, 2013, 2015, 2017, 2018, 2019, 2020, 2021) have been organized, as well as one open source system module development task (2006) and two strategic seminars (2010, 2012). These activities have made a substantial impact on advancing the research and development of machine translation in China. The conference has been a highly productive forum for the progress of this area and is considered a leading and important academic event in the natural language processing field in China.

This year, the 18th session (CCMT 2022) took place in Lhasa, Xizang, C. This conference continued the tradition of being the most important academic event dedicated to advancing machine translation research in China. It hosted the 12th Machine Translation Evaluation Campaign, featured two keynote speeches delivered by Nan Duan (Microsoft Research Asia) and Qun Liu (Huawei Noah's Ark Lab), and included two tutorials delivered-by Tong Xiao, Yinqiao Li, and Bei Li (Northeastern University) and Longyue Wang and Xing Wang (Tencent). The conference also organized five panel discussions, bringing attention to unsupervised and low-resource machine translation, the industry of machine translation, the frontier of machine translation, and the forum for PhD students. A total of 42 submissions (including 16 English papers and 26 Chinese papers) were received for the conference. All papers were carefully reviewed in a double-blind manner and each paper was evaluated by at least three members of an international Program Committee. From the submissions, eight English papers were accepted. These papers address all aspects of machine translation, including improvement of translation models and systems, translation quality estimation, document-level machine translation, low-resource machine translation, etc. We would like to express our thanks to every person and institution involved in the organization of this conference, especially the members of the Program Committee, the machine translation evaluation campaign, the invited speakers, the local organization team, our generous sponsors, and the organizations that supported and promoted the event. Last but not least, we greatly appreciate Springer for publishing the proceedings.

August 2022

Tong Xiao
Juan Pino

Organization

General Chairs

Fangbing Meng   Tibet University, China
Jiajun Chen   Nanjing University, China

General Vice Chairs

Tianlu Chen   Tibet University, China
Pingcuo Daji   Tibet University, China
Gesan Doji   Tibet University, China

Program Committee Co-chairs

Tong Xiao   Northeastern University, China
Juan Pino   Meta AI, USA

Evaluation Chairs

Muyun Yang   Harbin Institute of Technology, China
Yating Yang   Xinjiang Technical Institute of Physics and
     Chemistry, Chinese Academy of Sciences,
     China

Organizing Co-chairs

Nyima Tashi   Tibet University, China
Jiajun Zhang   Institute of Automation, Chinese Academy of
     Sciences, China

General Secretary

Jian Cheng   Tibet University and University of Electronic
     Science and Technology of China, China

Tutorial Co-chairs

Shujian Huang   Nanjing University, China
Zhaopeng Tu   Tencent, China

Student Forum Co-chairs

Maoxi Li	Jiangxi Normal University, China
Zhou Hao	Byte Dance, China

Front-Trends Forum Co-chairs

Rui Wang	Shanghai Jiao Tong University, China
Zhongjun He	Baidu, China

Industrial Application Forum Chairs

Chong Feng	Beijing Institute of Technology, China
Guoping Huang	Tencent, China

Publication Co-chairs

Zhixing Tan	Tsinghua University, China
Kehai Chen	Harbin Institute of Technology, Shenzhen, China

Sponsorship Co-chairs

Hao Yang	Huawei, China
Xiang Li	Xiaomi, China

Publicity Co-chairs

Junhui Li	Soochow University, China
Yongpeng Wei	Lingosail, China
Dingguo Gao	Tibet University, China

Program Committee

Hailong Cao	Harbin Institute of Technology, China
Kehai Chen	Harbin Institute of Technology, Shenzhen, China
Yidong Chen	Xiamen University, China
Yufeng Chen	Beijing Jiaotong University, China
Jinhua Du	Investments AI, AIG, UK
Quan Du	NiuTrans, China
Xiangyu Duan	Soochow University, China
Xiaocheng Feng	Harbin Institute of Technology, China
Shengxiang Gao	Kunming University of Science and Technology, China

Zhengxian Gong	Soochow University, China
Junliang Guo	MSRA, China
Bojie Hu	Tencent, China
Guoping Huang	Tencent, China
Hui Huang	University of Macau, China
Shujian Huang	Nanjing University, China
Junhui Li	Soochow University, China
Liangyou Li	Huawei, China
Maoxi Li	Jiangxi Normal University, China
Xiang Li	Xiaomi, China
Yachao Li	Northwest Minzu University, China
Lemao Liu	Tencent, China
Qun Liu	Huawei, China
Yang Liu	Tsinghua University, China
Cunli Mao	Kunming University of Science and Technology, China
Fandong Meng	Tencent, China
Haitao Mi	Tercent, China
Jinsong Su	Xiamen University, China
Xu Tan	Microsoft, China
Zhaopeng Tu	Tencent, China
Longyue Wang	Tencent, China
Mingxuan Wang	ByteDance, China
Qiang Wang	Straight Flush, China
Xing Wang	Tencent, China
Changxing Wu	East China Jiaotong University, China
Shuangzhi Wu	ByteDance, China
Jun Xie	Alibaba, China
Jinan Xu	Beijing Jiaotong University, China
Hongfei Xu	Zhengzhou University, China
Baosong Yang	Alibaba, China
Muyun Yang	Harbin Institute of Technology, China
Heng Yu	Shopee, China
Biao Zhang	University of Edinburgh, UK
Chunliang Zhang	Northeast University, China
Dakun Zhang	SYSTRAN, France
Jiajun Zhang	Institute of Automation, Chinese Academy of Sciences, China
Wen Zhang	Xiaomi, China
Muhua Zhu	Meituan, China
Toshiaki Nakazawa	University of Tokyo, Japan
Yves Lepage	

Organizer

Chinese Information Processing Society of China, China

Co-organizer

Qinghai Normal University, China

Sponsors

Diamond Sponsors

Global Tone Communication Technology Co., Ltd.

Volctrans

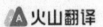

Platinum Sponsors

NiuTrans Research

Youdao

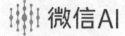

WeChat AI

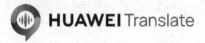

HUAWEI Translate

Gold Sponsors

OPPO Corporation

Magic Data Technology

Baidu

Cloud Translation

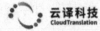

Xiaomi Corporation

Silver Sponsor

New Tranx Technology

Contents

PEACook: Post-editing Advancement Cookbook

Shimin Tao, Jiaxing Guo, Yanqing Zhao, Min Zhang, Daimeng Wei,
Minghan Wang, Hao Yang[✉], Miaomiao Ma, and Ying Qin

2012 Labs, Huawei Technologies CO., LTD., Beijing, China
{taoshimin,guojiaxin,zhaoyanqing,zhangmin186,weidaimeng,
wangminghan,yanghao30,mamiaomiao,qinying}@huawei.com

Abstract. Automatic post-editing (APE) aims to improve machine translations, thereby reducing human post-editing efforts. Training on APE models has made a great progress since 2015; however, whether APE models are really performing well on domain samples remains as an open question, and achieving this is still a hard task. This paper provides a mobile domain APE corpus with 50.1 TER/37.4 BLEU for the En-Zh language pair. This corpus is much more practical than that provided in WMT 2021 APE tasks (18.05 TER/71.07 BLEU for En-De, 22.73 TER/69.2 BLEU for En-Zh) [1]. To obtain a more comprehensive investigation on the presented corpus, this paper provides two mainstream models as the Cookbook baselines: (1) Autoregressive Translation APE model (AR-APE) based on HW-TSC APE 2020 [2], which is the SOTA model of WMT 2020 APE tasks. (2) Non-Autoregressive Translation APE model (NAR-APE) based on the well-known Levenshtein Transformer [3]. Experiments show that both the mainstream models of AR and NAR can effectively improve the effect of APE. The corpus has been released in the CCMT 2022 APE evaluation task and the baseline models will be open-sourced.

Keywords: Automatic post-editing · Autoregressive translation APE · Non-autoregressive translation APE

1 Introduction

MT automatic post-editing (APE) is the task of automatically correcting errors in a machine translated text. As pointed out by (Chatterjee et al., 2020), from the application point of view, the task is motivated by its possible uses to:

- Improve MT output by exploiting information unavailable to the decoder, or by performing deeper text analysis that is too expensive at the decoding stage;
- Cope with systematic errors of an MT system whose decoding process is not accessible;
- Provide professional translators with improved MT output quality to reduce (human) post-editing efforts;
- Adapt the output of a general-purpose MT system to the lexicon/style requested in a specific application domain (Fig. 1).

© The Author(s), under exclusive license to Springer Nature Singapore Pte Ltd. 2022
T. Xiao and J. Pino (Eds.): CCMT 2022, CCIS 1671, pp. 1–11, 2022.
https://doi.org/10.1007/978-981-19-7960-6_1

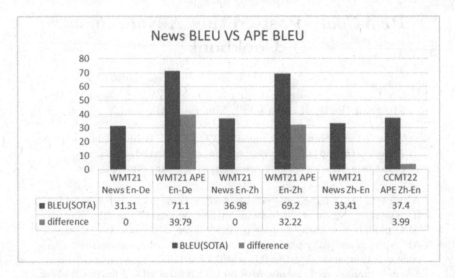

Fig. 1. News BLEU vs. APE BLEU; for BLEU gap with News SOTA, the PEACook corpus presents a much smaller gap than WMT 2021 APE corpora

From 2015 to 2021, APE has been paid with much more attentions. [4–6] called WMT2015 the "stone age of APE", which was the pilot run for APE shared tasks, with the main objective of identifying the state-of-the-art approach and setting a standard for the evaluation of APE systems in future competitions. Later, WMT16, 17 and 18 were considered as the golden years of APE, and all systems were neural-based end-to-end solutions and involved multi-source models. From 2019 to 2021, participants started to explore three directions: (i) Optimized Transformer architecture in the APE task; (ii) How to effectively inject more information with multi-sourced architecture; (iii) Better ways of using synthetic data. In conclusion, the performance improvements of APE models are more and more significant, making it closer to human PE, "things are getting really interesting" [7].

Although APE research in WMT has made remarkable progresses, there are still several problems:

- The progress for APE in to-En is not fully investigated. Since 2015, WMT has released 11 datasets in 7 APE shared tasks; however, there is only one to-En (De-En) dataset.
- The APE baseline for MT-PE BLEU is not closely related with the SOTA translation model. The gap of BLEU scores for the En-Zh direction is $(69.2 - 36.98 = 32.2)$, for WMT21 APE BLEU is 69.2 and for WMT21 NEWS SOTA is 36.98.
- Previously released corpora are collected from wiki, rather than any specific domain. As such, domain-specific APE is not fully investigated.

This paper presents a Zh-En APE dataset, the first To-En dataset since NMT became the mainstream model. The corpus is collected from a specific domain (Mobile) rather than from wiki or open domains. Moreover, the BLEU score of the APE corpus is 37.4, with only a small gap compared to the WMT News SOTA translation system $(37.4 - 36.9 = 0.5)$.

In addition to the APE corpus, we provide two types of APE model baselines, autoregressive (AR-APE) model baseline and non-autoregressive (NAR-APE) model baseline for APE. The AR model is built based on the work of HW-TSC APE [2], which is the WMT 2020 APE SOTA architecture. And the NAR model is built based on the Levenshtein Transformer [3]. With pre-training and fine-tuning strategies, experiments show that both models are better than the baseline approach (direct translation). However, compared with the blackbox MT model baselines, only the AR-APE model obtained positive gains; the NAR-APE model obtained negative gains. This indicates that the application of NAR-APE models requires more exploration.

In summary, to better analyze the effectiveness of APE in the improvement of machine translation and the decrease of human-editing efforts, this work makes the following contributions:

– A high quality corpus for APE tasks. The corpus is the first APE to-En dataset in NMT, which is more practical than previously proposed datasets.
– Two mainstream baseline models: AR-APE model based on the WMT2020 SOTA architecture, and NAR-APE model based on Levenshtein Transformer. AR-APE is better than the MT baseline, while NAR-APE is worse than it.
– A fine-tuning cookbook for AR-APE and NAR-APE, providing step-by-step methods for training customized APE models.

2 Related Work

2.1 APE Problem and APE Metrics

Table 1. Statistics of WMT and CCMT APE Corpora

Conference	Language pair	Domain	MT type	Baseline BLEU	Baseline TER
WMT 2015	En-ES	News	PBSMT	n/a	23.84
WMT 2016	En-De	IT	PBSMT	62.11	24.76
WMT 2017	En-De	IT	PBSMT	62.49	24.48
WMT 2017	De-En	Medical	PBSMT	79.54	15.55
WMT 2018	En-DE	IT	NMT	74.73	16.84
WMT 2019	En-DE	IT	NMT	74.73	16.84
WMT 2019	En-Ru	IT	NMT	76.2	16.16
WMT 2020	En-DE	Wiki	NMT	50.21	31.56
WMT 2020	En-Zh	Wiki	NMT	23.12	59.49
WMT 2021	En-DE	Wiki	NMT	71.07	18.05
WMT 2021	En-Zh	Wiki	NMT	69.2	22.7
CCMT 2022(PEACook)	Zh-En	Mobile	NMT	37.4	51.9

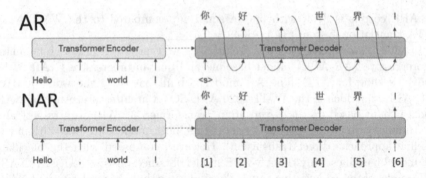

Fig. 2. AR and NAR models for machine translation and APE [8]

Table 2. Comparison of metrics for PEACook and WMT 21 datasets

Metrics	Split	WMT21 En-DE	WMT21 En-Zh	PEACook
(Domain)		Wiki	Wiki	Mobile
BLEU	train	70.8	40.1	38.6
	dev	69.1	62.4	39.2
	test	71.1	69.2	37.4
TER	Train	18.1	44.9	50.1
	dev	18.9	28.1	49.2
	test	18.5	22.7	51.9

APE Problem. The first APE shared task was held in the WMT 2015 [4]. The training and development datasets used in the task were triplets consisting of source (SRC), target (MT) and human post-edit (PE), in which (Fig. 2):

– SRC: The source is a tokenized source sentence, mainly in English.
– MT: The target is a tokenized German/Chinese translation of the source, which was produced by a generic, black-box neural MT system unknown to participants.
– PE: The human post-edit is a tokenized manually-revised version of the target, which was produced by professional translators.

An APE system aims to build models and predict the PE of the test set where only SRC and MT are provided. Human post-edits of the test target instances were left apart for the evaluation of system performance.

APE Metrics. Automatic evaluation is carried out by computing the distance between the predicted PEs produced by each system and the human PE references. Case-sensitive TER [9] and BLEU [10] are used as primary and secondary evaluation metrics, respectively.

TER is an estimation of the minimum edit-distance (deletions, insertions, substitutions and shifts of the positions of words) divided by the total number

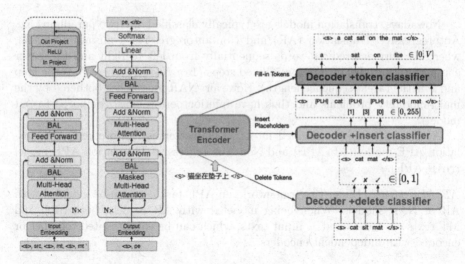

Fig. 3. AR-APE architecture of HW-TSC's APE model [2] and NAR-APE Architecture of Levenshtein Transformer [3]

of words in a target sequence. The systems with the lowest TER are the best, since their predictions are closer to the references. BLEU, which has an additional advantage of dealing with n-grams, is also an important metric to evaluate APE models. The third metric is Repetition Rate, which measures the repetitiveness inside a text by looking at the rate of non-singleton n-gram types ($n = 1...4$) and combining them using the geometric mean. In addition, the Repetition Rate is important in SMT, while in NMT, recent research by WMT [11] shows it is not closely related with APE performance. So, TER and BLEU become the standard metrics for APE tasks. Baseline metrics of APE tasks in WMT and CCMT in each year are shown in Table 1.

2.2   APE Baselines

Theoretically, an APE model is a parameterized function f with SRC and MT pairs as inputs and with PE texts as outputs. Since the PE texts normally have variable lengths, the task is inherently modeled as a generative problem with the sequence-to-sequence framework, resulting in a similar pipeline to the translation function t:

$$APE\_Model := f(src, mt) \rightarrow pe$$
$$:\approx t([src; mt]) \rightarrow pe, \tag{1}$$

where $[;]$ is the concatenation operation.

In this case, the model can be trained under the MLE framework with the cross-entropy loss:

$$\mathcal{L}_{APE} = CrossEntropy(\hat{pe}, pe), \tag{2}$$

where $\hat{PE}$ is the model predicted PE.

Nowadays, translation models are typically classified into two paradigms, i.e. Autoregressive Translation (AR) and Non-autoregressive Translation (NAR), where the former predicts words sequentially from left to right and the latter can perform parallel generation in fixed steps (1 or N $\ll$ T, where N is the step and T is the target sequence length). However, NAR models are bothered by the multi-modality problems and thus have inferior performance compared to AR models.

APE models can be divided into two mainstreams, Autoregressive Translation APE model (AR-APE) and Non-Autoregressive Translation APE model (NAR-APE).

AR-APE Model. Under this framework, an APE task can also be modeled with AR or NAR models. When being modeled with AR models, both SRC and MT texts are considered as input texts, which can be concatenated together or encoded with independent encoders:

$$P(pe|src, mt; \theta) = \prod_{j=1}^{n} P(y_j|y_{<j}, src, mt; \theta), \tag{3}$$

where θ is model parameters, y_j is current predicted token and $y_{<j}$ are previously predicted tokens.

As the SOTA model for both En-De and En-Zh in WMT 2020, HW-TSC APE model is built based on Transformer [12] and is pre-trained on the WMT News translation corpora. Different from previous works' models using pretrained multi-lingual language model (LM) [13], HW-TSC APE uses a pre-trained NMT model, which is more intuitive to APE and translation scenarios [14].

In terms of fine-tuning strategies, it was found that fine-tuning the model only on the officially released corpus could easily encounter a bottleneck. Therefore, data augmentation was used by introducing external translations as additional MT candidates or pseudo PEs to create more diversified features. The experimental results demonstrate the effectiveness of such an approach. The architecture of HW-TSC's APE model is shown in left of Fig. 3.

NAR-APE Model. Different from AR-APE models which predict words one by one from left to right, NAR-APE models predict the whole sequence or chunks of tokens in parallel, which improves the decoding efficiency but compromises the performance. This paradigm can also be extrapolated to APE tasks:

$$P(pe|src, mt; \theta) = \prod_{j=1}^{n} P(y_j|src, mt; \theta), \tag{4}$$

where θ is model parameters, and y_j is predicted token for each position. NAR has a vital drawback, namely the multi-modality problem. To conquer the problem, Levenshtein Transformer (LevT) [15] was proposed to learn from an expert policy: Levenshtein Distance Algorithm, which models the conversion of a sequence with a series of insertion and deletion operations. Same as other NAR works, Knowledge Distillation is also used in the training of Levenshtein Transformer. The decoding process of LevT is shown in right of Fig. 3.

Table 3. Five typical PE cases in PEACook corpus

src	mt	pe	PEType
存储环境温度: -10℃┬45℃ (14° F ┬13° F)	Storage temperature: −10 °C ┬45 °C (14 °F ┬13 °F)	Storage temperature: −10 °C to +45 °C (14°F to 113 °F)	coherence
键盘待机时间短、电池耗电快。	The standby time of the keyboard is short, and the battery power consumption is high	The standby time of the keyboard is short and the batteries drain quickly	grammar & syntax
将手表关机，并断开充电器连接。	Power off your watch and disconnect it from the charger	Power off your watch and disconnect it from the charger	no pe
HUAWEI M-Pencil第二代手写笔书写没有反应	The second generation of HUAWEI M-Pencil stylus does not respond	There is no response when I use the HUAWEI M-Pencil (2nd generation) to write or draw on the screen	lexicon
说明: 当前积分系统为Beta版本，在正式版上线后你的积分可能会有变化。	Note: The current bonus point system is a beta version. Your bonus points may change after the official version goes live	Note: Currently, the points contribution system is a beta version. Your points may change after the official version goes live	named entity

3 PEACook Corpus

3.1 PEACook Corpus Details

The PEACook corpus presented in this paper consists of training, dev and test datasets, with each consisting of 5000, 1000, and 1000 sentences, respectively. After detailed analysis, it was found that the PEACook corpus is more practical than the corpora provided in WMT21 En-De/Zh, shown in many aspects: 1) Its BLEU score gap is smaller than that of WMT, indicating that more PE patterns should be learned, as shown in Table 2. 2) Its domain is much narrower, requiring the model to perform domain adaptation during post editing.

PEACook Case Analysis. According to [16, 17] and [18], domain transfer with post-editing cases can be divided into five major categories, including coherence, grammar & syntax, lexicon, named entity and no pe. Detailed cases can be found in Table 3.

4 Baseline Model Experiments

4.1 Pre-training AR-APE Model

To build the AR-APE model, we need to first pre-train a standard translation model. Here, a Transformer-large is pre-trained on the WMT-19 corpus by strictly following the pipeline in [19]. When the pretrained model is directly evaluated, the BLEU score on the hypothesis and PE is only 15.8 (TER = 72.6), indicating that there is still large room for the model to improve over fine-tuning.

4.2   Fine-Tuning AR-APE Model

To further improve the AR-APE model performance, we propose three fine-tuning strategies as shown in Table 4: 1) We directly fine-tune the model on the (SRC, PE) pairs without using MT, which is to essentially perform domain adaptation. This baseline strategy helps the model to improve by +21.7 points on the BLEU score. 2) Src and MT texts are concatenated as input, while PE as output. This strategy brings +23.1 BLEU improvements compared to the baseline. 3) The last strategy is the series connection of the two, which obtains the best performance in our experiments, with +24.6 BLEU and −0.227 TER.

4.3   Pre-training NAR-APE Model

As mentioned in previous sections, we also provide an NAR baseline, which is a Levenshtein Transformer (LevT) model. Same as what we do in our AR-APE experiments, we pre-train the LevT on the WMT-19 corpus and knowledge distillation corpus, following the procedure in [15]. Then, we directly translate the src text with the LevT, with max decoding iterations being 10. The obtained baseline results are as follows: BLEU = 14.2 and TER = 0.727.

Table 4. Performances of fine-tuning AR-APE model with three strategies

Strategies	Approach	TER	BLEU
Baseline	PT on (src, ref$_{news}$)	0.726	15.8
Strategy 1	FT on (src, pe)	0.521 (−0.205)	37.5 (+21.7)
Strategy 2	FT on (src+mt, pe)	0.509 (−0.217)	38.9 (+23.1)
Strategy 3	FT on (src,pe), than, FT on (src+mt, pe)	0.499 (−0.227)	40.4 (+24.6)

4.4   Fine-Tuning NAR-APE Model

Again, NAR-APE model is fine-tuned on the in-domain PEACook corpus. Here, we present two types of evaluation strategies. The first one is to directly generate PE with the fine-tuned model, i.e. translate from scratch with the fine-tuned model. The second strategy is to generate PE with SRC and MT as input, applying the property of LevT partial decoding, i.e. post-editing on the MT by posing MT texts as decoder inputs. Performances of both strategies are shown in Table 5.

Although the performance of the NAR-APE model is not as good as the AR-APE model, LevT still brings improvements when editing MT (Strategy 2), indicating that NAR models have potentials in APE tasks thanks to their flexibility in the decoding.

Table 5. Performances of fine-tuning NAR-APE model with three strategies

	Approach	TER	BLEU
Baseline	PT on (src, ref_{news})	0.727	14.2
Strategy 1	FT on (src, pe), than, decode with (src,)	0.53 (−0.197)	34.1 (+19.9)
Strategy 2	FT on (src, pe), than, decode with (src, mt)	0.531 (−0.196)	36.1 (+21.9)

The performance comparisons between AR-APE/NAR-APE models and MT-PE baselines are shown in Fig. 4.

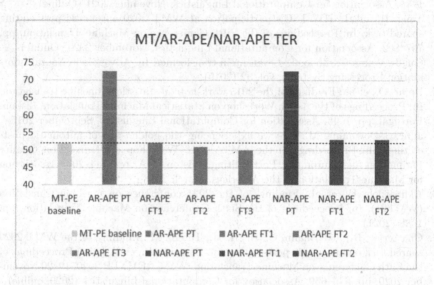

Fig. 4. TER scores of MT-PE baseline model, AR-APE model and NAR-APE model

5 Conclusion

This paper provides PEACook, which is the first from Chinese to English APE corpus. PEACook corpus is more practical than the WMT APE corpus, for higher TER and lower BLEU, which is closely related with WMT News SOTA performance results.

Also, AR-APE and NAR-APE baseline models with different fine-tuning strategies are provided for further investigation in the area. Experimental results demonstrated that the performances are relatively better than those using conventional machine translation approaches. The AR-APE model is better than the corpus MT-PE baseline, while the NAR-APE model is worse than the corpus MT-PE baseline.

The future research directions include (1) How to improve NAR-APE models, since the performance of NAT Translation models is closer to AT models in the WMT News translation task, with great advantages in decoding speed. (2) Knowledge-guided domain adaption for NAT models. Domain transfer is one important direction of APE, and much domain knowledge hasn't been fully applied in APE corpus. How to distill these knowledge from corpus and inject into AR/NAR-APE models is also very interesting and useful.

References

1. Akhbardeh, F., et al.: Findings of the 2021 conference on machine translation (WMT21). In: Proceedings of the Sixth Conference on Machine Translation, pp. 1–88. Association for Computational Linguistics, November 2021 (Online)
2. Yang, H., et al.: HW-TSC's participation at WMT 2020 automatic post editing shared task. In: Proceedings of the Fifth Conference on Machine Translation, pp. 797–802. Association for Computational Linguistics, November 2020 (Online)
3. Gu, J., Wang, C., Zhao, J.: Levenshtein transformer. In: Advances in Neural Information Processing Systems, vol. 32 (2019)
4. Bojar, O., et al.: Findings of the 2015 workshop on statistical machine translation. In: Proceedings of the Tenth Workshop on Statistical Machine Translation, Lisbon, Portugal, pp. 1–46. Association for Computational Linguistics, September 2015
5. Junczys-Dowmunt, M.: Are we experiencing the golden age of automatic post-editing? In: Proceedings of the AMTA 2018 Workshop on Translation Quality Estimation and Automatic Post-Editing, Boston, MA, pp. 144–206. Association for Machine Translation in the Americas, March 2018
6. Akhbardeh, F., et al.: Findings of the 2021 conference on machine translation (WMT21). In: Proceedings of the Sixth Conference on Machine Translation, pp. 1–88 (2021)
7. Chatterjee, R., Federmann, C., Negri, M., Turchi, M.: Findings of the WMT 2020 shared task on automatic post-editing. In: Barrault, L., et al. (eds.) Proceedings of the Fifth Conference on Machine Translation, WMT@EMNLP 2020, 19–20 November 2020, pp. 646–659. Association for Computational Linguistics (2020, online)
8. Gu, J., Bradbury, J., Xiong, C., Li, V.O.K., Socher, R.: Non-autoregressive neural machine translation. In: International Conference on Learning Representations (2018)
9. Snover, M., Dorr, B.J., Schwartz, R., Micciulla, L.: A study of translation edit rate with targeted human annotation (2006)
10. Papineni, K., Roukos, S., Ward, T., Zhu, W.-J.: BLEU: a method for automatic evaluation of machine translation. In: Proceedings of the 40th Annual Meeting of the Association for Computational Linguistics, Philadelphia, Pennsylvania, USA, pp. 311–318. Association for Computational Linguistics, July 2002
11. Chatterjee, R., Freitag, M., Negri, M., Turchi, M.: Findings of the WMT 2020 shared task on automatic post-editing. In: Proceedings of the Fifth Conference on Machine Translation, pp. 646–659. Association for Computational Linguistics, November 2020 (Online)
12. Vaswani, A., et al.: Attention is all you need. In: Guyon, I., et al. (eds.) Advances in Neural Information Processing Systems 30: Annual Conference on Neural Information Processing Systems 2017, Long Beach, CA, USA, 4–9 December 2017, pp. 5998–6008 (2017)

13. Devlin, J., Chang, M.-W., Lee, K., Toutanova, K.: BERT: pre-training of deep bidirectional transformers for language understanding. In: Burstein, J., Doran, C., Solorio, T. (eds.) Proceedings of NAACL-HLT 2019, Minneapolis, MN, USA, 2–7 June 2019, Volume 1 (Long and Short Papers), pp. 4171–4186. Association for Computational Linguistics (2019)

14. Lopes, A.V., Farajian, M.A., Correia, G.M., Trénous, J., Martins, A.F.: Unbabel's submission to the WMT2019 APE shared task: Bert-based encoder-decoder for automatic post-editing. CoRR, abs/1905.13068 (2019)

15. Gu, J., Wang, C., Zhao, J.: Levenshtein transformer. In: Wallach, H.M., Larochelle, H., Beygelzimer, A., d'Alché-Buc, F., Fox, E.B., Garnett, R. (eds.) Advances in Neural Information Processing Systems 32: Annual Conference on Neural Information Processing Systems 2019, NeurIPS 2019, Vancouver, BC, Canada, 8–14 December 2019, pp. 11179–11189 (2019)

16. Chollampatt, S., Susanto, R.H., Tan, L., Szymanska, E.: Can automatic post-editing improve NMT? arXiv preprint arXiv:2009.14395 (2020)

17. Wang, M., et al.: HW-TSC's participation at WMT 2020 quality estimation shared task. In: Proceedings of the Fifth Conference on Machine Translation, pp. 1056–1061. Association for Computational Linguistics, November 2020 (Online)

18. Yang, H., et al. Hw-TSC's submissions to the WMT21 biomedical translation task. In: Proceedings of the Sixth Conference on Machine Translation, pp. 879–884 (2021)

19. Ng, N., Yee, K., Baevski, A., Ott, M., Auli, M., Edunov, S.: Facebook fair's WMT19 news translation task submission. In: Bojar, O., et al. (eds.) Proceedings of the Fourth Conference on Machine Translation, WMT 2019, Florence, Italy, 1–2 August 2019 - Volume 2: Shared Task Papers, Day 1, pp. 314–319. Association for Computational Linguistics (2019)

Hot-Start Transfer Learning Combined with Approximate Distillation for Mongolian-Chinese Neural Machine Translation

Pengcong Wang[1,3], Hongxu Hou[2,3(✉)], Shuo Sun[1,2,3], Nier Wu[1,2,3], Weichen Jian[1,2,3], Zongheng Yang[1,2,3], and Yisong Wang[1,2,3]

[1] College of Computer Science, Inner Mongolia University, Hohhot, China
32009109@mail.imu.edu.cn
[2] National and Local Joint Engineering Research Center of Intelligent Information Processing Technology for Mongolian, Hohhot, China
cshhx@imu.edu.cn
[3] Inner Mongolia Key Laboratory of Mongolian Information Processing Technology, Hohhot, China

Abstract. When parallel training data is scarce, it will affect neural machine translation. For low-resource neural machine translation (NMT), transfer learning is very important, and the use of pre-training model can also alleviate the shortage of data. However, the good performance of common cold-start transfer learning methods is limited to the cognate language realized by sharing its vocabulary. Moreover, when using the pre-training model, the combination of general fine tuning methods and NMT will lead to a serious problem of knowledge forgetting. Both methods have some defects, so this paper optimizes the above two problems, and applies a new training framework suitable for low correlation language to Mongolian-Chinese neural machine translation. Our framework includes two technologies: a) word alignment method under hot-start, which alleviates the problem of word mismatch between the transferred subject and object in transfer learning. b) approximate distillation,not only retains the pre-trained knowledge, but also solves the forgetting problem, so that the encoder of NMT has stronger language representation ability. The results show that BLEU is increased by 3.2, which is better than ordinary transfer learning and multilingual translation system.

Keywords: Transfer learning · Pre-training · Machine translation

1 Introduction

Despite the rapid development of neural machine translation [1] recently, its main improvements and optimizations can not be easily applied to language pairs with insufficient resources. Basic training procedure of NMT does not work well with only a few bilingual data [2], and collecting bilingual resources is difficult for many languages. With fewer parallel corpora and sparse data, it is easy to cause over fitting problems in the training process. The trained model has poor robustness and generalization ability.

© The Author(s), under exclusive license to Springer Nature Singapore Pte Ltd. 2022
T. Xiao and J. Pino (Eds.): CCMT 2022, CCIS 1671, pp. 12–23, 2022.
https://doi.org/10.1007/978-981-19-7960-6_2

In order to solve this problem, unsupervised and transfer learning [3] methods are generally used to improve the quality of the model with the help of external resources. However, the unsupervised method has no annotation set, so the cross entropy method cannot be used for tuning. Back-translation [4] will produce false corpus, and the increase of false corpus will also produce noise, resulting in inaccurate translation. The concept of transfer learning is: We pre-train an NMT model on a high-resource language pair (parent language pair), and then continue training on the model using the bilingual data of another low-resource language pair (child language pair). This method can alleviate the poor performance of the model caused by less corpus, but it also has some shortcomings.

Some studies [5] show that the most important problem in transfer learning is the vocabulary mismatch between the transfer subject and the transfer object, which seriously limits the translation performance. We regard the source language in the parent language pair as the transfer subject, and the source language in the child language pair as the transfer object. If the words of the subject and object can be correctly corresponding during the transfer, the performance of transfer learning will be greatly improved. In previous studies [6], transfer learning is divided into hot-start method and cold-start method according to whether there is training data of child language pairs when training the parent model. The cold-start method does not use sublanguage for data. In contrast, in the hot-start method, we have available sublanguage pair training data when training the parent model. We can use sublanguage pair knowledge to solve this problem. In this paper, a cross-lingual word embedding method is used to convert words, and a semi-supervised method is used to correctly correspond the two languages without shared sub words. It can alleviate the word mismatch mentioned above and effectively improve the translation quality.

The pre-train models have demonstrated their excellent performance in various natural language processing tasks including translation tasks. Now the common training paradigm is "pre-train + fine-tune", which means that specific downstream tasks are tuning on the pre-trained model, so that additional knowledge can be obtained when training downstream tasks.

However, compared with other tasks that directly fine-tune the pre-trained model, NMT has two obvious characteristics, the availability of large training data (10 million or more) and the high capability of the baseline NMT model (i.e., Transformer). These two features need a lot of updating steps in the training process in order to adapt to the large capacity model well. However, too many updates will lead to disastrous forgetting [7]. Too many updates in training will forget the general knowledge before training. Since the output of the pre-train model and the encoder output of NMT are essentially language models, this paper does not use the "pre-train + fine-tune" method, but chooses the approximate distillation method to integrate the pre-trained knowledge into the encoder, so as to enhance the language representation ability of the NMT encoder and avoid the forgetting problem caused by a large number of updates.

This work proposes a new framework to adapt the transfer learning of neural machine translation to low-resources languages:

– Cross-lingual word embedding under hot-start is used to alleviate the problem of word mismatch between the transfer subject and the transfer object.

- The approximate distillation method is used to ensure that the NMT model can retain the previously trained knowledge and enhance the generalization ability of the NMT encoder.

2 Background

2.1 NMT

Neural Machine Translation is essentially an encoder decoder system. Typical NMT structures include RNN, LSTM, Transformer, etc. The function of encoder is to encode the source language sequence and extract the information in the source language. Then the information is converted to the target language by the decoder, so as to complete the translation of the language.

The training task is to map the source language sequence $X = \{x_1, x_2...x_n\}$ to the target language sequence $Y = \{y_1, y_2...y_m\}$. The sequence length can be different. In this case here, n and m are the length of source sequence and target sequence respectively. The model is trained on a parallel corpus by optimizing for the cross-entropy loss with the stochastic gradient descent algorithm.

$$L_{nmt} = -\sum_{i=1}^{m} \log p(\theta)(y_i|y_{<i}, X) \tag{1}$$

$p(\theta)$ is probability, θ is a set of parameters: source/target word embedding, encoder, decoder, and output layer. The training objective is to minimize the loss in equation (1) to obtain the optimal translation results. In Transformer, the encoder is similar to the decoder in structure. The decoder is essentially a language model of language y. Similarly, the encoder with an additional output layer can also be seen as a language model. Therefore, it is natural to transfer the pre-trained knowledge to the encoder and decoder of NMT.

2.2 Transfer Learning

Generally speaking, transfer learning refers to reusing knowledge from other fields/tasks when facing new problems [8]. Especially when there is not enough training data to solve this problem, transfer learning can play a better role. Because the hidden layer of neural network can implicitly learn the general representation of data, the weight of hidden layer can be copied to another network to transfer knowledge.

In NMT, the earliest transfer learning method was proposed by Zoph et al. [3]. In their work, the parent model was first trained on high resource language pairs. Then, the source word embedding is copied together with the rest of the model, and the ith parent language word embedding is assigned to the ith child language word. Because the parent and child source languages have different vocabularies, this is equivalent to embedding the parent source words and randomly assigning them to the child source words. In other words, even if a word exists in both parent and child vocabularies, it is unlikely that it will be assigned the same embedding in both models (Fig. 1).

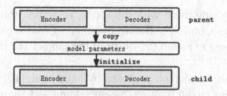

Fig. 1. Schematic diagram of transfer learning

For transfer learning, directly transferring the parameters of the parent model to the child model is not the optimal solution. Because the input language changes from the parent language to the child language, it is equivalent to introducing a completely different data space. The migrated model parameters cannot quickly adapt to the data space of the new language, and the translation effect will become worse. Previous studies have shown that the translation effect of transfer learning is closely related to the correct alignment of word vectors. The higher the alignment, the better the transfer effect.

2.3 Pre-train Techniques

In recent years, unsupervised pre-train of large neural models has recently completely changed natural language processing technology. The most representative model is BERT [9]. Generally, there are two methods to use BERT's feature, fine-tune and feature. For the fine-tune method, a simple classification layer is added to the pre-trained model, and all parameters of downstream tasks are jointly fine-tuned, while the feature method keeps the pre-trained parameters unchanged. In most cases, the performance of the fine-tune method is better than feature method.

The basic steps of the tuning method in NMT scenarios: train the language model on a large number of unlabeled text data, then initialize the NMT encoder with the pre-trained language model, and use a marked data set for tuning. However, this process may lead to catastrophic forgetting. After fine-tuning, the model performance on the language modeling task will be significantly reduced. This may hinder the ability of the model to use pre-trained knowledge. To solve this problem, we introduce a distillation method to improve the model.

3   Methods

3.1   Word Alignment Under Hot-Start

The biggest challenge of cross language transfer is vocabulary mismatch. When we replace only one source language, the NMT encoder will see a completely different input sequence. The pre-trained encoder weight does not match with the source embedding. Therefore, when we want to reuse the parent model parameters to train child language pairs, we need to solve the vocabulary mismatch between the transfer subject and the transfer object. However, the cold-start method is not applicable to the two languages that have nothing to do with subwords. Therefore, this paper uses the hot-start method to solve this problem. Before training, a Cross-lingual word embedding alignment method is used to match the words of the subject and object and align them correctly.

In this work, we use the method proposed by Patra et al. [10] and integrate it with transfer learning. Before model training, by embedding and aligning the words of the two languages, the parent model can recognize the transfer of child language pairs during training, so that the parameter migration can quickly adapt to the data distribution of the new language, which is impossible for the cold-start method.

Set $X = \{x_1, x_2...x_n\}$ and $Y = \{y_1, y_2...y_m\}$, They are two groups of word embedding from the source language and the target language respectively. Then set $S = \{(x_s^1, y_s^1)...(x_s^k, y_s^k)\}$, S represent the word embedding that has been bilingual aligned. We combine unsupervised distribution matching, alignment of known word pairs and weak orthogonal constraints to learn the linear mapping matrix W that maps X to Y (Fig. 2).

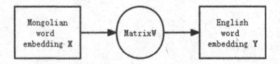

Fig. 2. Cross-lingual word embedding mapping from child language to parent language.

Unsupervised Method: Given X and Y, the objective of unsupervised loss is to match the distributions of these two embedding spaces. We used an adversarial distribution matching target, similar to the work of Conneau et al. [11]. Specifically, a source to target mapping matrix W is learned to trick a discriminator D, which is trained to distinguish between WX and Y. We parameterize our discriminator with MLP, or optimize the mapping matrix and discriminator with corresponding objectives:

$$L_{D|W} = -\frac{1}{n} \sum_{x_i \in X} \log\left(1 - D(WX_i)\right) - \frac{1}{m} \sum_{x_i \in Y} \log D(X_i) \qquad (2)$$

$$L_{W|D} = -\frac{1}{n} \sum_{x_i \in X} \log D(Wx_i) \qquad (3)$$

Aligning Known Word Pairs: Given aligned bilingual word embeddings S. Our task is to minimize a similarity function (f_s) and maximize the similarity between the corresponding matched word pairs. Specifically, loss is defined as:

$$L_{W|S} = -\frac{1}{|S|} \sum_{(x_i^s, y_i^s) \in S} f_s(Wx_i^s, y_i^s) \qquad (4)$$

Weak orthogonal constraint: Given an embedding space X, Patra et al. define a consistency loss that maximizes a similarity function f_a between x and $W^T W x$, $x \in X$

[10]. This cyclic consistency loss $L_{W|O}$ encourages orthogonality of the W matrix based on the joint optimization:

$$L_{W|O} = -\frac{1}{|X|} \sum_{x_i \in X} f_a(x_i, W^T W x_i) \tag{5}$$

The above loss terms are used in conjunction with supervised and unsupervised losses, allowing the model to adjust the trade-off between orthogonality and accuracy based on joint optimization. This is particularly useful in embedded spaces that do not conform to orthogonality constraints. The final loss function of the mapping matrix is:

$$L = L_{W|D} + L_{W|S} + L_{W|O} \tag{6}$$

It enables the model to utilize the available distribution information from the two embedded spaces, so as to use all available monolingual data. On the other hand, it allows the correct alignment of tag pairs in the form of a small seed dictionary. Finally, orthogonality is encouraged. We can think of and as opposed to each other. Co optimization of the two helps the model strike a balance between them.

3.2 Approximate Distillation

The transfer learning initializes the child model with the trained parent model parameters, and then fine-tune the new training set. Since the new training set is generally a low-resource language and the corpus is relatively small, it may not be able to fully learn the source language knowledge of the sub language pairs. The commonly used auxiliary method adopts the pre-train model to learn the source language knowledge, and then initializes the knowledge to NMT for fine tune. Moreover, the use of fine-tune of large pre-train model will reduce the speed of NMT [12]. In this regard, we use distillation method to integrate the knowledge obtained from the pre-train model into the NMT encoder, retain the previous knowledge, and improve the language representation ability of the encoder.

As shown in the figure, first use the pre-train language model (PLM) to train the source language monolingual, and the trained knowledge is stored in the hidden layer in the form of matrix. Then, the hidden layer of the PLM is taken as the teacher [13], and the hidden layer state of the translation model encoder is taken as the student for knowledge fusion. (The PLM and NMT encoder are essentially language models, so it is reasonable to integrate the knowledge of the two language models.)

$$L_{ad} = -\left\| \hat{h}^{lm} - h_l \right\|_2^2 \tag{7}$$

L_{ad} is the mean square error loss of the two hidden layer states, $\hat{h}^{lm}$ is the state of the last hidden layer of the PLM, and h_l is the state of the lth hidden layer of the encoder. By punishing the loss of mean square error between the PLM and the state of the hidden layer of NMT encoder, the states of the two hidden layers are gradually close. In the experiment, the hidden state of the PLM is frozen, and the last layer (top layer) of the encoder is set to h_l. We find that adding the supervision signal to the top

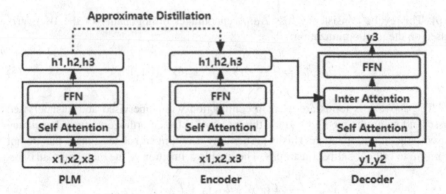

Fig. 3. The frame of approximate distillation.

encoder layer is the best. During training, distillation loss can be used together with traditional cross entropy loss (Fig. 3):

$$L_{all} = \alpha \cdot L_{nmt} + (1 - \alpha) \cdot L_{ad} \tag{8}$$

L_{nmt} is the cross entropy loss of the translation model. In the above formula, the total loss L_{all} combines L_{nmt} and L_{ad}, and α is a hyperparameter to balance the translation preference of the translation system [14]. In this way, the knowledge of PLM and the NMT can be combined to make better use of the pre-trained knowledge, so that the NMT encoder can obtain stronger representational capacity and generalization ability.

4   Experiment

4.1   Settings

We conducted experiments on English-Chinese (en-zh) and a low-resource translation task (mo-zh). For the en-zh task, the train set consists of 2 million bilingual sentences from the casic2015 corpus. We use NIST02 as the validation set and nist03-06 as the test set. For low-resource tasks, the dataset is provided by ccmt2019, as shown in Table 1. Mongolian monolingual comes from Wikipedia and news, with a total of 700 m words.

Table 1. Dataset distribution

Language	Train set	Validation set	Test set
mn-zh	256,754	2,000	2,000

All NMT models in our experiments follow the basic 6-layer transformer architecture of Vaswani et al. [1]. Each source language adopts byte pair encoding [15], 30K merge operation, while the target language adopts 50k bpe merge encoding. The training was conducted using sockeye [16] and Adam optimizer with default parameters.

The maximum sentence length is set to 100 and the batch size is set to 4,096 words. When the confusion on a verification set does not improve on the 12 checkpoints, the training is stopped. We set the checkpoint frequency of the parent model to 10,000 updates and the child model to 1,000 updates.The teacher model of knowledge distillation is trained by Bert, and the model in the experiment is $BERT_{base}$, which follows the structure proposed by Devlin et al. [9], l = 12, h = 768, a = 12, total parameters = 110 m. Set the hyperparameter α to 0.5 during knowledge fusion.

We first train the collected Mongolian and English monolingual corpus into word embedding. In order to learn cross language mapping, we use a semi-supervised framework, and the parameters basically follow the settings of Patra et al. [10]. The unsupervised method uses muse, the data set is composed of Mongolian and English dictionaries in the corpus, and the weak supervised method uses a set of aligned word embedding. After learning the final mapping matrix, the words in the source language are mapped to the target space, and their nearest neighbors are selected as the final result according to the CSLS [11] distance. We compared it with the multilingual translation model. In multilingual training, we trained a single and shared NMT model [17]. For each subtask, we learned the joint BPE vocabulary of all source and target languages in the parent/subtask through 32K merge operations. The training data of subtasks are oversampled, so the proportion of parent/child training samples of each small batch is about 1:1.

4.2 Results and Analysis

Results: From Table 2, in low-resource tasks, our method improved the scores of 3.2 and 1.7 BLEU respectively compared with traditional transformer and multilingual translation system.

Table 2. Comparison of experimental results.

System	Method	BLEU
Vaswani et al. [1]	Transformer base	27.4
Johnson et al. [17]	Multilingual	28.9
Ours	+Transfer Learning(cold-start)	28.7
	+Cross-lingual Word Embedding	29.5
	+Asymptotic Distillation	30.6

Analysis: In the first part of our experiment, we adopted the cold-start method of transfer learning, and directly transferred parameters without using sublanguage pairs. It is observed from the experiment that the cold-start method is also effective for low-resource languages, but it is less effective than the hot-start method using cross-lingual word embedding. It also further shows that the higher the degree of lexical matching between the subject and object of transfer, the better the effect of transfer learning. Finally, the approximate distillation method is added. Compared with the Transformer, it has a 3.2 BLEU improvement. We believe that the distillation method can enable the encoder of NMT to fuse additional information.

4.3 Ablation Test

In this section, we will further study our method in detail, compare it with their similar variants, and conduct general ablation studies.

Pre-trained Word Embedding Type. In Table 3, we analyze the cross-lingual impact of pre-trained embedding. We try not to transfer word embedding in transfer learning, but use pre-trained monolingual word embedding to replace the original word embedding. We observe that monolingual embedding without cross language mapping also improves transfer learning, but it is significantly worse than our proposed mapping to parent (en) embedding. You can also use learning mapping on the target (zh) side. Target mapping embedding is not compatible with the pre trained encoder, but directly guides the sub model to establish the connection between the new source and target. It also improves the system, but our method is still the best of the three embedding types.

Table 3. The experimental performance of different types of cross-lingual word embedding.

Pre-trained embedding	BLEU%
None	4.8
Monolingual	6.3
Cross-lingual (en-mo)	7.7
Cross-lingual (zh-mo)	7.2

Encoder vs Decoder. As shown in Table 4, the effect of integrating the pre-trained knowledge into the encoder is good, but the effect is low in the decoder. Since BERT contains bidirectional information, the fusion of pre-trained knowledge into decoder may lead to inconsistency between training and reasoning. Gpt-2 uses limited self attention, where each token can only focus on its left context. Therefore, it is natural to introduce gpt-2 into the NMT decoder. It may be that the decoder is not a typical language model, it only contains information from the source language.

Vocabulary Size. Table 5 shows the effect of different vocabulary sizes on translation. We changed the number of source side BPE merges and fixed the target vocabulary. The better result is to use 20K or 30K merges, which indicates that the vocabulary should be small in order to maximize the quality of translation. Fewer BPE merges result in more

Table 4. Different Transformer modules and different PLM were used for approximate distillation ablation test.

PLM to module	BLEU
BERT to transformer encoder	29.5
BERT to transformer decoder	26.8
GPT-2 to transformer encoder	28.3
GPT-2 to transformer decoder	27.7

language independent tags. Cross-lingual embedding makes it easier to find overlaps in the shared semantic space. However, if the vocabulary is too small, we may lose too many language specific details necessary in the translation process.

Table 5. Baseline translation results for different vocabulary sizes.

BPE merges	BLEU
20k	27.1
30k	27.4
40k	26.6
50k	26.3

4.4 Case Analysis

Src	ᠬᠠᠷ ᠲᠣᠯᠢ ᠣᠨᠠᠯ ᠲᠠᠯᠠᠪ ᠨᠠᠷ ᠲᠠᠨᠤ ᠬᠠᠮᠣᠭ ᠶᠢ ᠦᠷᠭᠦᠯᠵᠢ , ᠪᠢᠳᠠ ᠠᠴᠠ ᠨᠠᠷ ᠨᠠᠷ ᠲᠠᠨᠤ ᠲᠢᠢ ᠬᠣᠨ ᠬᠣᠨ ᠠᠪᠣᠯᠠᠯ ᠠᠪᠣᠪᠠᠩ ᠪᠣᠯᠵᠠᠢ ..
Ref	玉米 几乎 都 倒 在 地里 ， 我们 如数家珍 般 一个 一个 掰回 来 的 。
Baseline	额尔敦施几乎都倒在地里，我们家的宝贝泥烧碎了一个一个掰回来。
Transfer Learning	几乎所有的宝贝儿都躺在地里，我们把宝贝儿一个一个地折回来了。
Ours	玉米几乎都躺在地里，我们像宝贝一样一个一个掰回来的。

Fig. 4. Translation effects of different tasks.

It can be seen from the figure that the translation of this method basically conforms to the standard translation in terms of accuracy and fluency, so as to control the details of translation. In the case analysis, the words   and "宝贝" in Mongolian are very similar and easy to be confused. Translating these two words correctly makes the translation more accurate. And the words "几乎" and "掰" more reflect the fluency of language and express more accurately. It is proved that this method can improve the accuracy and fluency of translation (Fig. 4).

5 Conclusion

The main contributions of this paper include: we propose a transfer learning framework based on hot-start. On the basis of transfer learning, we alleviates the problem of vocabulary mismatch between two languages without shared subwords.Meanwhile, in order to give full play to the role of the PLM and improve the generalization ability of the NMT encoder, we use the approximate distillation method to guide the NMT model to learn the output probability distribution of the PLM.In this way, the NMT model can master the knowledge probability distribution of the PLM and the NMT encoder at the same time. Experiments show that this method has a significant impact on low-resource translation tasks.

References

1. Vaswani, A., et al.: Attention is all you need. In: Advances in Neural Information Processing Systems, vol. 30 (2017)
2. Koehn, P., Knowles, R.: Six challenges for neural machine translation. arXiv preprint arXiv:1706.03872 (2017)
3. Zoph, B., Yuret, D., May, J., Knight, K.: Transfer learning for low-resource neural machine translation. arXiv preprint arXiv:1604.02201 (2016)
4. Marie, B., Rubino, R., Fujita, A.: Tagged back-translation revisited: why does it really work? In: Proceedings of the 58th Annual Meeting of the Association for Computational Linguistics, pp. 5990–5997 (2020)
5. Aji, A.F., Bogoychev, N., Heafield, K., Sennrich, R.: In neural machine translation, what does transfer learning transfer? Association for Computational Linguistics (2020)
6. Neubig, G., Hu, J.: Rapid adaptation of neural machine translation to new languages. arXiv preprint arXiv:1808.04189 (2018)
7. Goodfellow, I.J., Mirza, M., Xiao, D., Courville, A., Bengio, Y.: An empirical investigation of catastrophic forgetting in gradient-based neural networks. arXiv preprint arXiv:1312.6211 (2013)
8. Freitag, M., Al-Onaizan, Y.: Fast domain adaptation for neural machine translation. arXiv preprint arXiv:1612.06897 (2016)
9. Devlin, J., Chang, M.-W., Lee, K., Toutanova, K.: BERT: pre-training of deep bidirectional transformers for language understanding. arXiv preprint arXiv:1810.04805 (2018)
10. Patra, B., Moniz, J.R.A., Garg, S., Gormley, M.R., Neubig, G.: Bilingual lexicon induction with semi-supervision in non-isometric embedding spaces. arXiv preprint arXiv:1908.06625 (2019)
11. Conneau, A., Lample, G., Ranzato, M.A., Denoyer, L., Jégou, H.: Word translation without parallel data. arXiv preprint arXiv:1710.04087 (2017)
12. Edunov, S., Baevski, A., Auli, M.: Pre-trained language model representations for language generation. arXiv preprint arXiv:1903.09722 (2019)
13. Zhu, Y., Wang, Y.: Student customized knowledge distillation: bridging the gap between student and teacher. In: Proceedings of the IEEE/CVF International Conference on Computer Vision, pp. 5057–5066 (2021)
14. Yang, J., et al.: Towards making the most of BERT in neural machine translation. Proc. AAAI Conf. Artif. Intell. **34**, 9378–9385 (2020)

15. Sennrich, R., Haddow, B., Birch, A.: Neural machine translation of rare words with subword units. arXiv preprint arXiv:1508.07909 (2015)
16. Hieber, F., et al.: Sockeye: a toolkit for neural machine translation. arXiv preprint arXiv:1712.05690 (2017)
17. Johnson, M., et al.: Google's multilingual neural machine translation system: enabling zero-shot translation. Trans. Assoc. Comput. Linguist. **5**, 339–351 (2017)

Review-Based Curriculum Learning
for Neural Machine Translation

Ziyang Hui, Chong Feng$^{(\boxtimes)}$, and Tianfu Zhang

School of Computer Science and Technology, Beijing Institute of Technology,
Beijing 100081, China
{huiziyang,fengchong,tianfuzhang}@bit.edu.cn

Abstract. For Neural Machine Translation (NMT) tasks with limited domain resources, curriculum learning provides a way to simulate the human learning process from simple to difficult to adapt the general NMT model to a specific domain. However, previous curriculum learning methods suffer from catastrophic forgetting and learning inefficiency. In this paper, we introduce a review-based curriculum learning method, targetedly selecting curriculum according to long time interval or unskilled mastery. Furthermore, we add general domain data to curriculum learning, using the mixed fine-tuning method, to improve generalization and robustness of translation. Extensive experimental results and analysis show that our method outperforms other curriculum learning baselines across three specific domains.

Keywords: Neural machine translation · Domain adaptation · Review-based curriculum learning

1 Introduction

Recently, constructing high-quality domain-specific neural machine translation (NMT) models has become a research hotspot. Due to the scarcity of domain-specific parallel corpora, it is currently impossible to train robust domain-specific NMT models from scratch. Domain adaptation uses general domain data and unlabeled-domain data to improve the translation of in-domain models. It focuses on two problems, catastrophic forgetting and overfitting [1]. Common NMT domain adaptation methods can be divided into two categories [2]: data-centric methods, including back translation and data selection; model-centric methods, including training objective-centric methods, architecture-centric methods and decoding-centric methods. These methods can alleviate the catastrophic forgetting and overfitting problems to varying degrees.

Curriculum learning (CL) is also used to solve the above problems. It imitates the way that humans learn curriculum from easier to harder [3], which results in better generalization of the NMT model. Two main questions of CL are how to rank the training examples, and how to modify the sampling procedure based on this ranking [4]. The above questions can be abstracted to difficulty measurer

© The Author(s), under exclusive license to Springer Nature Singapore Pte Ltd. 2022
T. Xiao and J. Pino (Eds.): CCMT 2022, CCIS 1671, pp. 24–36, 2022.
https://doi.org/10.1007/978-981-19-7960-6_3

and training scheduler [5]. Usually, difficulty measurers are task-specific, however, the existing predefined training schedulers are data/task agnostic. Training schedulers can be divided into discrete and continuous schedulers, and we focus on the improvement of the discrete schedulers in this paper. One-Pass [3] and Baby Step [6] are two discrete schedulers, which divide the sorted data into shards from easy to hard and then start training with the easiest shard. The difference between two methods is that at each learning phase, One-Pass only uses the current shard but Baby Step merges previously used shards into the current shard. One-Pass may suffer from the problem of catastrophic forgetting, while Baby Step has more generalization but takes longer to train when the number of shards increases.

From practical experience, humans usually review the previous curriculums when they learn. One-Pass can be compared to not reviewing the curriculums they have learned before, and Baby Step is analogous to reviewing all the previous curriculums at each phase. However, it is enough for humans to strengthen their memory by reviewing only some of the previous curriculums at each learning phase. In this paper, we imitate the way humans review curriculums, and propose this review-based CL method. Aiming at the problems of the existing discrete scheduler method, we design two review methods which select the previous curriculums that need to be reviewed and add them to the current training set. The first method calculates time interval of the previous curriculums between their last learning phase and the current phase, and selects curriculums with a larger time interval. The second method is based on the model's mastery of the previous curriculums, calculating the increment of curriculum scores between two close phases to select curriculums which are not proficiently mastered. Figure 1 shows the difference among the curriculum shards used at each phase for One-Pass, Baby Step and Review. The columns represent the curriculum shards and the rows represent the curriculum shards used at each learning phase. The darker color of each square, the less similar it is to the specific domain.

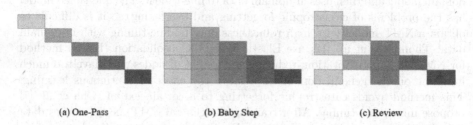

(a) One-Pass   (b) Baby Step   (c) Review

Fig. 1. Comparison of shards used at each phase for different curriculum learning methods.

With applying to NMT domain adaptation, the above methods still have the problem of forgetting. So we refer to the practice of mixed fine-tuning [7], bringing general domain data into each phase of CL after training the general model. The general domain can be seen as the learning foundation that humans already have when learning curriculums. Although it is not completely consistent with the distribution of specific domains, the knowledge contained in general domain can help NMT model learn common information, enhance the robustness and avoid forgetting happens.

We test our approach on TED talks for German-English and Chinese-English pairs and patent abstracts for German-English pairs. Experimental results show that our approach significantly improves compared to baseline methods, and alleviates the problem of occupying too long training time for Baby Step as well.

2   Related Work

From a data-driven perspective, CL is essentially similar to the instance weighting approach in domain adaptation. It makes NMT model pay more attention to the loss of certain training examples, and allows the model to adapt or forget certain pairs. Zhang et al. [8] design different difficulty measurers and training schedulers applying to NMT, and point out that no strategy can perfectly outperform the others, but they did not further analyze the effect of other hyperparameters in CL. Zhang et al. [9] use Baby Step method in NMT domain adaptation for the first time. They take in-domain data as the first curriculum shard, and analyze the effect of two distinct data selection methods and distinct number of shards on NMT model. However, they did not consider the negative impact of slower convergence speed and the problem of forgetting due to fine-tuning with in-domain data and unlabeled-domain data. Xu et al. [10] proposed a dynamic CL method, using training loss decline of two iterations as difficulty measurer and a function of BLEU value on the development set as training scheduler. This method achieves better performance in low-resource scenarios but no improvement when in-domain data is rich.

From a model-driven perspective, CL is also related to training objective-centric methods. Fine-tuning [11] is a classical method which first trains a general domain model and then uses in-domain data to fine-tune it. The fine-tuned model has the problems of catastrophic forgetting and overfitting, so it is difficult to obtain a NMT model with high robustness only by fine-tuning with in-domain data. Thompson et al. [12] use Elastic Weight Consolidation (EWC) method for NMT domain adaptation, reducing the weight of nodes that have too much influence on the general domain to achieve the effect of continuous learning. This method avoids catastrophic forgetting to a certain extent. Chu et al. [7] propose mixed fine-tuning. After training the general NMT model, it uses data mixed with in-domain data and general domain data rather than in-domain data alone, which greatly improves the robustness of the model. We borrow the idea of mixed fine-tuning to add general domain data to CL for solving the problem of catastrophic forgetting.

3   Review-Based Curriculum Learning

In this paper, we propose review-based curriculum learning for NMT. It focuses on the improvement of discrete training scheduler. We define the number of review curriculums at each phase and how to choose the review curriculum. Also, we introduce general domain data to each phase to solve the forgetting problem for NMT domain adaptation. The overall method is shown in Fig. 2. The solid line pointed out from the curriculum shard represents that it is used at this phase, while the dotted line indicates that some of the curriculum shards need to be reviewed. These two parts are combined into a review subset for each phase, and then further mixed with the general domain data and in-domain data in a certain proportion to form the whole training set of each phase. At each phase, we continue training the NMT model until it is converged.

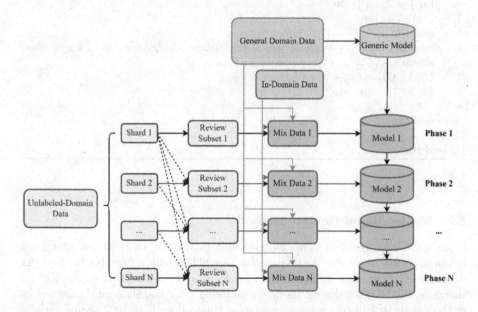

Fig. 2. Review-based curriculum learning method enhanced with general domain.

3.1   Time-Based Review Method

Commonly, humans usually forget curriculums which are learned a long time ago. Inspired by this phenomenon, we believe that the longer a curriculum has been since it was last learned, the more important it is to review it. We assume that the number of CL phases is T and the fixed data shard used at each phase is $C_i (1 \leq i \leq T)$ reaching a certain phase i, in addition to current shard C_i, the number of other curriculums to be reviewed is set to n_i. Apparently, the range of n_i between 1 and i−1. As Algorithm 1 shows, when reviewing curriculums at phase i, we calculate the difference value Δt_{c_i} between last used phase t_{c_j} and current phase i for curriculum $C_j(1 \leq j \leq i-1)$. Then we sort the difference values to choose the top n_i curriculum shards from largest to smallest and add them to phase i data re_{C_i}. Finally, the last used phase of the top n_i curriculum shards is updated to i. It is worth noting that phase 1 does not need to review, so $C_1^{re} = C_1$.

Algorithm 1. Time-based Review Method

Input: Number of curriculum phase T, each curriculum shard data $C_i(1 \leq i \leq T)$.
Output: Each curriculum phase data $C_1^{re}(1 \leq i \leq T)$.
1: $C_1^{re} \leftarrow C_1$
2: **for** i=2,3,...,T **do**
3:     **for** j=1,2,...,i-1 **do**
4:        $\Delta t_{c_i} \leftarrow$ i- t_{c_i}
5:     **end for**
6:     Sort $\Delta t_{c_i}(1 \leq j \leq$ i-1)from largest to smallest, choose the top n_i curric-ulum shards $C_{r_1}, C_{r_2}, ..., C_{r_{n_i}}$.
7:     $C_i^{re} \leftarrow C_{r_1} + C_{r_2} + ... + C_{r_{n_i}}$
8:     **for** k=1,2,...,n_i **do**
8:        $t_{c_{r_k}} \leftarrow i$
9:     **end for**
10:     $t_{c_i} \leftarrow i$
11: **end for**

3.2   Master-Based Review Method

From a different point of view, humans also review the curriculums which are not proficiently mastered. We change this thought into an achievable method. As Algorithm 2 shows, first we define the model's mastery of the previous curriculum shards as the BLEU value on them. Considering if we translate all the sentences in the shards, it will cost a long translation time, so we take 1000 sentence pairs from each curriculum shard at equal spacing as a representation of the shard and calculate the BLEU value. We think that compared to the last phase, the less curriculum shard improves, the more it needs to be reviewed. The master score is estimated as:

$$score_{C_j} = \frac{BLEU_{C_j}^i - BLEU_{C_j}^{i-1}}{BLEU_{C_j}^{i-1}}. \tag{1}$$

where $BLEU_{C_j}^i$ represents that the BLEU value of 1000 pairs from curriculum shard $C_j(1 \leq j \leq i-1)$ at phase i before training. If the score is smaller than others, we think that the NMT model has not learned this shard sufficiently, and conversely we consider this shard has improved more and does not need more attention. We select top n_i shards according to the master score from smallest to largest, and add them to phase i data C_i^{re}. Finally we calculate $BLEU_{C_j}^i$. Finally we calculate $BLEU_{C_j}^i$ and train new NMT model.

Algorithm 2. Master-based Review Method

Input: Number of curriculum phase T, each curriculum shard data $C_i (1 \leq i \leq T)$.
Output: Each curriculum phase data $C_i^{re} (1 \leq i \leq T)$.
1: $C_1^{re} \leftarrow C_1$
2: **for** i=2,3,...,T do **do**
3:    **for** j=1,2,...,i-1 do **do**
4:       Use current model to calculate $BLEU_{C_j}^i$
5:       Calculate master score of C_j by Equation 1.
6:    **end for**
7:    Sort $score_{c_j} (1 \leq j \leq i\text{-}1)$smallest to largest, choose the top n_i curriculum shards $C_{r_1}, C_{r_2}, ..., C_{r_{n_i}}$.
8:    $C_i^{re} \leftarrow C_{r_1} + C_{r_2} + ... + C_{r_{n_i}}$
9:    Use current model to calculate $BLEU_{C_j}^i$.
10:    Train the new NMT model.
11: **end for**

3.3   General Domain Enhanced Training

General domain can be seen as the inherent memory of humans, so in order to maintain a high level of generalization and robustness of NMT model, we add general domain data to each learning phase. In the experiments of Zhang [9], as training goes on, the weight of in-domain data is decrease due to the increment of unlabeled-domain data. Therefore, we assign weight to in-domain data individually, so that each phase uses a fixed proportion of general domain data, in-domain data and partially unlabeled-domain data:

$$train_t = w_{GD} * D_{GD} + w_{ID} * D_{ID} + w_{UD} * C_t^{re} \tag{2}$$

where D_{train_t} represents training set at phase t, w_{GD}, w_{ID} and w_{UD} represent the weight of general domain data D_{GD}, in-domain data D_{ID} and review unlabeled-domain data C_i^{re} separately.

4   Experiment

4.1   Data and Setup

General Domain Data. We use two general domain datasets in the experiment, Ger-man(de)-English(en) and Chinese(zh)-English. German-English general dataset includes Europarl, news commentary, OpenSubtitles and Rapid corpus, while Chinese-English includes CCMT2017, news commentary, UN Parallel Corpus. After tokenization (not to Chinese) and filtering sentence length up to 80 words, we get 19 million sentence pairs for German-English and 20 million sentence pairs for Chinese-English.

In-Domain Data. Chinese-English and German-English TED domain data are from Duh [13], and German-English patent domain data is from Junczys-Dowmunt et al. [14]. The concrete number of three domain corpora is shown in Table 1.

Table 1. Number of sentences in each dataset

Dataset	Training set	Development set	Test set
TED(zh-en)	166373	1958	1982
TED(de-en)	148460	1958	1982
Patent(de-en)	150000	2000	2000

Unlabeled-Domain Data. For unlabeled-domain data in two language directions, we use web-crawled bitext from the Paracrawl project [15]. After data cleaning and data selection, we get 20 million sentences for German-English and 8.3 million sentences for Chinese-English. For the final corpus size in the experiment, Zhang et al. [9] suggest 1024k pairs, and we follow this setup.

Curriculum Learning Setup. We refer to Zhang et al. [9] for some experiment set-tings. For difficulty measurer we use Moore-Lewis [16] method to build language models trained on in-domain and unlabeled-domain, and calculate the cross-entropy difference of sentence in unlabeled-domain dataset. KenLM [17] is used to build language models on the target side (English). Then, we set $n_i = \lfloor \log_2 i \rfloor$ setting is designed to review an appropriate number of curriculums to avoid forgetting or inefficient learning problem of not reviewing (like One-Pass) or reviewing all shards (like Baby Step). Finally, we set the number of curriculum phase to 5, which is different to Zhang et al. [9]. It is explained in experiment analysis.

Subword Model. We use general domain data to train sentencepiece [18] subword segmentation model. The vocab size is set to 32000 both for two languages. Since general domain is large enough to train a robust segmentation model, there is no need to retrain the subword model when we use the in-domain data and unlabeled-domain data.

NMT Setup. In all experiments, we use the OpenNMT [19] implementation of the Transformer [20], with 6 layers for both encoder and decoder and 8 attention heads. The word embedding size is set to 512. We use Adam [21] optimizer to adjust the learning rate automatically, with $\beta_1 = 0.9$ and $\beta_2 = 0.998$. We set batch size to 6000, and training stops when the perplexity on the development set has not improved for 5 checkpoints (2000 batches per checkpoint) at each phase. In addition, considering that the number of general domain data is much larger than the number of in-domain and unlabeled-domain data, we set the weights ($w_{GD} : w_{ID} : w_{UD}$) done to oversample in-domain data and maintain high learning ratio on the other two do-mains, which not only biases the final model distribution towards the specific domain, but also improves the robustness of the NMT model.

Evaluation Metric. We use BLEU as the evaluation metric, and calculate with sacreBLEU tool [22].

4.2   Main Results

Main experimental results is shown in Table 2. The model trained with large amount of general domain data (GEN) has BLEU scores of 35.98, 18.29 and 26.47. Fine tuning (FT) on in-domain data improves BLEU significantly by 3.25, 3.51 and 23.98. Mixed fine tuning (MFT) brings more robustness to NMT model, with improvement of 2.32, 2.17 and 0.94 BLEU score compared to fine tuning method.

For previous curriculum learning methods, One-Pass suffers from catastrophic for getting problem apparently, with BLEU scores of 31.09, 15.48 and 34.03. Although Baby Step improves this situation with BLEU scores of 36.97, 22.60 and 50.74, it does not work as well as fine tuning on TED (de-en) domain, and still has the problem of forgetting. Our two methods (T-Review and M-Review) perform better than OnePass and worse than Baby Step, because the NMT model does not focus on the indomain data all the time during the training process, and too much attention to the unlabeled-domain data may cause forgetting problem.

After we add general domain data into CL phases, all the CL methods mentioned perform better than original. T-Review+MFT performs best in all the methods with BLEU scores of 42.40, 24.49 and 52.29. Compared to MFT method, it improves BLEU by up to 0.9 score on patent (de-en). Also, compared to Baby Step method, it improves BLEU by up to 5.43 score on TED (de-en). We believe that general domain data enhances the generalization of the NMT model, so that instead of reviewing all the previous curriculum shards, we use only a part of shards that are necessary to be reviewed to improve the effect of NMT model.

As for the comparison of our two methods, T-Review+MFT performs slightly better than M-Review+MFT. Note that T-Review is not related to the NMT model while M-Review is related. The possible reason is that T-Review has a more logical review schedule for the shards and is able to review the curriculum evenly. We also compare the method of randomly selecting shards for review with MFT (Rand-Review+MFT). The result shows that even randomly select curriculums can be better than Baby Step+MFT and One-Pass+MFT, however, designed review curriculum rules are more effective such as T-Review and M-Review.

Table 2. Main experiment results

Method	TED(de-en)	TED(zh-en)	patent(de-en)
GEN	35.98	18.29	26.47
FT	39.23	21.80	50.45
MFT	41.55	23.97	51.39
One-Pass	31.09	15.48	34.03
One-Pass+MFT	42.24	24.08	52.19
Baby Step	36.97	22.60	50.74
Baby Step+MFT	42.05	24.06	51.97
Rand-Review+MFT	42.23	24.25	52.09
T-Review	35.35	21.05	47.67
T-Review+MFT	42.40	24.49	52.29
M-Review	35.64	21.17	47.45
M-Review+MFT	42.37	24.20	52.24

5   Analysis

5.1   Effect of Mixed Fine Tuning

We analyze the effect of MFT for CL. As shown in Table 3, we conduct the ablation studies on whether CL approach incorporate the general domain and whether indomain weight is fixed, with Baby Step and T-Review method. We can see that when the in-domain weight is fixed, T-Review outperforms original method by up to 3.29 BLEU score on TED (de-en), but Baby Step has an unstable effect as decreasing on TED (zh-en) and patent (de-en). When mixed with general domain only, T-Review increases by up to 4.19 BLEU score on TED (de-en) compared with original method, and this value is 3.81 for Baby Step. However, due to the reason that in-domain weight is unfixed and the Review method is not stable to review the in-domain shard, the effect of T-Review is worse than Baby Step.

When combining the general domain and fixing the in-domain weight, the robustness of NMT model is greatly improved. Relatively increasing the in-domain weight can learn the in-domain knowledge better with the help of general domain and solve the problem of overfitting. So T-Review+MFT performs better than Baby Step+MFT. It is worth noting that One-Pass+MFT is even more effective than Baby Step+MFT, which further proves that MFT does not require multiple repetitions of curriculms when applied to CL. Only the curriculums which need to be reviewed is enough.

Table 3. Ablation study results for general domain and in-domain fixed weight

Method	TED(de-en)	TED(zh-en)	patent(de-en)
Baby Step	36.97	22.60	50.74
+Fixed in-domain weight	39.00	21.93	50.66
+ General domain	40.78	23.49	51.42
+MFT(Fixed in-domain weight + General domain)	42.05	24.06	51.97
T-review	35.35	21.05	47.67
+Fixed in-domain weight	38.64	22.44	50.28
+ General domain	39.64	22.77	49.53
+MFT(Fixed in-domain	42.40	24.49	52.39

5.2 Low-Resource Scenario

We also explored the effects of using a review-based CL with MFT in a low-resource scenario. We set the number of patent (de-en) sentence pairs to 15k rather than 150k, in order to simulate the effect of extremely low-resource domain scenario. Table 4 shows that two Review+MFT methods have an average increment of 2.32, 0.55 and 0.53 BLEU score compared to MFT, One-Pass+MFT and Baby Step+MFT methods. This result indicates the effectiveness of using data from other rich resources to increase model robustness and also confirms that CL+MFT, especially review-based CL+MFT, could improve translation abilities of NMT models and avoid the problem of overfitting and catastrophic forgetting.

Table 4. Main experiment results

Method	patent(de-en)
MFT	45.35
One-Pass+MFT	47.12
Baby Step+MFT	47.14
Rand-Review+MFT	47.39
T-Review+MFT	47.68
M-Review+MFT	47.67

5.3 Data Sharding

We experiment with different number of shards setting and experiment on TED (de_en) domain with Baby Step+MFT and M-Review+MFT. As Fig. 3 shows, the two methods both achieve the best performance at the point of 5 shards. As the number of shards increases, the BLEU scores show a decreasing trend. Although Baby Step increases when the number of shards is 20, the BLEU score does not change too much. This result differs from the findings of Zhang et al. [9]. The possible reason is that our method is mixed with general domain and fixes weights of three domains, and increasing number of shards with the same number of unlabeled-domain data will reduce the number of data in each shard. This may result in the curriculum being repeated too many times at one phase, which may lead to overfitting. Further, considering the negative effects of too long training time of too many shards, we set the number of shards to 5 better than the number of other shards and Review is better than Baby Step.

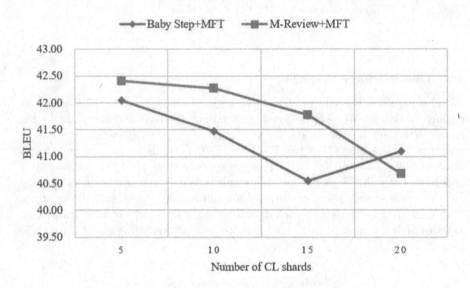

Fig. 3. Different number of curriculum learning shards

5.4   Training Efficiency

Table 5 shows the comparison of training steps for three CL methods. We can see that T-Review+MFT reduces training time by average of 18k steps and M-Review+MFT reduces an average of 12k steps both compared to Baby Step+MFT. It proves that review-based method with MFT can accelerate the convergence of NMT model. We argue that the number of curriculums learned at each phase has an impact on the convergence speed. More curriculums make the model less easy to converge, however, reviewing appropriate number of courses reduces training time and improves training efficiency.

Table 5. Training steps for three curriculum methods

Method	TED(de-en)	TED(zh-en)	patent(de-en)
Baby Step+MFT	92k	168k	144k
T-Review +MFT	84k	146k	118k
M-Review+MFT	86k	150k	132k

6   Conclusion

To address the problems of catastrophic forgetting and learning inefficiency of previous curriculum learning methods for NMT domain adaptation, this paper proposes a review-based curriculum learning method. We first select curriculum shards with long time interval or unskilled mastery to review in each learning phase, and add general domain data to improve the robustness of NMT model. The experimental results show that our method improves significantly compared to previous curriculum learning methods and the simulation of low-resource scenario also demonstrate the effectiveness.

For future work, we will explore more effective methods and more applications for review-based curriculum learning. Additionally, it is a meaningful job for adding dynamic weighting method to our approach.

References

1. Saunders, D.: Domain adaptation and multi-domain adaptation for neural machine translation: a survey. arXiv preprint arXiv:2104.06951 (2021)
2. Chu, C., Wang, R.: A survey of domain adaptation for neural machine translation. In: Proceedings of the 27th International Conference on Computational Linguistics, pp. 1304–1319 (2018)
3. Bengio, Y., Louradour, J., Collobert, R., Weston, J.: Curriculum learning. In: Proceedings of the 26th Annual International Conference on Machine Learning, pp. 41–48 (2009)
4. Weinshall, D., Cohen, G., Amir, D.: Curriculum learning by transfer learning: theory and experiments with deep networks. In: International Conference on Machine Learning, pp. 5238–5246. PMLR (2018)
5. Wang, X., Chen, Y., Zhu, W.: A survey on curriculum learning. IEEE Trans. Pattern Anal. Mach. Intell. (01), 1 (2021)
6. Spitkovsky, V.I., Alshawi, H., Jurafsky, D.: From baby steps to leapfrog: how "less is more" in unsupervised dependency parsing. In: Human Language Technologies: The 2010 Annual Conference of the North American Chapter of the Association for Computational Linguistics, pp. 751–759 (2010)
7. Chu, C., Dabre, R., Kurohashi, S.: An empirical comparison of domain adaptation methods for neural machine translation. In: Proceedings of the 55th Annual Meeting of the Association for Computational Linguistics (Volume 2: Short Papers), pp. 385–391 (2017)
8. Zhang, X., et al.: An empirical exploration of curriculum learning for neural machine translation. arXiv preprint arXiv:1811.00739 (2018)

9. Zhang, X., Shapiro, P., Kumar, G., McNamee, P., Carpuat, M., Duh, K.: Curriculum learning for domain adaptation in neural machine translation. In: Proceedings of the 2019 Conference of the North American Chapter of the Association for Computational Linguistics: Human Language Technologies, Volume 1 (Long and Short Papers), pp. 1903–1915 (2019)

10. Xu, C., et al.: Dynamic curriculum learning for low-resource neural machine translation. In: Proceedings of the 28th International Conference on Computational Linguistics, pp. 3977–3989 (2020)

11. Luong, M.T., Manning, C.D.: Stanford neural machine translation systems for spoken language domains. In: Proceedings of the 12th International Workshop on Spoken Language Translation: Evaluation Campaign (2015)

12. Thompson, B., Gwinnup, J., Khayrallah, H., Duh, K., Koehn, P.: Overcoming catastrophic forgetting during domain adaptation of neural machine translation. In: Proceedings of the 2019 Conference of the North American Chapter of the Association for Computational Linguistics: Human Language Technologies, Volume 1 (Long and Short Papers), pp. 2062–2068 (2019)

13. The Multitarget TED Talks Task. http://www.cs.jhu.edu/~kevinduh/a/multitarget-tedtalks/. Accessed Dec 2018

14. Junczys-Dowmunt, M., Pouliquen, B., Mazenc, C.: COPPA v2. 0: Corpus of parallel patent applications building large parallel corpora with GNU make. In: 4th Workshop on Challenges in the Management of Large Corpora Workshop Programme (2016)

15. Bañón, M., et al.: ParaCrawl: web-scale acquisition of parallel corpora. In: Proceedings of the 58th Annual Meeting of the Association for Computational Linguistics, pp. 4555–4567 (2020)

16. Moore, R.C., Lewis, W.: Intelligent selection of language model training data. In: Proceedings of the ACL 2010 Conference Short Papers, pp. 220–224 (2010)

17. Heafield, K.: KenLM: faster and smaller language model queries. In: Proceedings of the Sixth Workshop on Statistical Machine Translation, pp. 187–197 (2011)

18. Kudo, T., Richardson, J.: SentencePiece: a simple and language independent subword tokenizer and detokenizer for neural text processing. In: Proceedings of the 2018 Conference on Empirical Methods in Natural Language Processing: System Demonstrations, pp. 66–71 (2018)

19. Klein, G., Hernandez, F., Nguyen, V., Senellart, J.: The OpenNMT neural machine translation toolkit: 2020 edition. In: Proceedings of the 14th Conference of the Association for Machine Translation in the Americas (Volume 1: Research Track), pp. 102–109 (2020)

20. Vaswani, A., et al.: Attention is all you need. In: Advances in Neural Information Processing Systems, vol. 30 (2017)

21. KingaD, A.: A method for stochastic optimization. Anon. In: International Conference on Learning Representations. ICLR, SanDiego (2015)

22. Post, M.: A call for clarity in reporting BLEU scores. In: Proceedings of the Third Conference on Machine Translation: Research Papers, pp. 186–191 (2018)

Multi-strategy Enhanced Neural Machine Translation for Chinese Minority Languages

Zhanglin Wu[⊠], Daimeng Wei, Xiaoyu Chen, Ming Zhu, Zongyao Li,
Hengchao Shang, Jinlong Yang, Zhengzhe Yu, Zhiqiang Rao, Shaojun Li, Lizhi Lei,
Song Peng, Hao Yang, and Ying Qin

Huawei Beijing Research Center, Text Machine Translation Lab, Beijing 100038, China
{wuzhanglin2,weidaimeng,chenxiaoyu35,zhuming47,lizongyao,
shanghengchao,yangjinlong7,yuzhengzhe,raozhiqiang,lishaojun18,
leilizhi,pengsong2,yanghao30,qinying}@huawei.com

Abstract. This paper presents HW-TSC's submissions to CCMT 2022 Chinese
Minority Language Translation task. We participate in three language directions:
Mongolian→Chinese Daily Conversation Translation, Tibetan→Chinese Government Document Translation, and Uighur→Chinese News Translation. We
train our models using the Deep Transformer architecture, and adopt enhancement strategies such as Regularized Dropout, Tagged Back-Translation, Alternated Training, and Ensemble. Our enhancement experiments have proved the
effectiveness of above-mentioned strategies. We submit enhanced systems as primary systems for the three tracks. In addition, we train contrast models using
additional bilingual data and submit results generated by these contrast models.

Keywords: CCMT 2022 · Neural machine translation · Regularized dropout ·
Tagged back-translation · Alternated training · Ensemble · Second keyword ·
Another keyword

1 Introduction

CCMT 2022 Chinese Minority Language Translation Task is a challenging low-
resource task. How to maximize low-resource translation performances using multiple enhancement strategies is the subject of this task, which is also our long-term
research focus. We participate in the Mongolian→Chinese Daily Conversation Translation, Tibetan→Chinese Government Document Translation, and Uighur→Chinese
News Translation tracks. For each track, we submit a primary system result and a copy
of contrast translation. In the following chapters we will introduce our data processing
method, model training strategies, experiment results, and findings.

2 Dataset

Dataset Volume. We strictly comply with the task requirements and use only officially-
provided bilingual and monolingual data to train our primary systems. For our contrast
models, additional bilingual data is used. Table 1 presents the data size for each language pair after pre-processing.

T. Xiao and J. Pino (Eds.): CCMT 2022, CCIS 1671, pp. 37–44, 2022.
https://doi.org/10.1007/978-981-19-7960-6_4

Table 1. Data size for each language pair after pre-processing.

	Mongolian→Chinese	Tibetan→Chinese	Uygur→Chinese
Bilingual	1.24M	0.97M	0.16M
Monolingual	3.94M	3.94M	3.94M
Additional bilingual	4.97M	1.54M	6.89M

Data Pre-processing. The data pre-processing process is as follows:

1. Remove duplicate sentences.
2. Remove invisible characters.
3. Reverse xml escape character.
4. Convert full-width symbols to half-width symbols.
5. Use jieba word segmentation tool for Chinese sentences.
6. Use joint BPE [1], and the vocabulary size is set to 32k.
7. Filter out sentences with more than 150 tokens.
8. Filter out sentence pairs with token ratio greater than 4 or less than 0.25.

3   System Overview

Model. The Transformer [2] model adopts the full self-attention mechanism, which can realize algorithm parallelism, speed up model training, and improve translation quality. Deep Transformer [3] can further improve the transformer performance by applying layer normalization to the input of every sub-layer and increasing the number of encoder layers. Therefore, in all three tracks, we use the following model architecture:

1. Deep Transformer: Based on the Transformer-big model architecture, our Deep Transformer model features pre-layer-normalization, 25-layer encoder, 6-layer decoder, 16-head self-attention, 1024 dimensions of word embedding and 4096-hidden-state.

Regularized Dropout. Dropout [4] is a powerful and widely used technique for regularizing deep neural networks. Though it can help improve training effectiveness, the randomness introduced by dropouts may lead to inconsistencies between training and inference. Regularized Dropout [5] forces the output distributions of different sub models generated by dropout be consistent with each other. Therefore, we use Regularized Dropout to enhance the baseline for each track and reduce inconsistencies between training and inference.

3.1   Back-Translation

In order to utilize target-side monolingual data to improve model performance, we use Back-Translation [6] to expand the training corpus. There are many specific implementation methods [7–10] for Back-Translation. During the experiment, we verify the effectiveness of two methods, namely, Top-K Sampling Back-Translation [8] and Tagged Back-Translation [9], and finally choose to use Tagged Back-Translation according to the experimental results.

3.2   Alternated Training

Due to the scarcity of authentic bilingual data, pseudo-bilingual data plays an important role in improving translation quality, but it inevitably introduces noise and translation errors. In order to alleviate the noise and translation errors caused by pseudo-bilingual data and improve the translation quality, we use the Alternated Training strategy [11]. The basic idea is to alternately use pseudo-bilingual data and authentic bilingual data in the training process until there is no noticeable improvement in translation quality.

3.3   Ensemble

Ensemble [12] is a widely-used technique to integrate different models for better performance. It should be noted that when using the Ensemble strategy, increasing the number of models does not always lead to better performance and may even hurt the final accuracy. Therefore, for each track, we train four models using the same data, and then select the models used for ensemble according to the strategy we used in the WMT21 Biomedical Translation Task [13]. The core idea is traverse all combinations of models and find the best one in the dev set.

4   Experiments

In the training phase, we use the Pytorch-based Fairseq [14] open-source framework and use the Deep Transformer model as the benchmark system. Each model uses 8 GPUs for training, and the batch size is 1024. The update frequency is set to 4, and the learning rate is 5e-4. The label smoothing rate [15] is set to 0.1, the number of warmup steps is 4000, and the dropout is 0.3. Adam optimizer [16] with $\beta 1 = 0.9$ and $\beta 2 = 0.98$ is used. In addition, when applying Regularized Dropout, we follow the setting of Liang et al. [5], using reg_label_smoothed_cross_entropy as the loss function, and set reg-alpha to 5. In the inference phase, we use the Marian [17] tool to perform decoding. The beam size is set to 10, and the length penalties for Mongolian→Chinese, Tibetan→Chinese and Uyghur→Chinese machine translation are 1.0, 0.6, and 1.4 respectively. During the experiment, we find that there are super-long sentences in the development sets and test sets. Therefore, we segment sentences with more than 150 tokens based on punctuations indicating the end of a sentence before translation.

4.1   Mongolian → Chinese

With regard to the Mongolian→Chinese translation track, we found that a large portion of target-side text in the CCMT 2019 and CCMT 2020 development sets is also found in this year's training set, resulting in model overfitting. In order to fairly and accurately assess the model performance, we use a subset of CCMT 2020 development set. The subset contains only bitexts whose reference are not in the training set. During the training, we adopt enhancement strategies such as Regularized Dropout, Tagged Back-Translation, Alternated Training, and Ensemble. In addition, we train two contrast systems: contrast system b is fine-tuned on CCMT 2019 and CCMT 2020 development sets; while contrast system c is trained with additional bilingual data in the last step of alternated training, and ensembled by multiple models.

Table 2 presents the sacreBLEU [18] results for Mongolian→Chinese translations under different strategies. Using the CCMT 2020 subset for assessment, we found that Regularized Dropout, Tagged Back-Translation, Alternated Training, and Ensemble can all improve model performance. On the contrary, additional bilingual data used in contrast system c does not lead to further improvements. As a result, we fine-tune models on development sets in hope of further improving model performance on CCMT 2022 test set.

Table 2. BLEU scores of Mongolian→Chinese translation

	CCMT 2019	CCMT 2020	CCMT 2020 subset
Baseline	**69.15**	67.96	33.50
+ regularized dropout	68.21	69.88	37.44
+ tagged back-translation	54.56	67.04	45.77
+ alternated training	57.70	69.74	47.01
+ ensemble(primary a)	57.87	70.33	47.63
+ fine-tuning(contract b)	61.99	**72.96**	**52.63**
+ additional bilingual(contract c)	60.76	70.40	47.26

4.2 Tibetan→Chinese

With regard to the Tibetan→Chinese track, we train a baseline model with only bilingual data and use multiple enhancement strategies. We ensemble multiple models to generate the primary system. We also train a contrast system by ensemble models that use additional bilingual data in the last step of alternated training. Table 3 presents the experiment results, demonstrating that Regularized Dropout, Tagged Back-Translation, Alternated Training, and Ensemble all help improve model performance. In addition, adding additional bilingual data during training can lead to further improvement.

Table 3. BLEU scores of Tibetan→Chinese translation

	CCMT 2019	CCMT 2020
Baseline	47.85	61.45
+ regularized dropout	49.35	62.55
+ tagged back-translation	50.38	65.94
+ alternated training	53.56	66.97
+ ensemble(primary a)	54.46	67.96
+ additional bilingual(contract b)	**66.44**	**74.11**

4.3   Uyghur→Chinese

With regard to the Uyghur→Chinese track, we adopt the same training strategy as that in the Tibetan→Chinese track. Table 4 presents the experiment results. The results also demonstrate that all enhancement strategies mentioned, as well as additional bilingual data, can lead to model improvements.

Table 4. BLEU scores of Uyghur→Chinese translation

	CCMT 2019	CCMT 2020
Baseline	44.59	47.36
+ regularized dropout	48.26	51.71
+ tagged back-translation	54.89	59.59
+ alternated training	55.56	60.20
+ ensemble(primary a)	55.66	60.44
+ additional bilingual(contract b)	**59.06**	**64.28**

5   Analysis

5.1   The Effect of Different Back-Translation Methods

Past experience demonstrates that Tagged Back-Translation and Top-K Sampling Back-Translation are effective Back-Translation variants. We conduct comparative experiments on the two methods on the three minority language translation tracks. Experiment results shown in Table 5 indicate that Tagged Back-Translation can achieve better results in low-resource translation scenarios.

Table 5. BLEU scores of two different back-translation methods

	Mongolian→Chinese			Tibetan→Chinese		Uyghur→Chinese	
CCMT devset	2019	2020	2020 subset	2019	2020	2019	2020
Tagged back-translation	54.56	**67.04**	**45.77**	50.38	**65.94**	**54.89**	59.59
Top-k sampling back-translation	**54.63**	66.19	45.52	**51.64**	64.18	53.24	57.34

5.2   The Impact of Sentence Segmentation on the Translation Quality of Machine Translation

During experiments, we found development sets and test sets in all three language pairs contain some super-long sentences with more than 150 tokens. During training, we have filter out sentences more than 150 tokens. We assume that models cannot directly translate those super-long sentences well and do segmentation on those sentences based on punctuations that indicate the end of a sentence. Table 6 presents BLEU results before and after segmentation and demonstrate that segmentation is effective in improving Tibetan→Chinese and Uyghur→Chinese translation tasks. But we see no improvement on Mongolian→Chinese translation.

Table 6. Bleu scores of whether the baseline uses sentence segmentation.

CCMT devset	Mongolian→Chinese			Tibetan→Chinese		Uyghur→Chinese	
	2019	2020	2020 subset	2019	2020	2019	2020
Baseline	69.15	67.96	**33.50**	**47.85**	**61.45**	**44.59**	**47.36**
- sentence segmentation	**69.58**	**68.08**	33.47	45.88	59.91	42.84	45.82

5.3   Analysis of BLEU Scores of Mongolian→Chinese Machine Translation on the Development Set

We find an abnormal phenomenon during Mongolian→Chinese experiment: we see no consistent improvements on CCMT 2019 and CCMT 2020 development sets when using Regularized Dropout and Tagged Back-Translation. So we conduct an analysis on the overlapping between development sets and training set. We found that the majority of Chinese text in CCMT 2019 development set and half of Chinese text in CCMT 2020 development set are also in this year's training data (Table 7). So we construct a sub development set containing only sentences not in the training data, in hope of evaluating the model performance in a more fair way.

Table 7. The number of source sentences, target sentences and sentence pairs in the development set that appear in the training set.

	Source in Training Set	Target in Training Set	Sentence pair in Training Set
CCMT 2019	21	958	20
CCMT 2020	6	584	6

6   Conclusion

This paper presents our submissions to the CCMT 2022 Mongolian→Chinese, Tibetan→Chinese, and Uyghur→Chinese translation tasks. We train our models using the Deep Transformer architecture and employ enhancement strategies such as Regularized Dropout, Tagged Back-Translation, Alternated Training, and Ensemble. We also train contrast models with additional bilingual data. In addition, we conduct experiments on two Back-Translation variants (Tagged Back-Translation and Top-K Sampling Back-Translation), analyze how segmentation influences the translation quality of neural machine translation model, and find a better solution to the abnormal phenomenon on Mongolian→Chinese development sets.

References

1. Sennrich, R., Haddow, B., Birch, A.: Neural machine translation of rare words with subword units. In: Proceedings of the 54th Annual Meeting of the Association for Computational Linguistics (Volume 1: Long Papers), pp. 1715–1725 (2016)
2. Vaswani, A., Shazeer, N., Parmar, N., et al.: Attention is all you need. In: Advances in Neural Information Processing Systems, vol. 30 (2017)
3. Wang, Q., Li, B., Xiao, T., et al.: Learning deep transformer models for machine translation. In: Proceedings of the 57th Annual Meeting of the Association for Computational Linguistics, pp. 1810–1822 (2019)
4. Hinton, G.E., NitishSrivastava, A.K., Salakhutdinov, I.S.R.R.: Improving neural networks by preventing co-adaptation of feature detectors
5. Wu, L., Li, J., Wang, Y., et al.: R-drop: regularized dropout for neural networks. In: Advances in Neural Information Processing Systems (2021)
6. Burlot, F., Yvon, F.: Using monolingual data in neural machine translation: a systematic study. In: Proceedings of the Third Conference on Machine Translation: Research Papers, 144–155 (2018)
7. Edunov, S., Ott, M., Auli, M., et al.: Understanding back-translation at scale. Proc. Conf. Empirical Meth. Nat. Lang. Process. **2018**, 489–500 (2018)
8. Graça, M., Kim, Y., Schamper, J., et al.: Generalizing Back-Translation in Neural Machine Translation. In: Proceedings of the Fourth Conference on Machine Translation (Volume 1: Research Papers), pp. 45–52 (2019)
9. Caswell, I., Chelba, C., Grangier, D.: Tagged Back-Translation. In: Proceedings of the Fourth Conference on Machine Translation (Volume 1: Research Papers), pp. 53–63 (2019)
10. Abdulmumin, I., Galadanci, B.S., Isa, A.: Enhanced back-translation for low resource neural machine translation using self-training. In: ICTA 2020. CCIS, vol. 1350, pp. 355–371. Springer, Cham (2021). https://doi.org/10.1007/978-3-030-69143-1_28
11. Jiao, R., Yang, Z., Sun, M., et al.: Alternated training with synthetic and authentic data for neural machine translation. In: Findings of the Association for Computational Linguistics: ACL-IJCNLP 2021, pp. 1828–1834 (2021)
12. Garmash, E., Monz, C.: Ensemble learning for multi-source neural machine translation. In: Proceedings of COLING 2016, the 26th International Conference on Computational Linguistics: Technical Papers, pp. 1409–1418 (2016)
13. Yang, H., Wu, Z., Yu, Z., et al.: HW-TSC's submissions to the WMT21 biomedical translation task. In: Proceedings of the Sixth Conference on Machine Translation, pp. 879–884 (2021)
14. Ott, M., Edunov, S., Baevski, A., et al.: fairseq: a fast, extensible toolkit for sequence modeling. Proc. Conf. North Am. Chapter Assoc. Comput. Linguist. (Demonstrations) **2019**, 48–53 (2019)

15. Szegedy, C., Vanhoucke, V., Ioffe, S., et al.: Rethinking the inception architecture for computer vision. In: 2016 IEEE Conference on Computer Vision and Pattern Recognition, pp. 2818–2826. IEEE (2016)
16. Kingma, D.P, Ba, J.L.: Adam: a method for stochastic optimization (2015)
17. Junczys-Dowmunt, M., Grundkiewicz, R., Dwojak, T., et al.: Marian: fast neural machine translation in c++. In: ACL 2018–56th Annual Meeting of the Association for Computational Linguistics, Proceedings of System Demonstrations (2015)
18. Post, M.A.: Call for clarity in reporting BLEU scores. In: Proceedings of the Third Conference on Machine Translation: Research Papers, pp. 186–191 (2018)

Target-Side Language Model
for Reference-Free Machine Translation
Evaluation

Min Zhang[✉], Xiaosong Qiao, Hao Yang, Shimin Tao, Yanqing Zhao,
Yinlu Li, Chang Su, Minghan Wang, Jiaxin Guo, Yilun Liu, and Ying Qin

Huawei Translation Services Center, Beijing, China
{zhangmin186,qiaoxiaosong,yanghao30,taoshimin,zhaoyanqing,liyinglu,
suchang8,wangminghan,guojiaxin1,liuyilun3,qinying}@huawei.com

Abstract. With the rapid progress of deep learning in multilingual language processing, there has been a growing interest in reference-free machine translation evaluation, where source texts are directly compared with system translations. In this paper, we design a reference-free metric that is based only on a target-side language model for segment-level and system-level machine translation evaluations respectively, and it is found out that promising results could be achieved when only the target-side language model is used in such evaluations. From the experimental results on all the 18 language pairs of the WMT19 news translation shared task, it is interesting to see that the designed metrics with the multilingual model XLM-R get very promising results (best segment-level mean score on the from-English language pairs, and best system-level mean scores on the from-English and none-English language pairs) when the current SOTA metrics that we know are chosen for comparison.

Keywords: Target-side language model · Machine translation evaluation · Reference-free metric

1 Introduction

Traditional automatic metrics for machine translation (MT) score MT output by comparing it with one or more reference translations. Common such metrics include the word-based metrics BLEU [1] and METEOR [2], and the word embedding-based metrics BERTScore [3] and BLEURT [4]. However, reference sentences could only cover a tiny fraction of input source sentences, and non-professional translators can not yield high-quality reference translations [5].

These problems can be avoided through *reference-free* MT evaluation, meaning that only source texts are used in MT output evaluation and they are directly compared with system translations. Recently, with the rapid progress of deep learning in multilingual language processing [6,7], a lot of reference-free metrics have been proposed for such evaluation. Popović et al. [8] exploited a bag-of-word translation model for quality estimation, which sums over the likelihoods

© The Author(s), under exclusive license to Springer Nature Singapore Pte Ltd. 2022
T. Xiao and J. Pino (Eds.): CCMT 2022, CCIS 1671, pp. 45–53, 2022.
https://doi.org/10.1007/978-981-19-7960-6_5

of aligned word pairs between source and translation texts. Specia et al. [9] used language-agnostic linguistic features extracted from source texts and system translations to estimate quality. YiSi-2 [10] evaluates system translations by summing similarity scores over words pairs which are best-aligned mutual translations. Moreover, by introducing cross-lingual linear projection, Lo and Larkin [11] greatly improved the effect of YiSi-2. Prism-src [12] frames the task of MT evaluation as one of scoring machine translation output with a sequence-to-sequence paraphraser, conditioned on source text. COMET-QE [13,14] encodes segment-level representations of source text and translation text as the input to a feed forward regressor. Gekhman et al. [15] proposed a simple and effective Knowledge-Based Evaluation (KoBE) method by measuring the recall of entities found in source texts and system translations. To mitigate the misalignment of cross-lingual word embedding spaces, Zhao et al. [16] proposed post-hoc re-alignment strategies which integrate a target-side GPT [17] language model. Song et al. [18] proposed an unsupervised metric SentSim by incorporating a notion of sentence semantic similarity.

In this paper, we find out that assessing system translation only with a target-side language model could achieve very promising results. With a modified sentence perplexity calculation for system translations, we design a reference-free metric for segment-level and system-level MT evaluations respectively. And then we test the performances of the two metrics on all the 18 language pairs of WMT19 news translation shared task [19]. The experimental results demonstrate that our metrics with the pretrained model XLM-R [7] are very competitive for reference-free MT evaluations when compared with the current SOTA reference-free metrics that we know.

2   Target-Side Language Model Metrics

A statistical language model is a probability distribution over sequences of words [20]. Given such a sequence with m words, i.e., $s = (w_1, \ldots, w_m)$, it assigns a probability $P(s)$ to the whole sequence, which is defined as:

$$P(s) = P(w_1, \ldots, w_m) = \prod_{i=1}^{m} P(w_i | w_1, \ldots, w_{i-1}). \tag{1}$$

In order to overcome the data sparsity problem in building a statistical language model, a common solution is to assume that the probability of a word only depends on the previous n words. This is known as the n-gram model or unigram model when $n = 1$. So the probability $P(s)$ could be approximated as:

$$P(s) = \prod_{i=1}^{m} P(w_i | w_1, \ldots, w_{i-1}) \approx \prod_{i=1}^{m} P(w_i | w_{i-(n-1)}, \ldots, w_{i-1}). \tag{2}$$

With the advancements in deep learning [21], various neural language models are proposed to use continuous representations or embeddings of words to make their predictions [6,22]. Typically, a neural language model is constructed and trained as probabilistic classifiers for

$$P(w \mid context), \; for \; w \in V. \tag{3}$$

That is to say, the model is trained to predict a probability distribution over the vocabulary V, when some linguistic *context* is given.

In this paper, we adopt the masked language model [6] to design a reference-free metric for segment-level and system-level MT evaluations respectively.

For segment-level evaluation where a single system translation sentence s is provided, the metric SEG_LM is defined as:

$$SEG\_LM(s) = \frac{1}{m} \sum_{i=1}^{m} \log \frac{1}{P(w_i | s - w_i)}, \tag{4}$$

where m is the number of words in sentence s, w_i is the i-th word in s, and $P(w_i | s - w_i)$ the probability of w_i predicted by the masked language model when w_i is replaced by [MASK] in s.

It should be pointed out that the metric SEG_LM is slightly different from the log form of the sentence perplexity [20] (PPL), which is defined as:

$$\log PPL(s) = \log \sqrt[m]{\frac{1}{P(w_1, \ldots, w_m)}} = \frac{1}{m} \sum_{i=1}^{m} \log \frac{1}{P(w_i | w_1, \ldots, w_{i-1})}. \tag{5}$$

From the above definitions, it could be seen that the context for predicting the probability of w_i in PPL is different from SEG_LM.

For system-level evaluation where a set of system translation sentences S is given, the metric SYS_LM is defined as:

$$SYS\_LM(S) = \frac{1}{|S|} \sum_{s \in S} SEG\_LM(s), \tag{6}$$

which is the mean value of SEG_LM scores on each sentence in S.

Although source texts are not considered in our designed metrics, the experimental results on WMT19 in Sect. 3 will show that the metrics SEG_LM and SYS_LM are very promising for both segment-level and system-level reference-free MT evaluations.

3   Experiments

In this section, we evaluate the performance of our metrics SEG_LM and SYS_LM by correlating their scores with human judgments of translation quality for reference-free MT evaluations. The pretrained multilingual model XLM-R[1] is used as the masked language model for our metrics.

---

[1] https://huggingface.co/xlm-roberta-base.

Table 1. Segment-level metric results for the into-English language pairs of WMT19

Metrics	de-en	fi-en	gu-en	kk-en	lt-en	ru-en	zh-en	Avg
sentBLEU	0.056	0.233	0.188	0.377	0.262	0.125	0.323	0.223
LASIM	−0.024	–	–	–	–	0.022	–	–
LP	−0.096	–	–	–	–	−0.035	–	–
UNI	0.022	0.202	–	–	–	0.084	–	–
UNI+	0.015	0.211	–	–	–	0.089	–	–
YiSi-2	0.068	0.126	−0.001	0.096	0.075	0.053	0.253	0.096
YiSi-2+CLP	**0.116**	**0.271**	**0.249**	**0.370**	**0.281**	**0.121**	**0.340**	**0.250**
SEG_LM	0.115	0.265	0.214	0.135	0.280	0.120	0.183	0.187

Table 2. Segment-level metric results for the from-English language pairs of WMT19

Metrics	en-cs	en-de	en-fi	en-gu	en-kk	en-lt	en-ru	en-zh	Avg
sentBLEU	0.367	0.248	0.396	0.465	0.392	0.334	0.469	0.270	0.368
LASIM	–	0.147	–	–	–	–	−0.240	–	–
LP	–	−0.119	–	–	–	–	−0.158	–	–
UNI	0.060	0.129	0.351	–	–	–	0.226	–	–
UNI+	–	–	–	–	–	–	0.222	–	–
YiSi-2	0.069	0.212	0.239	0.147	0.187	0.003	−0.155	0.044	0.093
YiSi-2+CLP	0.299	0.329	0.459	**0.512**	**0.459**	0.314	0.078	0.158	0.326
SEG_LM	**0.443**	**0.343**	**0.492**	0.328	0.301	**0.471**	**0.457**	**0.297**	**0.392**

Table 3. Segment-level metric results for the none-English language pairs of WMT19

Metrics	de-cs	de-fr	fr-de	Avg
sentBLEU	0.203	0.235	0.179	0.206
YiSi-2	0.199	0.186	0.066	0.150
YiSi-2+CLP	**0.355**	**0.294**	**0.226**	**0.292**
SEG_LM	0.263	0.244	0.198	0.235

3.1 Datasets and Baselines

The source language sentences, and their system and reference translations are collected from the WMT19 news translation shared task [19], which contains predictions of 233 translation systems across 18 language pairs. Each language pair has about 3,000 source sentences, and each is associated with one reference translation and with the automatic translations generated by the participating systems. In this paper, all the 18 language pairs in WMT19 are chosen for reference-free MT evaluation.

A range of reference-free metrics are chosen to compare with our metrics: LASIM and LP [23], UNI and UNI+ [19], YiSi-2 [10] and YiSi-2+CLP [11], KoBE [15] and CLP-UMD [16]. To the best of our knowledge, the above metrics could cover most of the current SOTA metrics for reference-free MT evaluation. Reference-based baseline metrics BLEU and sentBLEU [24] are selected as references. It should be pointed out that only the results of our metrics SEG_LM and SYS_LM are calculated in this paper, and the results of the other metrics are from their respective papers.

3.2   Results

Evaluation Measures. Kendall's Tau and Pearson correlations [19] are used as measures for segment-level and system-level metric evaluations respectively.

Table 4. System-level metric results for the into-English language pairs of WMT19

Metrics	de-en	fi-en	gu-en	kk-en	lt-en	ru-en	zh-en	Avg
BLEU	0.849	0.982	0.834	0.946	0.961	0.879	0.899	0.907
LASIM	0.247	–	–	–	–	0.310	–	–
LP	0.474	–	–	–	–	0.488	–	–
UNI	0.846	0.930	–	–	–	0.805	–	–
UNI+	0.850	0.924	–	–	–	0.808	–	–
YiSi-2	0.796	0.642	0.566	0.324	0.442	0.339	0.940	0.578
YiSi-2+CLP	**0.898**	**0.959**	0.739	0.981	**0.935**	0.461	**0.980**	**0.850**
KoBE	0.863	0.538	**0.828**	0.899	0.704	**0.928**	0.907	0.810
CLP-UMD	0.625	0.890	−0.060	**0.993**	0.851	**0.928**	0.968	0.742
SYS_LM	0.856	0.932	0.748	0.696	0.932	0.869	0.480	0.788

Segment-level Results. Tables 1, 2 and 3 show the comparison results of the metrics for reference-free segment-level evaluations on the into-English, from-English and none-English language pairs of WMT19 respectively (Best results excluding sentBLEU are in bold).

From Table 1, it could be seen that the scores of our metric SEG_LM on the de-en, lt-en and ru-en language pairs are very close to the best values (only 0.001 gap). And as shown in Table 2, our metric not only gets the best mean score on the from-English language pairs, but also ranks first on 6 of all the 8 language pairs. The results in Table 3 show that our metric even gets better scores on all the none-English language pairs than the reference-based metric sentBLEU. Therefore, our metric SEG_LM is very promising for segment-level MT evaluation especially when the target-side language is not English.

Table 5. System-level metric results for the from-English language pairs of WMT19

Metrics	en-cs	en-de	en-fi	en-gu	en-kk	en-lt	en-ru	en-zh	Avg
BLEU	0.897	0.921	0.969	0.737	0.852	0.989	0.986	0.901	0.907
LASIM	–	0.871	–	–	–	–	0.823	–	–
LP	–	0.569	–	–	–	–.	−0.661	–	–
UNI	0.028	0.841	0.907	–	–	–	**0.919**	–	–
UNI+	–	–	–	–	–	–	0.918	–	–
YiSi-2	0.324	0.924	0.696	0.314	0.339	0.055	0.766	0.097	0.439
YiSi-2+CLP	0.773	0.963	0.906	**0.890**	**0.977**	0.761	0.473	0.449	0.774
KoBE	0.597	0.888	0.521	-0.340	0.827	−0.049	0.895	0.216	0.444
SYS_LM	**0.896**	**0.978**	**0.941**	0.683	0.897	**0.919**	0.819	**0.959**	**0.886**

Table 6. System-level metric results for the none-English language pairs of WMT19

Metrics	de-cs	de-fr	fr-de	Avg
BLEU	0.941	0.891	0.864	0.899
YiSi-2	0.606	0.721	0.530	0.619
YiSi-2+CLP	0.860	0.853	0.461	0.725
KoBE	**0.958**	0.485	−0.785	0.219
SYS_LM	0.885	**0.902**	**0.778**	**0.855**

System-level Results. Tables 4, 5 and 6 illustrate the comparison results of the metrics for reference-free system-level evaluations on the into-English, from-English and none-English language pairs of WMT19 respectively (Best results excluding BLEU are in bold).

As shown in the into-English results of Table 4, our metric SYS_LM again gets scores very close to the best values on the fi-en and lt-en language pairs. The results in Table 5 demonstrate that our metric gets the best mean score and 5 best scores on all the 8 from-English language pairs. Meanwhile, the results in Table 6 show that SYS_LM gets better scores than the SOTA metric YiSi-2+CLP on the system-level evaluations, although it does not outperform YiSi-2+CLP on the segment-level evaluations, as shown in Table 3. In addition, SYS_LM gets the best mean score on the none-English language pairs. Overall, the experimental results demonstrate that our metric SYS_LM is very competitive for system-level MT evaluations when the current SOTA metrics that we know are involved for comparison.

3.3   Discussion

In this section, an explanation for why target-side language model works is provided. For segment-level evaluation where the input is a source sentence s and a system translation sentence t, we design metrics to estimate the true probability $P(t|s)$. According to the conditional probability formula, we could have:

$$\log P(t|s) = \log \frac{P(s|t)P(t)}{P(s)} = \log P(s|t) + \log P(t) - \log P(s). \qquad (7)$$

The target-side language model is mainly to approximate the second term $\log P(t)$, and when there are no much differences in the first term $\log P(s|t)$, our target-side language model metric works for MT evaluation.

4 Conclusion

In this paper, a reference-free metric designed only with a target-side language model is proposed for segment-level and system-level MT evaluations respectively. With the pretrained multilingual model XLM-R as the target-side language model, the performances of our metrics SEG_LM and SYS_LM are evaluated on all the 18 language pairs of WMT19. The experimental results show that our metrics are very competitive (best mean score of segment-level evaluations on the from-English language pairs, and best mean scores of system-level evaluations on the from-English and none-English language pairs) when most of the current SOTA reference-free metrics are chosen for comparison. Furthermore, the reason why the target-side language model works is discussed. The fusion of our metrics and other metrics that are for the first term $\log P(s|t)$ in Eq. 7 will be our future work.

References

1. Papineni, K., Roukos, S., Ward, T., Zhu, W.J.: Bleu: a method for automatic evaluation of machine translation. In: Proceedings of the 40th Annual Meeting of the Association for Computational Linguistics, pp. 311–318. Association for Computational Linguistics, Philadelphia, Pennsylvania, USA (2002)
2. Lavie, A., Agarwal, A.: METEOR: an automatic metric for MT evaluation with high levels of correlation with human judgments. In: Proceedings of the Second Workshop on Statistical Machine Translation, pp. 228–231. Association for Computational Linguistics, Prague, Czech Republic (2007)
3. Zhang, T., Kishore, V., Wu, F., Weinberger, K.Q., Artzi, Y.: Bertscore: evaluating text generation with BERT. In: 8th International Conference on Learning Representations, ICLR 2020, Addis Ababa, Ethiopia, 26–30 April 2020. OpenReview.net (2020)
4. Sellam, T., Das, D., Parikh, A.: BLEURT: learning robust metrics for text generation. In: Proceedings of the 58th Annual Meeting of the Association for Computational Linguistics, pp. 7881–7892. Association for Computational Linguistics, Online (2020)
5. Zaidan, O.F., Callison-Burch, C.: Crowdsourcing translation: Professional quality from non-professionals. In: Proceedings of the 49th Annual Meeting of the Association for Computational Linguistics: Human Language Technologies, pp. 1220–1229. Association for Computational Linguistics, Portland, Oregon, USA (2011)

6. Devlin, J., Chang, M.W., Lee, K., Toutanova, K.: BERT: pre-training of deep bidirectional transformers for language understanding. In: Proceedings of the 2019 Conference of the North American Chapter of the Association for Computational Linguistics: Human Language Technologies, Vol. 1 (Long and Short Papers), pp. 4171–4186. Association for Computational Linguistics, Minneapolis, Minnesota (2019)

7. Conneau, A., et al.: Unsupervised cross-lingual representation learning at scale. In: Jurafsky, D., Chai, J., Schluter, N., Tetreault, J.R. (eds.) Proceedings of the 58th Annual Meeting of the Association for Computational Linguistics, ACL 2020, Online, pp. 8440–8451, 5–10 July 2020. Association for Computational Linguistics (2020)

8. Popović, M., Vilar, D., Avramidis, E., Burchardt, A.: Evaluation without references: IBM1 scores as evaluation metrics. In: Proceedings of the Sixth Workshop on Statistical Machine Translation, pp. 99–103. Association for Computational Linguistics, Edinburgh, Scotland (2011)

9. Specia, L., Shah, K., de Souza, J.G., Cohn, T.: QuEst - a translation quality estimation framework. In: Proceedings of the 51st Annual Meeting of the Association for Computational Linguistics: System Demonstrations, pp. 79–84. Association for Computational Linguistics, Sofia, Bulgaria (2013)

10. Lo, C.K.: YiSi - a unified semantic MT quality evaluation and estimation metric for languages with different levels of available resources. In: Proceedings of the Fourth Conference on Machine Translation (Volume 2: Shared Task Papers, Day 1), pp. 507–513. Association for Computational Linguistics, Florence, Italy (2019)

11. Lo, C.K., Larkin, S.: Machine translation reference-less evaluation using YiSi-2 with bilingual mappings of massive multilingual language model. In: Proceedings of the Fifth Conference on Machine Translation, pp. 903–910. Association for Computational Linguistics, Online (2020)

12. Thompson, B., Post, M.: Automatic machine translation evaluation in many languages via zero-shot paraphrasing. In: Proceedings of the 2020 Conference on Empirical Methods in Natural Language Processing (EMNLP), pp. 90–121. Association for Computational Linguistics, Online (2020)

13. Rei, R., et al.: Are references really needed? unbabel-IST 2021 submission for the metrics shared task. In: Proceedings of the Sixth Conference on Machine Translation, pp. 1030–1040 (2021)

14. Rei, R., Stewart, C., Farinha, A.C., Lavie, A.: COMET: a neural framework for MT evaluation. In: Proceedings of the 2020 Conference on Empirical Methods in Natural Language Processing (EMNLP), pp. 2685–2702 (2020)

15. Gekhman, Z., Aharoni, R., Beryozkin, G., Freitag, M., Macherey, W.: KoBE: knowledge-based machine translation evaluation. In: Findings of the Association for Computational Linguistics: EMNLP 2020, pp. 3200–3207. Association for Computational Linguistics (2020)

16. Zhao, W., Glavaš, G., Peyrard, M., Gao, Y., West, R., Eger, S.: On the limitations of cross-lingual encoders as exposed by reference-free machine translation evaluation. In: Proceedings of the 58th Annual Meeting of the Association for Computational Linguistics, pp. 1656–1671. Association for Computational Linguistics (2020)

17. Radford, A., Narasimhan, K., Salimans, T., Sutskever, I.: Improving language understanding by generative pre-training (2018)

18. Song, Y., Zhao, J., Specia, L.: SentSim: crosslingual semantic evaluation of machine translation. In: Proceedings of the 2021 Conference of the North American Chapter

of the Association for Computational Linguistics: Human Language Technologies, pp. 3143–3156. Association for Computational Linguistics (2021)

19. Ma, Q., Wei, J., Bojar, O., Graham, Y.: Results of the WMT19 metrics shared task: segment-level and strong MT systems pose big challenges. In: Proceedings of the Fourth Conference on Machine Translation (Volume 2: Shared Task Papers, Day 1), pp. 62–90. Association for Computational Linguistics, Florence, Italy (2019)

20. Rosenfeld, R.: Two decades of statistical language modeling: where do we go from here. In: Proceedings of the IEEE, vol. 88, pp. 1270–1278 (2000)

21. Hinton, G.E., Salakhutdinov, R.R.: Reducing the dimensionality of data with neural networks. Science **313**(5786), 504–507 (2006)

22. Mikolov, T., Chen, K., Corrado, G., Dean, J.: Efficient estimation of word representations in vector space. CoRR abs/1301.3781 (2013)

23. Yankovskaya, E., Tättar, A., Fishel, M.: Quality estimation and translation metrics via pre-trained word and sentence embeddings. In: Proceedings of the Fourth Conference on Machine Translation (Volume 3: Shared Task Papers, Day 2), pp. 101–105. Association for Computational Linguistics, Florence, Italy (2019)

24. Koehn, P., et al.: Moses: open source toolkit for statistical machine translation. In: Proceedings of the 45th Annual Meeting of the Association for Computational Linguistics Companion Volume Proceedings of the Demo and Poster Sessions, pp. 177–180. Association for Computational Linguistics, Prague, Czech Republic (2007)

Life Is Short, Train It Less: Neural Machine Tibetan-Chinese Translation Based on mRASP and Dataset Enhancement

Hao Wang[1], Yongbin Yu[1(⊠)], Nyima Tashi[2(⊠)], Rinchen Dongrub[2], Ekong Favour[1], Mengwei Ai[1], Kalzang Gyatso[2], Yong Cuo[2], and Qun Nuo[2]

[1] University of Electronic Science and Technology of China, Chengdu 610000, China
`ybyu@uestc.edu.cn`
[2] Engineering Research Center for Tibetan Information Processing, School of Information Science and Technology, Tibet University, Lhasa 850000, China
`nmzx@utibet.edu.cn`

Abstract. This paper highlights a multilingual pre-trained neural machine translation architecture as well as a dataset augmentation approach based on curvature selection. The multilingual pre-trained model is designed to increase the performance of machine translation with low resources by bringing in more common information. Instead of repeatedly training several checkpoints from scratch, this study proposes a checkpoint selection strategy that uses a cleaned optimizer to hijack a midway status. Experiments with our own dataset on the Chinese-Tibetan translation demonstrate that our architecture gets a 32.65 BLEU score, while in the reverse direction, it obtains a 39.51 BLEU score. This strategy drastically reduces the amount of time spent training. To demonstrate the validity of our method, this paper shows a visualization of curvature for a real-world training scenario.

Keywords: Neural machine translation · Dataset enhancement · Chinese-Tibetan translation · Curvature

1 Introduction

Many fields, such as education, publishing, and information security, have a strong demand for Chinese-Tibetan translation algorithms. During the last few years, neural machine translation (NMT) tasks have had a great deal of success thanks to the transformer architecture [11]. However, one of the key drawbacks of this approach is that transformer is greedy in terms of both quality and quantity of data. This study set out with the aim of investigating a training method including cross-language transferable pre-trained models and dataset

---

The demo of this paper is available at http://mt.utibet.edu.cn.

© The Author(s), under exclusive license to Springer Nature Singapore Pte Ltd. 2022
T. Xiao and J. Pino (Eds.): CCMT 2022, CCIS 1671, pp. 54–59, 2022.
https://doi.org/10.1007/978-981-19-7960-6_6

enhancement algorithm to achieve better results in low-resource Chinese-Tibetan translation tasks.

Many studies focus on cross-language unified models, which may increase translation quality in low-resource languages, on the assumption that a cross-language unified model will acquire common knowledge between languages to boost performance on unseen data [2,3]. Johnson et al. add an artificial token at the beginning of the sentence to set the required language [4]. Zhang et al. suggest that the off-target translation issue is the main reason for unexpected zero-shot performance. [12] Xiao et al. involve contrastive learning in their mRASP framework which achieve good results on other language pair yet misses the Tibetan language dataset [7].

The use of dataset enhancement as a solution to the data hungriness problem is another alternative. One of the merits of such methods is that most of them proceed in parallel with model architecture, saving time on model modifications. Aside from data augmentation, the back translation method [1,8] is a simple yet effective way to generate synthetic data to improve efficiency. Although this methodology is highly effective, it involved the use of additional monolingual data. Nguyen et al. [5] propose an interesting method that generates a diverse set of synthetic data to augment original data. This method is powerful and effective yet still required training multiple loops.

2 Prerequisite

2.1 Neural Machine Translation with mRASP

mRASP uses a standard Transformer with both 6 layers encoder and decoder pre-trained jointly on 32 language pairs. In this paper, we use the pre-trained mRASP model to finetune our Chinese-Tibetan translation model. Following the symbols in mRASP, we denote the Chinese-Tibetan parallel dataset as (L_{src}, l_{tgt}), the finetuned loss is

$$\mathcal{L}^{finetune} = \mathbb{E}_{(\mathbf{x}^i, \mathbf{x}^j) \sim \mathcal{D}_{src,tgt}} \left[-\log P_\theta \left(\mathbf{x}^i \mid \mathbf{x}^j \right) \right]. \tag{1}$$

where the θ is the pretrained mRASP model.

2.2 Diversification Method

Data diversification is a simple yet effective data augmentation method. It trains predictions from multiple bi-direction models to diversify training data which is ideal for the low-source Chinese-Tibetan translation task. This strategy is formulated as:

$$\mathcal{D} = (S, T) \bigcup \cup_{i=1}^k \left(S, M_{S \to T,1}^i(S) \right) \bigcup \cup_{i=1}^k \left(M_{T \to S,1}^i(T), T \right) \tag{2}$$

M denotes the model and k is the diversification factor. In this paper, we propose an accelerating hijack method to reduce this training burden significantly.

2.3   Curvature

In this work, we choose the curvature as the metric of the sharpness of the perplexity curve for the validation dataset in the whole training process. Denote K as the curvature, for a continuous curve it can be calculated as:

$$K = \frac{1}{r} = \frac{|f''(x_0)|}{\left(1 + (f'(x_0))^2\right)^{\frac{3}{2}}} \tag{3}$$

However, the valid perplexity averaged within an epoch is discrete and the direct finite difference may bring relatively large error. In this work, we use the curvature of the quadratic curve determined by the nearest three points to estimate the curvature of a valid perplexity curve [13].

3   Methodology

3.1   Overall Structure

In this work, mRASP pretrained on 32 language pairs is utilized to provide a good starting point than plain Transformer. The vocabulary for our 115k dataset is merged into the provided vocabulary of mRASP. Then the private Tibetan-Chinese parallel dataset is utilized to generate an enhanced dataset. As shown in Fig. 1, the whole fine-tune stage is divided into three parts based on the valid perplexity averaged on each epoch. We hijack the checkpoint from the key points and then continue training using a cleaned optimizer to generate k more checkpoints. Along with the main checkpoint, the enhanced dataset is generated to train the final model.

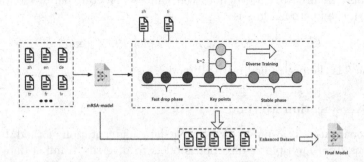

Fig. 1. The overall architecture of this work. The proposed work can be divided into three stages. (1) In the pre-trained stage, the multi-lingual pre-trained mRASP model is prepared for further finetune. (2) In the dataset enhancement stage, $m + 1$ checkpoints are trained and inference to generate an enhanced dataset. (3) The final translation model is finetuned based on mRASP at the enhanced dataset.

3.2 Curvature Based Checkpoint Hijack

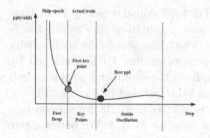 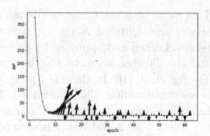

Fig. 2. The curvature change for an ideal training process. The green point denotes the first key point which is used to re-train. The red point denotes the best perplexity which is an ideal end-point. (Color figure online)

Fig. 3. Actual ppl change during training. The very first epoch is deleted for better visualization without changing the shape of the curve. The curvature is visualized as black arrows.

In this paper, we argue that it is not necessary to train the entire procedure for a large pre-trained model like mRASP. Figure 2 illustrates the perplexity of the valid set will go under three stages. In the fast drop stages, the perplexity will sharply drop to fit the new dataset. Then in the key points stage, the perplexity will gradually get smooth to the minimal value. The final stage is the stable oscillation stage where the perplexity will not change fast. Instead of training from scratch, the curvature is involved to quantify the key points. To ensure the model status is as far as possible from the best point, a few checkpoints before the first key checkpoint are averaged along with the key checkpoint to ensure maximum diversity (Fig. 3).

Formally, denote the training epoch as N. The calculated curvature for valid set is denoted as a sequence $\mathscr{A} := \{k_1, k_2, \ldots k_i, \ldots k_N\}, k_j \in \mathbb{R}$ where i denotes the very first key point. By setting the threshold for curvature as hyperparameter T, the key points can be formulated as:

$$\mathscr{S} := \{k \in \mathscr{A} \mid k_i \geq k_j, k_i \geq T, \forall i, j \in \mathbb{R}, i < j\}. \tag{4}$$

The generated parallel dataset is:

$$\mathcal{D} = (S, T) \bigcup \cup_{i=1}^{k} \left(S, \frac{1}{m} \sum_{i-m}^{i} M_{S \to T, i}^{i}(S) \right) \bigcup \cup_{i=1}^{k} \left(\frac{1}{m} \sum_{i-m}^{i} M_{T \to S, i}^{i}(T), T \right) \tag{5}$$

where m is the total averaged checkpoints numbers and i is the smallest index in $\mathscr{S}$.

4   Experiments

4.1   Dataset Description and Finetune Parameters

This paper uses the Chinese-Tibetan parallel dataset constructed by Tibet University and Qinghai Normal University. It contains high-quality parallel sentences checked and approved by professionals. The Chinese segment tool is Jieba and the Tibetan segment tool is based on perceptron and CRF developed by Tsering et al. [10] In the fine-tuning process, both the input and output length is restricted to 300. The optimizer is Adam and the learning rate is set to 1e−4. Label smoothing is set to 0.1 and mixed precision is used. The diversion factor k is set to 2 and the average checkpoint number m is 3. We perform our experiments in RTX 3090 and A5000 with fairseq [6].

4.2   Experiment Result

Table 1. BLEU score reported on test set

Task	Direction	BLEU	Epoch
Base [9]	zh-ti	30.46	X
	ti-zh	X	X
Train-scratch	zh-ti	27.17	90
	ti-zh	37.34	90
mRASP-finetuned	zh-ti	32.65	90
	ti-zh	39.51	90
Hijack-enhanced (our)	zh-ti	33.04	90(47)
	ti-zh	39.87	90(47)

Table 1 shows the BLEU score on the test set. Compared to baseline, the mRASP-based pre-trained model indeed performs better. For the training epochs, 90(47) means that we first train an entire loop and then use the best ppl as a stopping point so the next m training will stop at it. The hijack-enhanced dataset brings slightly better benefits than mRASP. However, it is worth mentioning that it only takes dozens of extra epochs to fine-tune, which is faster than the original diversity approach.

5   Conclusion

In this paper, a neural machine translation architecture is proposed for Chinese-Tibetan translation. The involvement of curvature selection reduces the training time significantly. The experiments demonstrate that a multilingual pre-trained model can boost low resources language translation performance. More discussion of curvature in neural networks is desirable for future work.

Acknowledgement. This paper is supported by the Chinese Tibetan English neural machine translation system, the artificial intelligence industry innovation task of the Ministry of industry and information technology with the open competition mechanism to select the best candidates to undertake key research projects. The authors thank you for the guidance of the reviewers!

References

1. Edunov, S., Ott, M., Ranzato, M., Auli, M.: On the evaluation of machine translation systems trained with back-translation. arXiv preprint arXiv:1908.05204 (2019)
2. Gu, J., Wang, Y., Cho, K., Li, V.O.: Improved zero-shot neural machine translation via ignoring spurious correlations. In: Proceedings of the 57th Annual Meeting of the Association for Computational Linguistics, pp. 1258–1268. Association for Computational Linguistics, Florence (2019)
3. Ji, B., Zhang, Z., Duan, X., Zhang, M., Chen, B., Luo, W.: Cross-lingual pre-training based transfer for zero-shot neural machine translation. In: Proceedings of the AAAI Conference on Artificial Intelligence, vol. 34, pp. 115–122 (2020)
4. Johnson, M., et al.: Google's multilingual neural machine translation system: enabling zero-shot translation. Trans. Assoc. Comput. Linguist. **5**, 339–351 (2017)
5. Nguyen, X.P., Joty, S., Kui, W., Aw, A.T.: Data diversification: a simple strategy for neural machine translation. In: Advances in Neural Information Processing Systems, vol. 32. Curran Associates, Inc. (2020)
6. Ott, M., et al.: Fairseq: a fast, extensible toolkit for sequence modeling. In: Proceedings of NAACL-HLT 2019: Demonstrations (2019)
7. Pan, X., Wang, M., Wu, L., Li, L.: Contrastive learning for many-to-many multilingual neural machine translation. arXiv preprint arXiv:2105.09501 (2021)
8. Sennrich, R., Haddow, B., Birch, A.: Improving neural machine translation models with monolingual data. arXiv preprint arXiv:1511.06709 (2015)
9. Cairang, T., Dongzhu, R., Zhaxi, N., Yongbin, Y., Quanxin, D.: Research on Chinese-Tibetan machine translation model based on improved byte pair encoding. J. Univ. Electron. Sci. Technol. **50**(02), 249–255+293 (2021)
10. Tsering, T., Dhondub, R., Tashi, N.: Research on Tibetan location name recognition technology under CRF. Comput. Eng. Appl. **55**(18), 111 (2019)
11. Vaswani, A., et al.: Attention is all you need. In: Advances in neural information processing systems, vol. 30 (2017)
12. Zhang, B., Williams, P., Titov, I., Sennrich, R.: Improving massively multilingual neural machine translation and zero-shot translation. In: Proceedings of the 58th Annual Meeting of the Association for Computational Linguistics, pp. 1628–1639. Association for Computational Linguistics (2020)
13. Zhang, P., Wang, C.B., Ye, L.: A type iii radio burst automatic analysis system and statistic results for a half solar cycle with nançay decameter array data. Astron. Astrophys. **618**, A165 (2018)

Improving the Robustness of Low-Resource Neural Machine Translation with Adversarial Examples

Shuo Sun, Hongxu Hou[(✉)], Nier Wu, Zongheng Yang, Yisong Wang, Pengcong Wang, and Weichen Jian

Inner Mongolia Key Laboratory of Mongolian Information Processing Technology, National & Local Joint Engineering Research Center of Intelligent Information Processing Technology for Mongolian, College of Computer Science, Inner Mongolia University, Hohhot, China
cshhx@imu.edu.cn

Abstract. Weak robustness and noise adaptability are major issues for Low-Resource Neural Machine Translation (NMT) models. That is, once some tiny perturbs are added to the input sentence, the model will produce completely different translation with high confidence. Adversarial example is currently a major tool to improve model robustness and how to generate an adversarial examples that can degrade the performance of the model and ensure semantic consistency is a challenging task. In this paper, we adopt reinforcement learning to generate adversarial example for low-resource NMT. Specifically, utilizing the actor-critic algorithm to modify the source sentence, the discriminator and translation model in the environment are used to determine whether the generated adversarial examples maintain semantic consistency and the overall deterioration of the model. Furthermore, we also install a language model reward to measure the fluency of adversarial examples. Experimental results on low-resource translation tasks show that our method highly aggressive to the model while maintaining semantic constraints greatly. Moreover, the model performance is significantly improved after fine-tuning with adversarial examples.

Keywords: Reinforcement learning · Adversarial example · Low-resource NMT

1 Introduction

Neural Machine Translation (NMT) [2,16,17] has made significant progress. However, even the best trained translation models still make unpredictable errors in practical applications [3]. Figure 1 illustrates the fragility of NMT. Robustness is the feature that a model can maintain some performance despite perturbations or noise. For machine translation tasks, robustness refers to the ability of the model to adapt to new corpus. The lack of model training and noise learning ability leads to the model generating a completely different translation after adding certain perturbations to the sentence, which seriously affects the model performance. The original method improves

T. Xiao and J. Pino (Eds.): CCMT 2022, CCIS 1671, pp. 60–71, 2022.
https://doi.org/10.1007/978-981-19-7960-6_7

the model robustness by manually compiling error features [7, 18], but it is too costly and some features are inapplicable for tasks of machine translation.

Adversarial example is a momentous tool for exploring the robustness of deep learning systems and it's initially applied in the field of computer vision [14]. Recently, some researchers utilizing adversarial examples to Natural Language Processing (NLP) tasks [4, 5, 19], which cur-

input	现代音乐最初是在意大利发展起来的。
output	᠊᠊᠊ ᠊᠊᠊ ᠊᠊ ᠊᠊᠊ ᠊᠊᠊ ᠊᠊᠊ ᠊᠊᠊ ᠊᠊ ᠊᠊᠊ ᠊᠊᠊ ᠊᠊ ··
perturb input	现代音乐最初是在意利发展的。
output	᠊᠊᠊ ᠊᠊᠊ ᠊᠊᠊ ᠊᠊᠊ ᠊᠊ ᠊᠊᠊ ᠊᠊᠊ ᠊᠊᠊ ᠊᠊᠊ ᠊᠊᠊ ᠊᠊᠊ ··

Fig. 1. Fragility of neural machine translation. Leaving out a Chinese character " 大 " and word "起来" lead to significant errors in Mongolian translation.

rently include character-level, word-level, phrase-level, and sentence-level adversarial examples. It makes the model produce error output by adding carefully designed perturbations to the input data. In general, the generation of adversarial examples implies that the model uses non-robust features, resulting in a less robust model as well. Adversarial training is performed by data augmentation methods, where adversarial examples are proportionally blended into the training set. In this way, the model obtained by training on the new dataset learns these non-robust features, resulting in a more robust model. Thus for machine translation tasks, we can quickly obtain a large amount of parallel data that can be applied for robustness analysis by using the input of an existing parallel corpus to generate adversarial examples along the output of the source text.

However, unlike images that directly use the gradient optimization to obtain adversarial examples, the sentence space in NLP is discrete, so it's difficult to disturb along the gradient update direction when generating adversarial examples for text. On the other hand, if the common noise introduction such as adding, deleting, and modifying words is used to perturb against the source input, the generated adversarial examples aren't only difficult to ensure sentence fluency and semantic consistency, but also may even degrade the model performance. Especially for low-resource translation tasks, its own lack of massively parallel corpus has led to poor model performance, poor robustness and weak adaptation to new corpus or sentences with noise. Therefore, to improve the robustness of low-resource translation tasks, this paper utilizes reinforcement learning to generate adversarial examples and uses discriminators as terminal signals in the environment to further constrain semantics. Furthermore, we also add a language model to evaluate the fluency of the adversarial examples. The method learns how to apply discrete perturbations at the token-level to directly reduce translation quality. The experimental results on the CCMT2019 Mongolian-Chinese and CWMT2017 Uighur-Chinese show that using the adversarial examples generated by this method to fine-tune the model can significantly improve its performance.

2 Background and Related Work

2.1 Neural Machine Translation

Neural machine translation (NMT) mainly utilizes the encoder-decoder structure to achieve semantic encoding of the source language and prediction of the target language. The specific way is to use an *Encoder* to encode the input source language $x = (x_1, ..., x_n)$ into a fixed vector, and then use *Decoder* to decode the vector to finally get the target language. For y_t, given its previous word sequence $y_{<t}$ and the source language sentence x, use $P(y|x)$ to determine the probability of the current target word $P(y_t|y_{<t}, x)$. The specific calculation process is shown in Eq. (1):

$$P(y_t|y_{<t}, x) \propto exp(y_t; r_t; C_t) \tag{1}$$

where r_t is the hidden layer state of the neural machine translation model *Encoder* at time t. C_t is the context state information of the generated word y_t defined according to the hidden layer node state of *Encoder*. NMT is trained using Maximum Likelihood Estimation (MLE). Given J training sentence pairs $\{x^i, y^i\}_{i=1}^{N}$, at each time step, NMT generates the target word y_t by maximizing the translation probability on the source sentence x. The training objective is to maximize the Eq. (2):

$$L_{MLE} = \sum_{i=1}^{N} logp(y^i|x^i) = \sum_{i=1}^{N} \sum_{t=1}^{M} logp(y_t^i|y_1^i...y_{t-1}^i, x^i) \tag{2}$$

2.2 Adversarial Example, Adversarial Attack and Adversarial Training in NLP

Adversarial Example can be described as $\hat{x}$, which is obtained by adding a restricted perturbation of δ to the original input sample (x, y) and cause model deterioration. For an original sample (x, y), there exists its adversarial sample set $A(x, y)$, and its expression is shown in Eq. (3):

$$A(x, y) = \{\hat{x}|R(\hat{x}, x) \leq \delta \wedge M(\hat{x}) \neq y\} \tag{3}$$

where $R(\hat{x}, x)$ represents the vector perturbed between the disturbed sample $\hat{x}$ and the original sample x. "Restricted perturbation" requires that $R(\hat{x}, x)$ to be constrained by δ. The model M is generally non-robust, which makes it possible that when the model inputs a sample $\hat{x}$ with minor perturbations, the resulting $M(\hat{x})$ is completely different from the original output $M(x)$. The generation of adversarial samples is usually associated with perturbations of non-robust features.

Adversarial Attack is the process of generating adversarial examples $\hat{x}_1, \hat{x}_2, ..., \hat{x}_n \in A(x, y)$ against model M and (x, y) sample. It aims to look for the non-robust and useful features to perturb x, and finally make the model produce error output. According to the attack environment, adversarial attack can be divided into black-box attack and white-box attack. For black-box attack, the attack algorithm can only access the output of M without knowing the parameters and structure information. For white-box attack, the attack algorithm can access all the information and parameters of M and generate adversarial examples based on the gradient of M to attack the network. In NLP task, due to the discreteness of sentence space, it is difficult to disturb effectively with gradient information, so white box attack is difficult.

Adversarial Training is the process in which adversarial examples are generated on the training set through adversarial attacks for data enhancement and the enhanced data is used to retrain model M, so it can be defined as an optimization problem, and the model is expected that both performance and robustness will be enhanced. The original non-robust features may become useless after adversarial training, thereby weakening the association between non-robust features and labels, and achieving the purpose of anti-disturbance model.

2.3   Genetic Algorithm-Based Adversarial Attack

GeneticAttack [1] is a black-box adversarial attack method that performs word-level perturbation on examples, and uses genetic algorithm to optimize the examples. Inspired by the theory of biological evolution, the core of genetic algorithm lies in population mutation, crossover and selection. The population of GeneticAttack consists of several sentences x, and the size of the population is limited by hyperparameters. The mutation operation is completed by synonym replacement, and synonyms are obtained through an independently obtained word-embedding matrix. In mutation operations, GeneticAttack additionally uses a language model to filter out inappropriate word substitutions. The crossover operation takes out two sentences in the population and randomly selects words from one of them in the position of each word to form a new sentence. The new sentence collection forms the next generation population. The selection fitness is the output $M(\hat{x})$.

2.4   Gradient-Based Adversarial Attack

HotFlip [6] is a typical white-box attack method, which uses gradient ascending to directly select the largest disturbance among the acceptable perturbations by limiting the degree of perturbation, thereby generating adversarial samples quickly and efficiently. HotFlip performs one-hot encoding on sentences, which are represented as a three-dimensional tensor, in which each word corresponds to a matrix, and each column in the matrix is a one-hot character vector. It has the advantage of allowing character substitutions to be represented using a tensor of the same size as the sentence, as well as a tensor representation of character substitutions from the gradient tensor. During character replacement, Hotflip directly selects the character closest to the gradient direction for replacement. The insertion and deletion operations are completed by character substitutions of words.

3   Adversarial Examples Based on Reinforcement Learning

Adversarial examples must be semantically consistent with the original input, while causing the model to produce incorrect output. GeneticAttack (Sect. 2.3) generates adversarial examples through synonym substitution, and the resulting perturbations are often tiny in semantic space, but the algorithm cannot effectively use gradient information to efficiently generate perturbations. HotFlip (Sect. 2.4) uses gradient information to make attacks extremely efficient. However, it can only attack the character-level model and produce several meaningless words, which will greatly reduce the overall fluency of the sentence.

Therefore, this paper utilizes Reinforcement Learning (RL) to generate adversarial examples by combining the advantages of above two methods. According to [20], it is regarded as a restricted Markov Decision Process (MDP), which edits the tokens at each position in the source sentence from left to right. Each editing decision depends on the impact of the existing modification on the semantics and the degradation expectation of the system output. Furthermore, inspired by GeneticAttack [1], we also add a Language Model (LM) to measure the fluency of adversarial examples. The generation strategy of adversarial examples is obtained through the continuous interactive feedback of the degree of attack on the translation model and the fluency of the examples.

3.1 Reinforcement Learning

As an momentous branch in the field of machine learning, reinforcement learning aims to study the use of agents to conduct model training through interacting with the environment and receiving "feedback" information, so as to "automatically" decide the optimal solution [8]. Figure 6 illustrates the process of reinforcement learning. At each time t, $Agent$ receive state s_t from $Environment$, and $Agent$ make action a_t on basis of s_t, while act on $Environment$ to generate reward r_t. $Agent$ reach the new state s_{t+1} according to r_t. Figure 7(a) shows the overall framework of the model, in which the $Environment$ (Sect. 3.2) and the $Agent$

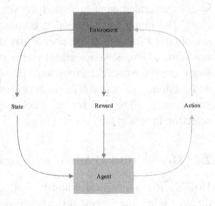

Fig. 2. Reinforcement learning.

(Sect. 3.3) are two significant parts. $Agent$ learns to modify the token of each position in the original sample sequentially from left to right, and uses a discriminator in the $Environment$ to determine whether the modified sample is semantically consistent with the original sample, at the same time, inputs the modified sample into the language model and translation model to evaluate the fluency of adversarial examples and whether reach the deterioration of the model. The specific process is as in Fig. 7(b).

3.2 Environment

This section details the environment state and the calculation of rewards.

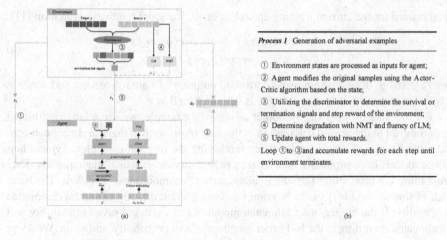

① Environment states are processed as inputs for agent;
② Agent modifies the original samples using the Actor-Critic algorithm based on the state;
③ Utilizing the discriminator to determine the survival or termination signals and step reward of the environment;
④ Determine degradation with NMT and fluency of LM;
⑤ Update agent with total rewards.
Loop ①to ③and accumulate rewards for each step until environment terminates.

Fig. 3. The architecture and specific process of our method.

State. The state of the *Environment* is described as $s_t = (x, t)$, where $x = (x^1, ..., x^N)$ are N sequences. Adding the begin and end tags (BOS and EOS) to each sequence $x^i = (x_1, x_2, ..., x_n)$ and padding them to the same length. $t \in (1, n)$ indicates the token position to be perturbed by *Agent*. *Environment* will consecutively loop for all token positions and update s_t based on *Agent*'s modification. *Environment* also yields reward signals until the end or intermediately terminated.

Reward Calculation. The reward r_t consists of a survival reward r_s for each step, a final degradation r_d and the fluency reward r_l when the *Agent* survives till the end. Therefore, the reward for each time step is calculated as follows:

$$r_t = \begin{cases} -1, terminated \\ \frac{1}{N}\sum_N \alpha \cdot r_s, survive \wedge t \in [1, n) \\ \frac{1}{N}\sum_N (\alpha \cdot r_s + \beta \cdot r_d + \gamma \cdot r_l), survive \wedge t = n \end{cases} \quad (4)$$

where α, β γ and are hyper-parameters. Since the adversarial examples must maintain semantic consistency with the original examples, the *Agent* must survive for its goal by also fooling the discriminator D, which determines terminal or survival signal by judging whether the modified sequence matches the original target translation y. Once D determines the pair as positive, its corresponding possibility is regarded as the reward, otherwise 0:

$$r_s = \begin{cases} P(positive|(\hat{x}, y); \theta_d), positive \\ 0, otherwise \end{cases} \quad (5)$$

When all sequences in x are intermediately terminated, the overall reward r_t yields -1. For example which is defined as "negative" during survival phase, it's subsequent rewards and actions will be disguised as zero. If the agent survives to the end, *Environment* generates an additional average reward r_d and fluency reward r_l as the final reward for the current training episode. For r_d, we adopt relative degradation [11]:

$$r_d = \frac{score(y, refs) - score(y', refs)}{score(y, refs)} \tag{6}$$

where y and y' denote original and perturbed output, $refs$ are references, and $score$ is a translation metric. If $score(y, refs)$ is 0 and return 0 as r_d.

For the sake of receiving smoother adversarial example, we use a language model to participate in the reward calculation in the $Environment$ so that the $Agent$ can consider the fluency of the examples when modifying the original examples. Typical language models have problems such as zero probability or statistical inadequacies. Katz smoothing is a probability formula to alleviate the "unsmoothness" problem. The basic idea of this method is if exists N-gram language model, directly using the discounted probability; If the higher-order language model is non-exist, the saved probability will be allocated according to the N-1 order language model probability, and so on. We adopt 3-gram and r_l represents the fluency score of sequence $\hat{x}$:

$$r_l = \sum_{t=1}^{n} P_{katz}\left(x_t | x_{t-2}^{t-1}\right) \tag{7}$$

$$P_{katz}\left(x_t | x_{t-2}^{t-1}\right) = \begin{cases} P_{ML}\left(x_t | x_{t-2}^{t-1}\right), & if \quad count\left(x_{t-2}^{t-1}\right) > 0 \\ \lambda P_{katz}^{(n-1)}\left(x_t | x_{t-1}\right), & if \quad count\left(x_{t-2}^{t-1}\right) = 0 \end{cases} \tag{8}$$

3.3 Agent

As it is shown in Fig. 7(a), $Agent$ uses Actor-Critic algorithm [9] to modify samples, the actor and critic share the same input layers and encoder. Actor takes in $Source$ and current token with its surrounding (x_{t-1}, x_t, x_{t+1}), then yields a binary distribution to determine whether to attack a token on step t, while critic emits a value $V(s_t)$ for every state. Once the $Actor$ determines that a token at specific location can be perturbed, it is replaced with one of the token's candidates within the distance of σ in the vocabulary. See [20] for more details about training and inferencing.

4 Experiment

4.1 Data Preprocessing

We test our adversarial example generations on Mongolian-Chinese (Mo-Zh) translation tasks of CCMT2019 and Uighur-Chinese (Ug-Zh) translation tasks of CWMT2017. In this paper, we use the open-source Chinese word splitting tool THULAC [10] to split the Chinese corpus, so that the corpus can be better adapted to the model and reduce the problem of poor model performance caused by word order to a certain extent. Moreover, Byte Pair Encoding (BPE) [13] encoding is used to process the Mongolian and Uighur corpus, which is firstly sliced into the corresponding smallest granularity. The training of the translation model is assisted by extracting the highest frequency character substrings into the newly generated dictionary. This approach slices the sentences into a granularity between words and characters, which can preserve the contextual semantics to a certain extent while alleviating the data sparsity problem.

4.2   NMT Model

This paper selects the state-of-the-art RNNSearch [2] and Transformer [15] as victim translation models. For RNN-Search, it's an encoder-decoder framework based on RNN, we set the hidden layer nodes and word-embedding dimensions to 512 and $dropout = 0.1$. By averaging the single model obtained from the last 20 checkpoints, we use adaptive to adjust the learning rate. For Transformer, we set $dropout = 0.2$ and the dimension of word embedding to 1024, with the learning rate and checkpoint settings consistent with RNNSearch.

4.3   Evaluating Indicator

We report de-tokenized BLEU with SacreBLEU [12] as the evaluation metric of adversarial examples and also test source semantic similarity with human evaluation (HE) ranging from 0 to 5 (Table 1) used by [11] by randomly sampling 20% of total sequences for a double-blind test.

Table 1. Human evaluation metrics.

0	Meaning of the two sentences is completely different
1	The topic is the same but the meaning is different
2	Some key messages are different
3	The key messages is the same, but the details differ
4	Meaning is essentially equal but some expressions are unnatural
5	Meaning is essentially equal and the expression is fluent and natural

4.4   Adversarial Attack Results and Analysis

We utilize GeneticAttack [1], HotFlip [6] and our method to generate adversarial examples for the test set respectively to attack the translation model. Table 2 illustrates the deterioration degree of adversarial examples to different translation tasks. We randomly select 20% of the adversarial examples for double-blind human evaluation to evaluate the semantic similarity between the adversarial example and the original example.

As it is shown in Table 2, GeneticAttack uses synonym replacement and genetic algorithm optimization to modify the original sample, resulting in less disturbance, but it lacks some semantic and fluency constraints compared with our method, which is easy to produce grammar problems, and low efficiency due to the inability to use gradient information effectively. Hotflip mainly uses gradient information to generate typo adversarial examples (such as " 香蕉 " → " 香交 ") to improve the model's ability to adapt and correct typos. Although the efficiency is high, it may produce some meaningless words which greatly reduce the overall smoothness of the sentence. Our method uses the actor-critic to modify the token of each position of the original example from left to right, uses the discriminator to restrict the semantics of the confrontation sample, and the language model and the translation model are utilized to evaluate its fluency

Table 2. Experiment results for Mo-Zh and Ug-Zh MT attacks. We list BLEU for perturbed test sets generated by each adversarial example generation method. An ideal adversarial example shouldachieve low $BLEU$ and high HE.

Model	Mo→Zh		Zh→Mo		Ug→Zh		Zh→Ug	
	BLEU↓	HE↑	BLEU↓	HE↑	BLEU↓	HE↑	BLEU↓	HE↑
RNNSearch	26.51	–	22.25	–	28.24	–	23.18	–
GeneticAttack	20.27	1.98	18.56	2.34	22.12	2.06	19.67	2.43
HotFlip	19.15	2.60	18.03	2.91	20.76	2.47	18.32	2.98
Ours	22.14	3.36	20.75	3.73	23.47	3.26	21.48	3.84
Transformer	30.44	–	25.57	–	32.67	–	26.32	–
GeneticAttack	24.02	2.16	22.13	2.91	26.43	2.21	22.18	2.94
HotFlip	23.17	2.67	21.21	3.14	24.67	2.74	21.35	3.13
Ours	26.87	3.45	23.12	3.62	26.98	3.47	23.69	3.88

and the overall deterioration of the model. Therefore, our model stably generate adversarial examples without significant change in semantics and any handcrafted semantic constraints by the same training setting among different models and tasks, achieving stably model degradation and high HE.

4.5   Adversarial Training Results and Analysis

Due to *Agent* can effectively generate adversary examples that retain semantic information, we can directly use these samples to tune the original translation model. Given the original training data, Transformer models of different methods are used to generate equal number of adversarial examples, which are then paired with the initial target sentences.

Table 3. Fine-tuning with adversarial examples.

Model	Mo→Zh		Zh→Mo		Ug→Zh		Zh→Ug	
	BLEU↑	Promote	BLEU↑	Promote	BLEU↑	Promote	BLEU↑	Promote
Transformer	30.44	–	25.57	–	32.67	–	26.32	–
GeneticAttack	31.19	0.75	26.13	0.56	33.46	0.79	26.93	0.61
HotFlip	32.07	1.63	26.41	0.84	34.39	1.72	27.24	0.92
Ours	33.29	2.85	27.33	1.76	35.41	2.79	28.11	1.79

We directly train the model by mixing the augmented sentence pairs with the original sentence pairs. As shown in Table 3, utilizing the adversarial examples generated by GeneticAttack and HotFlip to adversarial training enable improve the performance of the model, but the effect is unapparent. The reason is they aren't guaranteeing semantic consistency and sentence fluency, and has a poor effect attack on the model. Our method can not only guarantee the semantics, but also have strong aggression against the translation model. The results of fine-tuning using the adversarial examples show that the robustness of the model can be significantly improved.

4.6   Ablation Study

Table 4 shows the results of ablation study. Line 1 represent only use discriminator (D) rewards to guide *Agent* optimization. It is clear that NMT reward r_d plays a critical role since removing it impairs model performance (line 2 and line 3). The language model reward is also shown to be benefit for improving performance (line 4) but seem to have relatively smaller contributions than r_d.

Table 4. The results of ablation study, "○" means utilize this module and "×" means not.

ID	D	NMT	LM	MO-ZH
1	○	×	×	28.35
2	○	○	×	33.02
3	○	×	○	28.94
4	○	○	○	33.29

5   Conclusion

This paper adopts a novel approach to generate adversarial examples for low-resource machine translation tasks. It can expose the defects of the translation model without manual error features, and ensure the semantic consistency with the original examples. The experimental results on CCMT2019 Mongolian-Chinese and CWMT2017 Uighur-Chinese show that this method achieves stable model degradation on different attacked models. Furthermore, we use adversarial examples to fine-tune the model, and the performance is significantly improved after adversarial training.

References

1. Alzantot, M., Sharma, Y., Elgohary, A., Ho, B., Srivastava, M.B., Chang, K.: Generating natural language adversarial examples. In: Riloff, E., Chiang, D., Hockenmaier, J., Tsujii, J. (eds.) Proceedings of the 2018 Conference on Empirical Methods in Natural Language Processing, Brussels, Belgium, 31 October–4 November 2018, pp. 2890–2896. Association for Computational Linguistics (2018). https://doi.org/10.18653/v1/d18-1316
2. Bahdanau, D., Cho, K., Bengio, Y.: Neural machine translation by jointly learning to align and translate. In: 3rd International Conference on Learning Representations, ICLR 2015, San Diego, CA, USA, 7–9 May 2015, Conference Track Proceedings (2015). http://arxiv.org/abs/1409.0473
3. Belinkov, Y., Bisk, Y.: Synthetic and natural noise both break neural machine translation. In: 6th International Conference on Learning Representations, ICLR 2018, Vancouver, BC, Canada, 30 April–3 May 2018, Conference Track Proceedings. OpenReview.net (2018). https://openreview.net/forum?id=BJ8vJebC-
4. Cheng, M., Yi, J., Chen, P., Zhang, H., Hsieh, C.: Seq2sick: Evaluating the robustness of sequence-to-sequence models with adversarial examples. In: The Thirty-Fourth AAAI Conference on Artificial Intelligence, AAAI 2020, The Thirty-Second Innovative Applications of Artificial Intelligence Conference, IAAI 2020, The Tenth AAAI Symposium on Educational Advances in Artificial Intelligence, EAAI 2020, New York, NY, USA, 7–12 February 2020, pp. 3601–3608. AAAI Press (2020). https://ojs.aaai.org/index.php/AAAI/article/view/5767

5. Ebrahimi, J., Lowd, D., Dou, D.: On adversarial examples for character-level neural machine translation. In: Bender, E.M., Derczynski, L., Isabelle, P. (eds.) Proceedings of the 27th International Conference on Computational Linguistics, COLING 2018, Santa Fe, New Mexico, USA, 20–26 August 2018, pp. 653–663. Association for Computational Linguistics (2018). https://aclanthology.org/C18-1055/

6. Ebrahimi, J., Rao, A., Lowd, D., Dou, D.: Hotflip: white-box adversarial examples for text classification. In: Gurevych, I., Miyao, Y. (eds.) Proceedings of the 56th Annual Meeting of the Association for Computational Linguistics, ACL 2018, Melbourne, Australia, 15–20 July 2018, Volume 2: Short Papers, pp. 31–36. Association for Computational Linguistics (2018). https://aclanthology.org/P18-2006/

7. Karpukhin, V., Levy, O., Eisenstein, J., Ghazvininejad, M.: Training on synthetic noise improves robustness to natural noise in machine translation. In: Xu, W., Ritter, A., Baldwin, T., Rahimi, A. (eds.) Proceedings of the 5th Workshop on Noisy User-generated Text, W-NUT@EMNLP 2019, Hong Kong, China, 4 November 2019, pp. 42–47. Association for Computational Linguistics (2019). https://doi.org/10.18653/v1/D19-5506

8. Keneshloo, Y., Shi, T., Ramakrishnan, N., Reddy, C.K.: Deep reinforcement learning for sequence to sequence models. CoRR abs/1805.09461 (2018). http://arxiv.org/abs/1805.09461

9. Konda, V.R., Tsitsiklis, J.N.: Actor-critic algorithms. In: Solla, S.A., Leen, T.K., Müller, K.. (eds.) Advances in Neural Information Processing Systems, NIPS Conference, Denver, Colorado, USA, 29 November–4 December 1999, vol. 12, pp. 1008–1014. The MIT Press (1999). http://papers.nips.cc/paper/1786-actor-critic-algorithms

10. Li, Z., Sun, M.: Punctuation as implicit annotations for Chinese word segmentation. Comput. Linguist. 35(4), 505–512 (2009). https://doi.org/10.1162/coli.2009.35.4.35403

11. Michel, P., Li, X., Neubig, G., Pino, J.M.: On evaluation of adversarial perturbations for sequence-to-sequence models. In: Burstein, J., Doran, C., Solorio, T. (eds.) Proceedings of the 2019 Conference of the North American Chapter of the Association for Computational Linguistics: Human Language Technologies, NAACL-HLT 2019, Minneapolis, MN, USA, 2–7 June 2019, Volume 1 (Long and Short Papers), pp. 3103–3114. Association for Computational Linguistics (2019). https://doi.org/10.18653/v1/n19-1314

12. Post, M.: A call for clarity in reporting BLEU scores. In: Bojar, O., et al. (eds.) Proceedings of the Third Conference on Machine Translation: Research Papers, WMT 2018, Belgium, Brussels, 31 October–1 November 2018, pp. 186–191. Association for Computational Linguistics (2018). https://doi.org/10.18653/v1/w18-6319

13. Sennrich, R., Haddow, B., Birch, A.: Neural machine translation of rare words with subword units. In: Proceedings of the 54th Annual Meeting of the Association for Computational Linguistics, ACL 2016, August 2016, Berlin, Germany, Volume 1: Long Papers, pp. 7–12 (2016). https://doi.org/10.18653/v1/p16-1162

14. Szegedy, C., et al.: Intriguing properties of neural networks. In: Bengio, Y., LeCun, Y. (eds.) 2nd International Conference on Learning Representations, ICLR 2014, Banff, AB, Canada, 14–16 April 2014, Conference Track Proceedings (2014). http://arxiv.org/abs/1312.6199

15. Vaswani, A., et al.: Attention is all you need. In: Advances in Neural Information Processing Systems 30: Annual Conference on Neural Information Processing Systems 2017, 4–9 December 2017, Long Beach, CA, USA, pp. 5998–6008 (2017). http://papers.nips.cc/paper/7181-attention-is-all-you-need

16. Wu, L., Tian, F., Qin, T., Lai, J., Liu, T.: A study of reinforcement learning for neural machine translation. In: Proceedings of the 2018 Conference on Empirical Methods in Natural Language Processing, Brussels, Belgium, 31 October– 4 November 2018, pp. 3612–3621 (2018). https://www.aclweb.org/anthology/D18-1397/

17. Yang, Z., Chen, W., Wang, F., Xu, B.: Improving neural machine translation with conditional sequence generative adversarial nets. In: Proceedings of the 2018 Conference of the North American Chapter of the Association for Computational Linguistics: Human Language Technologies, NAACL-HLT 2018, New Orleans, Louisiana, USA, 1–6 June 2018, Volume 1 (Long Papers), pp. 1346–1355 (2018). https://www.aclweb.org/anthology/N18-1122/

18. Zhao, Y., Zhang, J., He, Z., Zong, C., Wu, H.: Addressing troublesome words in neural machine translation. In: Riloff, E., Chiang, D., Hockenmaier, J., Tsujii, J. (eds.) Proceedings of the 2018 Conference on Empirical Methods in Natural Language Processing, Brussels, Belgium, 31 October–4 November 2018, pp. 391–400. Association for Computational Linguistics (2018). https://doi.org/10.18653/v1/d18-1036

19. Zhao, Z., Dua, D., Singh, S.: Generating natural adversarial examples. CoRR abs/1710.11342 (2017). http://arxiv.org/abs/1710.11342

20. Zou, W., Huang, S., Xie, J., Dai, X., Chen, J.: A reinforced generation of adversarial examples for neural machine translation. In: Jurafsky, D., Chai, J., Schluter, N., Tetreault, J.R. (eds.) Proceedings of the 58th Annual Meeting of the Association for Computational Linguistics, ACL 2020, 5–10 July 2020, pp. 3486–3497. Association for Computational Linguistics (2020). https://doi.org/10.18653/v1/2020.acl-main.319

Dynamic Mask Curriculum Learning for Non-Autoregressive Neural Machine Translation

Yisong Wang, Hongxu Hou[✉], Shuo Sun, Nier Wu, Weichen Jian,
Zongheng Yang, and Pengcong Wang

National & Local Joint Engineering Research Center of Intelligent Information
Processing Technology for Mongolian, Inner Mongolia Key Laboratory of Mongolian
Information Processing Technology, College of Computer Science,
Inner Mongolia University, Hohhot, China
wangyisong06@126.com, cshhx@imu.edu.cn

Abstract. Non-autoregressive neural machine translation is gradually becoming a research hotspot due to its advantages of fast decoding. However, the increase of decoding speed is often accompanied by the loss of model performance. The main reason is that the target language information obtained at the decoder side is insufficient, and the mandatory parallel decoding leads to a large number of mistranslation and missing translation problems. In order to solve the problem of insufficient target language information, this paper proposes a dynamic mask curriculum learning approach to provide target side language information to the model. The target side self-attention layer is added in the pre-training phase to capture the target side information and adjust the amount of information input at any time by way of curriculum learning. The fine-tuning and inference phases disable the module in the same way as the normal NAT model. In this paper, we experiment on two translation datasets of WMT16, and the BLEU improvement reaches 4.4 without speed reduction.

Keywords: Non-autoregressive model · Curriculum learning · Mask ratio

1 Introduction

Neural machine translation (NMT) [1–3] has become a popular direction of research and has achieved great results. However, the mainstream autoregressive neural machine translation (AT) models have high decoding latency and exist in exposure bias [4]. Therefore, Gu et al. [5] proposed non-autoregressive neural machine translation (NAT), which uses parallel decoding to generate all tokens at once and improves the decoding speed significantly. However, this method can't obtain enough contextual information for the model to learn, and the generated translations suffer from a large number of mistranslation, missing translation and multi-modality problems.

T. Xiao and J. Pino (Eds.): CCMT 2022, CCIS 1671, pp. 72–81, 2022.
https://doi.org/10.1007/978-981-19-7960-6_8

Ding et al. [6] proposed that there are differences between the distillation data and the raw data, and simply using distillation data in one direction will result in poor translation of low-frequency words. Therefore, adding the knowledge distillation data in the opposite direction, which utilizes the target side data and solves the low-frequency word problem, but generating distillation data using only the target side data does not allow the decoder to obtain more information on the target side. Ran et al. [7] proposed that the decoding stage makes use of reordering information. Reorder the source copy token so that the position of each token is aligned with the target language token. Although makes use of word alignment information at the target side, but semantic information is not sufficiently obtained. Guo et al. [8] proposed fine-tuning by curriculum learning (FCL-NAT), which transfers the knowledge learned from the AT model to the NAT model by way of curriculum learning. However, this approach requires training the AT model first and then fine-tuning it using curriculum learning. This approach greatly increases the training time and consumes a lot of resources.

Obtain more linguistic information at the target side, some researchers have proposed a semi-autoregressive model with multiple iterations of decoding. Therefore, Gu et al. [9] proposed Levenshtein Transformer (LevT), which modifies the translation by three operations: delete, insert, and replace placeholders. More contextual information can be obtained during the translation adjustment process. The mask prediction method proposed by Ghazvininejad et al. [10] replaces a token with a lower probability with a mask and re-predicts it after each generation. It stops after two iterations unchanged or after reaching the maximum number of iterations. Although the above method can provide enough target side information for the model by multiple iterations, the increase in the number of iterations is accompanied by a decrease in the decoding speed, which can even degrade to the autoregressive model level and lose the advantage of NAT. Qian et al. [11] proposed GLAT, which uses the token of partial ground truth translation to replace the source copy token, and the model obtained by training in this way can achieve better performance. It is illustrated that, the performance of the model can be improved without losing speed by incorporating more target side information based on the model decoded in a single iteration.

In this paper, we propose a **dynamic mask** method based on **curriculum learning** (DMCL) to generate ground truth translations with mask for model training, so that the decoder can obtain more linguistic information on the target side. Specifically, the number of masks for the ground truth translations is dynamically increased in each training phase by means of curriculum learning, and the ground truth translations with mask are input to the decoder side. The target self-attention layer is added at the decoder side to obtain the target language information and fuse it with the self-attention layer information. The target language information provided can be limited by the mask ground truth token to prevent relying too much on the target self-attention part in the training phase. The number of masks is dynamically adjusted using a curriculum learning approach so that the model can be trained from easy to difficult, and the training process is smoother and achieves better model performance. In the fine-tuning phase, the target self-attention is removed, and the model is identical to the common NAT model. The experimental results show that the maximum improvement of BLEU value is more than 4.4 without losing decoding speed. It is noted that the DMCL approach in this paper is also applicable to the model with multiple iterations of decoding.

2 Background

2.1 Non-autoregressive Neural Machine Translation

The non-autoregressive model is based on the hypothesis that all words in the target language are independent of each other, and generates all target language words in parallel [5]. The generation process can be expressed as follows:

$$P(y|x) = P(T_y|x) \cdot \prod_{t=1}^{T_y} P(y_t|x, z) \tag{1}$$

where T_y denotes the length of the target sentence, x denotes the source language sentence, and y denotes the target language sentence. From the Eq. (1), it can be seen that although the hidden variable of z is involved in the decoding stage, the latent variables are also derived from the source side language. Therefore, this approach does not fully utilize the target side language information in the training phase, but forcibly decodes the translation based on the latent variables. In contrast, the DMCL proposed in this paper can provide part of the target side information in the pre-training stage, so that the model learns richer target side information.

2.2 Curriculum Learning

Curriculum learning is a strategy to train a model from easy to difficult. This asymptotic training approach allows the model to be smoother during the training phase while achieving better results. Platanios et al. [12] proposed a new training framework that decides the next phase of input to the model based on the difficulty of the training data and the current model capabilities. There are two important metrics under this training framework, data difficulty and model competence. The data difficulty can be calculated based on the sentence length or the average word occurrence probability. The model competence uses a predefined incremental function. The input data difficulty at each stage is less than the current model competence. In this paper, the same idea is adopted, and DMCL determines the amount of target side language information provided in the next step based on the current status of the model. The DMCL strategy adjusts the amount of target side language information provided to enable the model to achieve better results compared to the strategy that doesn't use the course learning approach.

3   Method

In this section, a detailed description of the model structure of DMCL-NAT and the dynamic mask curriculum learning training strategy will be illustrated.

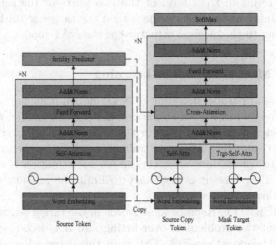

Fig. 1. The model structure of DMCL-NAT. Where trgt-self-attention is added to this paper. Residual connectivity is dispensed with in the figure.

3.1   Model

The encoder side of the model is identical to the Transformer's encoder, and the fertility predictor is added to the encoder side to predict the target sentence length. DMCL -NAT adds language information on the target side mainly at the decoder side. It also gradually reduces the amount of incorporated information in a curriculum learning manner, thus achieving an easy-to-hard training strategy. Firstly, the symbolic representation is defined, and the source language token sequence is denoted as $X = \{x_1, x_2, x_3, ..., x_n\}$, and the target language token sequence is denoted as $Y = \{y_1, y_2, y_3, ..., y_T\}$. The main structure of the model is shown in Fig. 1. The input to the decoder side has two parts, one part of the copy from the source language according to the fertility predictor denoted as $X^* = \{x_1, x_2, x_2...x_T\}$, and the other part replaces the token in the ground truth translation with the mask according to the mask ratio. The input is the mask target token denoted as $Y^* = \{y_1, y_2, [MASK], [MASK], ...y_T\}$. The DMCL strategy will be described in detail on the next section. The two part inputs are embedding and their respective self-attention modules:

$$H_{self-attn} = MultiHead(Emb(x^*), Emb(x^*), Emb(x^*)) \qquad (2)$$

$$H_{tart-self-attn} = MultiHead(Emb(y^*), Emb(y^*), Emb(y^*)) \qquad (3)$$

where $Emb(\cdot)$ denotes the word embedding. After obtaining the self-attention results of the two parts, the two parts are fused and expressed as:

$$H = 0.5 * (H_{self-attn} + H_{tart-self-attn}) \tag{4}$$

where H is the result of the fusion of the two parts of the self-attention. In the model fine-tuning and inference phase then the target self-attention layer is disabled, returning to the original structure of the NAT model.

3.2 Dynamic Mask Curriculum Learning

Due to the feature of parallel decoding of NAT model, if all the target language information is directly introduced at the decoder side, the model will completely rely on the target self-attention part in the training phase, and the originally self attention part can't be adequately trained, resulting in the model losing the ability to generate translations after the target self-attention is removed in the inference phase. Therefore, it is necessary to limit the amount of information provided in the target language.

Inspired by BERT [13], Replace some words in the target sentence with mask tokens. To prevent the problem of over-fitting and not decoding properly, the mask ratio should be more than 50%. Therefore, this paper adopts the curriculum learning method to dynamically adjust the proportion of tokens in mask, and its value range should be $[0.5, 1]$.

The mind of curriculum learning is to let the model train from easy to difficult. When the mask is less, more contextual semantic information can be provided to the model, and as the mask ratio keeps increasing, the ground truth translation information that the model can refer to keeps decreasing. Therefore, the adjustment function for the mask ratio should be an increasing function overall. Platanios et al. [12] proposed a function taking values between 0 and 1 and increasing with the number of training steps:

$$ratio(t) = min(1, \sqrt[p]{\frac{t}{T}(1 - c_0^p) + c_0^p}) \tag{5}$$

where c_0 is the starting value, t is the current number of training steps, and T is the total number of curriculum learning steps. When $p = 1$, it is a linear increasing function, and when $p = 2$, $ratio(t)$ increases gradually less as t increases. From the existing course learning experience, generally $p = 2$ works best.

However, this way of taking values still has drawbacks. The main reason is that the mask ratio cannot be adjusted in time for different training conditions and can only be trained in a predefined way. Therefore, dynamically adjusting the mask ratio according to the current training condition of the model can make the model achieve better results. Therefore, this paper proposes a dynamic adjustment strategy that follows the change of last step loss. The equation is as follows:

$$ratio(loss) = min(1, \sqrt[2]{\frac{loss_{min}}{loss}(1 - c_0^2) + c_0^2}) \tag{6}$$

where *loss* denotes the loss obtained by the model for the previous stage of calculation, and $loss_{min}$ denotes the loss when the autoregressive model reaches the convergence state, c_0 is the minimum mask ratio. As can be seen from the Eq. (6), as the loss decreases indicates that the current model can reach a better learning state, so the mask ratio can be increased appropriately, and when the loss increases during the training process indicates that the current stage is difficult to train, the mask ratio can be reduced appropriately.

3.3   Train and Inference

Train: The model is divided into pre-training and fine-tuning phases during training. The pre-training process is shown in Fig. 2. In the pre-training phase, which can also be called the mask curriculum learning phase, the mask ratio is dynamically adjusted according to the current training status of the model, and some of the target side language information is added so that the model can learn more target side language information. Can be expressed as:

$$P(y|x, y^*) = P(T_y|x) \cdot \prod_{t=1}^{T_y} P(y_t|x, y^*, z) \tag{7}$$

where y^* denotes the ground truth translation with mask token and T_y denotes the target sentence length. However, due to the existence of target self-attention there is still the problem of partial information leakage. Therefore, the fine-tuning phase removes target self-attention completely and doesn't introduce the ground truth translation information. The fine-tuning process can be expressed as Eq. (1).

Inference: The method in this paper only modifies the model structure in the training phase, and the fine-tuned model no longer relies on the target side information provided by target self-attention. The inference stage is the same as in Eq. (1). The sentence length is obtained according to the fertility prediction and the decoder needs the latent variable z copied from the source language. In addition, this paper also uses the noise parallel decoding (NPD) [5] method to generate the translation, the candidate set is increased according to the

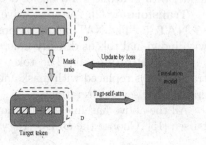

Fig. 2. Dynamic mask curriculum learning process. The shaded area indicates the token that was masked

sentence length in the inference stage, and then the optimal result is selected from all the candidate sets as the final translation, which can make a better decision on the sentence length. Therefore, the inference stage is the same as the ordinary NAT model, and the model performance is further improved without affecting the decoding speed.

4 Experiment

4.1 Data Preparation

In this paper, experiments were conducted on two sets of language pairs. The WMT16 RO-EN dataset is v6 version containing a total of 220K sentence pairs. For the WMT16 EN-DE dataset (2M sentence pairs), 1M sentence pairs were selected as the training set. On the RO-EN and EN-DE tasks, all the corpus was preprocessed by Byte Pair Encoding (BPE) [14], and the BPE dictionary size was set to 32K for both.

4.2 Configuration

For all the above datasets, the experimental model configurations all follow the settings of Vaswani et al. [2]. The decoder and encoder were each set to n-layers $= 6$, where the attention module d-model $= 512$, n-heads $= 8$. The warm-up steps were all set to 4000. The learning rate was set to 0.0005, and the learning rate update followed the inverse square root annealing algorithm. For the RO-EN dataset, a total of 6W steps are trained, and for the EN-DE dataset, a total of 30W steps are trained, where the DMCL pre-training are set to half of the total training steps.

4.3 Baseline

The experimental baseline in this paper is derived from the autoregressive model, the non-autoregressive model with single decoding, and the semi-autoregressive model with multiple iterations of decoding.

Transformer [2]: Autoregressive model strong baseline.

NAT [5]: The NAT model proposed by Gu et al. assumes parallel decoding with individual tokens directly independent of each other.

Mask Predict [10]: The token with lower probability in each generated translation is replaced with mask and re-predicted. The final translation is generated after several iterations.

All the above baseline and methods in this paper are implemented based on fairseq [15]. Choose the BLEU [16] value to evaluate the model performance.

4.4 Results

The main results of the experiments are shown in Table 1. The DMLM approach can significantly improve the performance of the NAT model. Compared with the multiple iteratives decoding model, the method in this paper retains the original fast decoding advantage of the NAT model and significantly reduces the performance difference with the multiple iteratives decoding model. Compared with the vanilla NAT model, significant improvements are obtained on the RO-EN dataset, with a maximum performance gain of more than 4.4. In addition, great potential is shown on large corpora of millions.

Table 1. Results on the WMT16 RO-EN and EN-DE benchmarks. m denotes the noise parallel decoding window size. DMCL-NAT is the method proposed in this paper. The bolded results indicate the best performance of single decoding.

Models		WMT2016			Speedup
		RO-EN	EN-RO	EN-DE	
AT Model	Transformer	36.64	34.65	22.13	1.0×
Iterative NAT	Mask-Predict (iter = 10)	35.22	32.96	18.43	2.6×
Fully NAT	NAT	26.46	25.32	12.56	15.7×
	NAT (m = 5)	28.83	27.07	12.92	7.6×
Ours	DMCL-NAT	30.47	28.81	14.74	15.7×
	DMCL-NAT (m = 5)	**33.27**	**31.76**	**15.44**	7.6×

In this paper, only the target self-attention layer is added to the pre-training process of the model, and the amount of target language information input is adjusted by adjusting the number of masks in the input ground truth translation. Therefore the method can be applied to a variety of NAT models.

5   Analysis

5.1   Mask Strategy

In this paper, two points of view are evaluated to verify the effectiveness of DMCL. Firstly, the mask ratio is fixed to a certain value. In addition, a strategy of mask ratio adjustment with the idea of curriculum learning is adopted, which gradually increases from 0.5 to 1. There are four incremental functions set in Table 3.

Table 2. Performance on WMT16 RO-EN with fixed mask ratio.

Mask ratio	BLEU
0.5	29.78
0.6	29.91
0.7	30.00
0.8	29.57
0.9	28.36
Ours	**30.47**

The experimental results are shown in Table 2 and Table 3. The optimal performance is reached when the fixed mask ratio is 0.7. When the incremental function is used, the inverse quadratic incremental function achieves the maximum value and is stronger than the model performance when the ratio is fixed. But this DMCL strategy proposed in this paper obtains a significantly better model performance than all the above approaches. The main reason is that dynamically adjusting the amount of information input allows the model to obtain the most appropriate amount of information and achieve better training results. So the DMCL strategy proposed in this paper is effective.

Table 3. Performances on WMT16 RO-EN with incremental mask ratio.

Functions	Description	BLEU
Linear	$\frac{t}{T}(1 - c_0) + c_0$	29.85
Sqrt	$\sqrt[2]{\frac{t}{T}(1 - c_0^2) + c_0^2}$	30.23
Exponent	$e^{-log\frac{t}{T}(1-c_0)+c_0}$	29.72
Ladder-like	$\lfloor\frac{5*t}{T}\rfloor * 0.1 + c_0$	29.82
Ours		**30.47**

Table 4. Performance on WMT16 RO-EN when DMCL applied to Mask Predict.

Model	BLEU
Transformer	36.64
Mask Predict (iter $= 10$)	35.22
Mask Predict+DMLM (iter $= 10$)	35.87

5.2 Method Generality

Since the method in this paper is to add target self-attention at the decoder side and then pre-train the model by DMCL. So the method is also applicable to the non-autoregressive translation model with multiple iterations of decoding. To test this hypothesis, the multiple iterations decoding model Mask Predict was chosen as the base model and experiments were conducted on the RO-EN task. The experimental results are shown in the Table 4, after adding the method of this paper to Mask Predict, the BLEU value has improved by 0.65. The reason why the improvement is not as large as that of the model with single decoding is that DMCL provides linguistic information on the target side in the training phase, while the same information on the target side is available during the iteration of Mask Predict. Therefore, the impact of DMCL is weakened.

6 Conclusion

In this paper, we propose a new method that can incorporate the target side language information in the NAT model, while dynamically adjusting the ratio of mask substitution in the ground truth translation in a curriculum learning approach, and controlling the amount of target language information provided by the ground truth translation can achieve a progressive learning process from easy to difficult. The method significantly improves the performance of the single decoding model without speed loss. Also, experiments are conducted in this paper based on the Mask Predict model, and it is demonstrated that the method is also applicable to models with multiple iterations of decoding. Providing target side information at the decoder side can effectively improve NAT model performance, and future research will focus on exploring more appropriate curriculum learning strategies and ways to apply the approach to other generative tasks.

References

1. Bahdanau, D., Cho, K., Bengio, Y.: Neural machine translation by jointly learning to align and translate. arXiv preprint arXiv:1409.0473 (2014)
2. Vaswani, A., et al.: Attention is all you need. Adv. Neural. Inf. Process. Syst. **30**, 5998–6008 (2017)
3. Gehring, J., Auli, M., Grangier, D., Yarats, D., Dauphin, Y.N.: Convolutional sequence to sequence learning. In: International Conference on Machine Learning, pp. 1243–1252. PMLR (2017)
4. Yu, L., Zhang, W., Wang, J., Yu, Y.: SeqGAN: sequence generative adversarial nets with policy gradient. In Proceedings of the AAAI Conference on Artificial Intelligence, vol. 31, No. 1 (2017)
5. Gu, J., Bradbury, J., Xiong, C., Li, V.O., Socher, R.: Non-autoregressive neural machine translation. arXiv preprint arXiv:1711.02281 (2017)
6. Ding, L., Wang, L., Liu, X., Wong, D.F., Tao, D., Tu, Z.: Rejuvenating low-frequency words: making the most of parallel data in non-autoregressive translation. arXiv preprint arXiv:2106.00903 (2021)
7. Ran, Q., Lin, Y., Li, P., Zhou, J.: Guiding non-autoregressive neural machine translation decoding with reordering information. In: Proceedings of the AAAI Conference on Artificial Intelligence, vol. 35, No. 15, pp. 13727–13735 (2021)
8. Junliang Guo, X., Tan, L.X., Qin, T., Chen, E., Liu, T.-Y.: Fine-tuning by curriculum learning for non-autoregressive neural machine translation. In: Proceedings of the AAAI Conference on Artificial Intelligence, vol. 34, pp. 7839–7846 (2020)
9. Gu, J., Wang, C., Zhao, J.: Levenshtein transformer. arXiv preprint arXiv:1905.11006 (2019)
10. Ghazvininejad, M., Levy, O., Liu, Y., Zettlemoyer, L.: Mask-predict: parallel decoding of conditional masked language models. arXiv preprint arXiv:1904.09324 (2019)
11. Qian, L., et al.: Glancing transformer for non-autoregressive neural machine translation. arXiv preprint arXiv:2008.07905 (2020)
12. Antonios Platanios, E., Stretcu, O., Neubig, G., Poczos, B., Mitchell, T.M.: Competence-based curriculum learning for neural machine translation. arXiv preprint arXiv:1903.09848 (2019)
13. Devlin, J., Chang, M.W., Lee, K., Toutanova, K.: BERT: pre-training of deep bidirectional transformers for language understanding. arXiv preprint arXiv:1810.04805 (2018)
14. Sennrich, R., Haddow, B., Birch, A.: Neural machine translation of rare words with subword units. arXiv preprint arXiv:1508.07909 (2015)
15. Ott, M., et al.: fairseq: a fast, extensible toolkit for sequence modeling. In: Proceedings of NAACL-HLT 2019: Demonstrations (2019)
16. Papineni, K., Roukos, S., Ward, T., Zhu, W.J.: BLEU: a method for automatic evaluation of machine translation. In: Proceedings of the 40th annual meeting of the Association for Computational Linguistics, pp. 311–318 (2002)

Dynamic Fusion Nearest Neighbor Machine Translation via Dempster-Shafer Theory

Zongheng Yang[1,2], Hongxu Hou[1,2(✉)], Shuo Sun[1,2], Nier Wu[1,2],
Yisong Wang[1,2], Weichen Jian[1,2], and Pengcong Wang[1,2]

[1] College of Computer Science, Inner Mongolia University, Hohhot, China
cshhx@imu.edu.cn
[2] Inner Mongolia Key Laboratory of Mongolian Information Processing Technology,
Hohhot, China

Abstract. kNN-MT has been recently proposed, uses a token-level k-nearest neighbor approach to retrieve similar sentences, obtaining knowledge guidance from an external memory module, and then combined with the prediction results of the translation model, which greatly improves the accuracy of machine translation. However, kNN-MT uses simple linear interpolation in the fusion of retrieval probability and translation probability, which can not dynamically adjust the fusion ratio according to the matching degree of the retrieved sentences. Moreover, different fusion ratios need to be explored in different translation scenarios, and the translation effect will be affected when the retrieved sentences have a low matching degree or contain noise. In this paper, we propose an approach via Dempster-Shafer theory (DST) to dynamically fuse different probability distributions to suit different scenarios. We demonstrate that our approach is more significantly improved and more robust than the traditional kNN-MT, and we explore the application of kNN-MT in low-resource translation scenarios for the first time.

Keywords: kNN-MT · Dynamic fusion · Translation

1 Introduction

Over the past few years, with the development of deep learning, neural machine translation has come a long way. In order to further improve the translation accuracy, more and more researches have started to express the training data as some kind of external knowledge rather than as model parameters, which is called non-parametric method. Since this method requires search to obtain external knowledge, it is also called search-based model. The representative methods are as follows: Nearest neighbor language models (kNN-LM) [1], which introduces kNN to the language model for the first time and gains tremendous enhancements; k-nearest-neighbor machine translation (kNN-MT) [2], which extends kNN-LM to translation model, has made a qualitative leap in bilingual translation, multilingual translation, and especially domain adaptation translation tasks compared with traditional methods; As well as Adaptive *k*NN-MT implemented by [3] on this basis, a meta-k network is trained by artificially constructing features for generating the number of nearest neighbors *k*, instead of artificially specifying them; And Fast *k*NN-MT [4] introduces hierarchical retrieval to improve the retrieval efficiency thus improving the slow translation speed of *k*NN-MT.

*k*NN-MT bulids an external memory module on top of the ordinary NMT, storing the context representation of the corresponding sentence as well as the target word. The idea of *k*NN-MT is to retrieve sentences similar to the current sentence in the memory module when translating the current word, and get reference and guidance from the translation memory by the words corresponding to the similar sentences. Then it is fused with the translation result of NMT to get the final result.

Although *k*NN-MT has demonstrated its powerful capability in high-resource languages as well as domain adaptation, there are still two problems. On the one hand, *k*NN-MT has not been studied in low-resource scenarios due to its particular reliance on the representational power of pre-trained translation models and the retrieval effect of similar sentences. On the other hand, in the fusion of NMT with an external memory module, the fusion ratio is controlled by a hyperparameter λ, i.e., how much information the NMT model obtains from the external memory module. However, it poses some problems, due to the long-tail effect of the dataset, some sentences have more similar sentences while some sentences have less similar sentences. Using the same fusion ratio for all data will cause the problem that some sentences do not acquire enough information and some sentences introduce noise. We illustrate this with a concrete example in Fig. 1. Moreover, it is experimentally demonstrated that the model translation results are very sensitive to the selection of hyperparameter λ, which affects the robustness of the model.

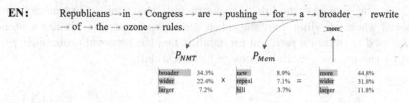

Fig. 1. Example of failure of probability interpolation between p_{NMT} and p_{Mem}, while translating DE-EN.

To solve this problem, we propose a dynamic fusion method via Dempster-Shafer theory, which drops the fixed fusion method with linear interpolation, and gives different fusion results for different retrieval probabilities and translation probabilities. The problem of high confidence in retrieval probability, but too low fusion ratio, i.e., better prediction of retrieval probability, but biased final translation result due to too low fusion ratio, and vice versa, is alleviated. Moreover, our method improves the robustness of the model to cope with translation in complex scenarios. More importantly, we explore the application of kNN-MT in low-resource translation scenarios for the first time, demonstrating the effectiveness of non-parametric methods in low-resource scenarios. We validate the effectiveness of our methodology for multi-domain datasets, including IT, Medical, Koran, Law, and the CCMT'19 Mongolian-Chinese low-resource dataset. Our method obtains an increase of 0.41-1.89 BLUE, and the robustness of the model is improved.

2   Background

The main approach of kNN-MT involves the building of memory modules and the fusion of external knowledge with the predicted results of the NMT model. In terms of memory module construction, unlike [5] and [6] which construct sentence-level and fragment-level memory datastore, kNN-MT constructs token-level memory datastore. Its advantage is better retrieval and higher matching, but the memory module size is the total number of tokens in the target language, which leads to low retrieval efficiency. In terms of construction method, kNN-MT selects an offline construction method, therefore a pre-trained model with strong knowledge representation capability is required. The memory module is stored as a key-value pair of a context vector and a target token, and is constructed by feeding the training data into the model in a single forward pass. Given a bilingual corpus $(x, y) \in (\mathcal{X}, \mathcal{Y})$ the decoder decodes y_t based on the source language x and the words $y_{<t}$ that have been generated. Assuming that the hidden layer state of the pre-trained model is $f(x, y_{<t})$, the key of the datastore is $f(x, y_{<t})$ and the value is y_t, then the construction process is:

$$(\mathcal{K}, \mathcal{V}) = \{(f(x, y_{<t}), y_t), \forall y_t \in y \mid (x, y) \in (\mathcal{X}, \mathcal{Y})\} \qquad (1)$$

Once the memory module is constructed, the similar sentences can be retrieved when decoding, and the token corresponding to the similar sentences can be used to obtain a retrieval probability, i.e., the retrieval probability p_{Mem} given by the memory module through historical data.

$$p_{Mem}(y_i \mid x, \hat{y}_{1:i-1}) \propto \sum_{(k_i, v_i \in \mathcal{N})} \mathbb{1}_{y_i = v_i} exp\left(\frac{-d(k_j, f(x, \hat{y}_{1:i-1}))}{T}\right) \qquad (2)$$

The retrieval probability represent external knowledge guidance, and kNN-MT fuses the external knowledge with the model knowledge by simple linear interpolation to obtain the final probability distribution.

$$p(y_t \mid x, \hat{y}_{1:i-1}) = \lambda p_{NMT}(y_t \mid y_{<t}, x) + (1 - \lambda) p_{Mem}(y_t \mid y_{<t}) \qquad (3)$$

3 Method

In this section, we mainly introduce our proposed method, and our method is mainly applied in the inference stage of the model. We discard linear interpolation and use DST (Dempster-Shafer theory) in the fusion process of p_{NMT} and p_{Mem}, and our method is shown in Fig. 2. Since p_{Mem} only generates probabilities for a few relevant words of the similar neighbors in the actual calculation process, and the probabilities of other irrelevant words are all 0, resulting in a very hard distribution of p_{Mem}, and more 0 probabilities will have a very significant impact on the DST results, so we use label smoothing for p_{Mem} to make the distribution of p_{Mem} smoother.

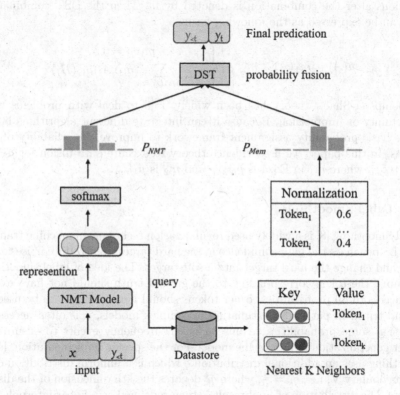

Fig. 2. Schematic diagram of our approach, the retrieval process occurs at the decoder, where similar sentences are retrieved in the memory module based on the context vector. The retrieval probability is obtained by normalizing the target token and then dynamically fused with the translation probability using the DST algorithm.

3.1 Dempster-Shafer Theory

Dempster-Shafer theory [7] is a generalization of probability theory and a very effective method for data fusion. DST extends the basic event space in probability theory to power sets of basic elements by replacing a single probability value of a basic element with a probability range. DST is based on the mathematical theory proposed by Demster and Schaeffer, and is a more general formulation of Bayesian theory. DST proposes a framework that can be used to represent incomplete knowledge and update credibility. If a set is defined as $\Theta = \{\theta_1, \theta_2, ..., \theta_N\}$ and all elements in the set are independent and mutually exclusive, Θ is called the frame of discernment framework. Under this premise, the DST combination rules are provided.

Let m_1 and m_2 be the two probability assignment functions on the same discernment framework. The corresponding focal elements are A_i $(i = 1, 2, ..., k)$ and B_j $(j = 1, 2, ..., l)$, respectively, and the new probability assignment (BPA) functions after the combination is denoted by m. Then the DST combination rule can be expressed as the following form:

$$m(A) = m_1(A) \oplus m_2(A) \begin{cases} m(\phi) = 0 \\ \frac{1}{1-k} \sum_{A_i \cap B_j = A} m_1(A_i) m_2(B_j) \end{cases} \tag{4}$$

Dempster-Shafer theory has been widely used to deal with problems with uncertainty or imprecision. Because it can integrate different algorithms based on its basic probability assignment framework to improve the reliability of the results. In this paper, we use evidence theory to execute data fusion for p_{NMT} and p_{Mem}, where m_1 in Eq. 4 is p_{NMT} and m_2 is p_{Mem}.

3.2   Label Smoothing

Label Smoothing [8] is a widely used regularization technique in machine translation. LS penalizes the high confidence in the hard target to introduce noise to the label and change the hard target into a soft target. The idea of label smoothing is simple: the token corresponding to the ground truth should not have exclusive access to all probabilities; other tokens should have a chance to be used as ground truth. In parameter estimation of complex models, it is often necessary to assign some probabilities to unseen or low-frequency events to ensure the better generalization ability of the model. For the specific implementation, label smoothing uses an additional distribution q which is a uniform distribution over the vocabulary V, i.e., $q_k = \frac{1}{v}$, where q_k denotes the kth dimension of the distribution. The distribution of final result is then redefined as a linear interpolation of y_j and q:

$$y_j^{ls} = (1 - \alpha) \cdot y_j + \alpha \cdot q \tag{5}$$

Here, α denotes a coefficient to control the importance of the distribution q, and y_j^{ls} denotes the learning target after using label smoothing. The schematic diagram is shown in Fig. 3.

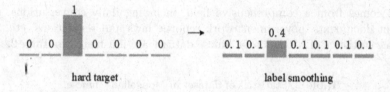

Fig. 3. Targets with Label Smoothing when $\alpha = 0.1$.

Label smoothing can also be seen as an adaptation of the loss function with the introduction of additional prior knowledge (i.e., the part related to q). But this prior knowledge is not fused with the original loss function by means of linear interpolation.

The process of generating the final probability can be summarized by the following procedure, where the LS denotes a label smoothing, DST denotes Dempster-Shafer theory, p_{Mem} denotes the retrieval probability obtained from the memory module, and p_{NMT} denotes the translation probability of the NMT model.

$$p\left(y_t \mid y_{<t}\right) = DST\left(p_{NMT}, LS\left(p_{Mem}\right)\right) \tag{6}$$

4   Experiment

We validate the effectiveness of our method in two translation scenarios: (1) domain adaptation. (2) Mongolian-Chinese low resource language.

4.1   Experimental Setup

Data. We use the following datasets for training and evaluation:

MULTI-DOMAINS: We use the multi-domains dataset [9], re-split by [10] for the domain adaptation experiments. It includes German-English parallel data for train/valid/test sets in four domains: **Medical**, **Law**, **IT** and **Koran**. The sentence statistics of MULTI-DOMAINS datasets are illustrated in Table 1.

Table 1. Statistics of dataset in different domains.

	Train	Valid	Test
IT	222,927	2,000	2,000
Medical	248,009	2,000	2,000
Koran	17,982	2,000	2,000
Laws	467,309	2,000	2,000

Low-resource: We use the CCMT'19 Mongolian-Chinese dataset to evaluate the performance of our method in low-resource scenarios. The bilingual parallel corpus comes from a comprehensive field, including daily conversations, government documents, government work reports, laws and regulations, etc. The sentence statistics of Mongolian-Chinese dataset are illustrated in Table 2.

Table 2. Statistics of dataset in Mongolian-Chinese.

	Train	Valid	Test
Mo-Zh	247,829	1,000	1,000

Models. For the domain adaptation experiments, we use the WMT'19 German-English news translation task winner [11], available via the FAIRSEQ library [12]. It is a Transformer encoder-decoder model [13] with 6 layers, 1,024 dimensional representations, 8,192 dimensional feedforward layers and 8 attention heads. Apart from WMT'19 training data, this model is trained on over 10 billion tokens of back translation data and fine-tuned on newstest test sets from years prior to 2018.

For low-resource translation, we train a Mongolian-Chinese translation model based transformer. The corpus is subworded using subword-nmt[1] [14], using a Adam optimizer [15] with a warmup step of 10,000, epoch of 30 and setting early stop. Other settings are kept the same as transformer-base.

Our experiments are based on the fairseq[2] sequence modeling toolkit to train NMT models, using the faiss[3] [16] toolkit for external memory module construction and high-speed retrieval. We implement our approach on the open source code of adaptive-knn-mt[4], which implements the original kNN-MT based on fairseq and has a good code structure.

4.2   Result and Analysis

For the domain adaptive task, the main results are shown in Table 3. Consistency improvement is obtained for all four domains of our method. The BLEU scores are improved by 1.89, 0.51, 0.48, and 0.55 compared to kNN-MT. The minimum improvement is in the Koran domain and the highest is in the IT domain.

For the low-resource task, the experimental results are shown in Table 4, and it can be found that kNN-MT can also obtain a huge improvement on the translation result in the low-resource domain, and our method is also improved compared with kNN-MT.

Analysis. Compared with kNN-MT our method is more flexible in the probabilistic fusion stage, which is reflected in the results to obtain a consistent improvement of BLEU. The biggest improvement in the domain adaptive experiments is in the IT domain, and by analyzing the translation results we speculate

---

[1] https://github.com/rsennrich/subword-nmt.
[2] https://github.com/pytorch/fairseq.
[3] https://github.com/facebookresearch/faiss.
[4] https://github.com/zhengxxn/adaptive-knn-mt.

Table 3. BLEU scores of Base NMT model, kNN-MT and our method on domain adaptive experiments with hyperparameters k of 8, 4, 8 and 4, respectively. The linear interpolation ratios α for kNN-MT are 0.7, 0.8, 0.7, and 0.7.

Model	IT	Medical	Koran	Laws
Base-NMT	32.05	36.25	14.38	41.78
kNN-MT	36.68	51.27	17.55	57.55
Ours	**38.57**	**51.78**	**18.03**	**58.1**

Table 4. BLEU scores of Base NMT model, kNN-MT and our method on Mongolian-Chinese low-resource experiments with hyperparameter $k = 4$.

Model	Valid	Test
Base-NMT	27.85	36.56
kNN-MT	31.19	42.29
Ours	**33.64**	**42.77**

that it may be due to the presence of more low-frequency special nouns in the IT domain. kNN-MT introduces noise in the retrieval process, while our method performs better in the translation of low-frequency words.

In the low-resource scenario since the test sets of Mongolian-Chinese are mostly simple short sentences, while the valid sets have more long and difficult sentences. Therefore, the improvement of our method on the test sets is not as large as that on the valid sets, which also reflects the effectiveness of our method in complex translation scenarios to some extent. Since DST can produce different results according to different probabilities and expose more information after using label smoothing for p_{Mem}, it increases the generalization and robustness of the model.

4.3   Robustness

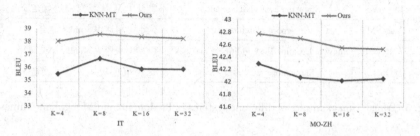

Fig. 4. Robustness experiments of kNN-MT and our method at different hyperparameters k.

To verify the robustness of our method, we test the accuracy of translation under different hyperparameters k. The experimental results are shown in Fig. 4. We find that the BLEU scores of kNN-MT fluctuate more in the case of not optimal k values, indicating that the performance of kNN-MT is more sensitive to the noise brought by k. And the performance of our method is also affected during the increase of k, but with less fluctuation. It indicates that a relatively good performance can be maintained at different noise intensities.

We also evaluate the robustness of our method in the domain-mismatch setting, where we consider a scenario that the user inputs an out-of-domain sentence (e.g. Medical domain) to a domain-specific translation system (e.g. IT domain) to evaluate the robustness of different methods. Specifically, in IT→Medical setting, We use hyperparameters and datastore in the IT domain, and then use Medical test set to test the model with IT datastore. As shown in Table 5, the retrieved results are highly noisy so that the kNN-MT encounters drastic performance degradation. In contrast, our method could filter out some noise and therefore prevent performance degradation as much as possible.

Table 5. Robustness Evaluation, where the test sets are from Medical/IT domains and the datastore are from IT/Medical domains respectively.

Model	IT→Medical	Medical→IT
Base-NMT	36.25	32.05
kNN-MT	15.81	12.31
Ours	**24.1**	**19.56**

4.4 Case Study

	IT	Mo-Zh
Source	Weitere Suchergebnisse anzeigen	ᠪᠤᠤ ᠮᠠᠨ ᠤ ᠬᠠᠵᠠᠭᠤ <unk>
Reference	Show the next search results	不要 让 机遇 从 我们 身边 溜走 。
Base-NMT	View more search results	不要 让 机遇 从 <unk> 溜走 。
kNN-MT	Show & Location Find additional matches	不要 让 机遇 从 <unk> 溜走 。
Ours	Show more search results	不要 让 机遇 从 我们 身边 溜走 。

Fig. 5. Translation examples of different systems in IT domain and Mongolian-Chinese.

As shown in Fig. 5, we show examples of translations in the IT domain and Mongolian-Chinese. We can observe that kNN-MT can produce mistranslations in some cases, and our method can generate translations with more fidelity and fluency in this case. Moreover, our method can alleviate the $\langle unk \rangle$ problem to a certain extent. In the Mongolian-Chinese example, both the Base NMT model and kNN-MT can not translate correctly when the corpus contains $\langle unk \rangle$, which also shows that our method is more robust and higher error tolerance.

5   Conclusion

In this paper we propose dynamic fusion of kNN-MT. By using Dempster-Shafer theory instead of fixed linear interpolation to dynamically fuse the two probability distributions from NMT model and memory modules. Through experiments in domain adaptation, we verify that our method has some improvement on kNN-MT and validate that our method is more robust. In addition, we explore the possibility of applying kNN-MT in low-resource scenarios for the first time. In the future, we will deeply explore the application of non-parametric methods in low-resource scenarios.

References

1. Khandelwal, U., Levy, O., Jurafsky, D., Zettlemoyer, L., Lewis, M.: Generalization through memorization: nearest neighbor language models. In: 8th International Conference on Learning Representations, ICLR 2020, Addis Ababa, Ethiopia, 26–30 April 2020. OpenReview.net (2020). https://doi.org/10.48550/arXiv.1911.00172
2. Khandelwal, U., Fan, A., Jurafsky, D., Zettlemoyer, L., Lewis, M.: Nearest neighbor machine translation. In: 9th International Conference on Learning Representations, ICLR 2021, Virtual Event, Austria, 3–7 May 2021. OpenReview.net (2021). https://doi.org/10.48550/arXiv.2010.00710
3. Zheng, X., et al.: Adaptive nearest neighbor machine translation. In: Zong, C., Xia, F., Li, W., Navigli, R. (eds.) Proceedings of the 59th Annual Meeting of the Association for Computational Linguistics and the 11th International Joint Conference on Natural Language Processing, ACL/IJCNLP 2021, (Volume 2: Short Papers), Virtual Event, 1–6 August 2021, pp. 368–374. Association for Computational Linguistics (2021). https://doi.org/10.18653/v1/2021.acl-short.47
4. Meng, Y., et al.: Fast nearest neighbor machine translation. CoRR abs/2105.14528 (2021). https://arxiv.org/abs/2105.14528
5. Eriguchi, A., Rarrick, S., Matsushita, H.: Combining translation memory with neural machine translation. In: Nakazawa, T., et al. (eds.) Proceedings of the 6th Workshop on Asian Translation, WAT@EMNLP-IJCNLP 2019, Hong Kong, China, 4 November 2019, pp. 123–130. Association for Computational Linguistics (2019). https://doi.org/10.18653/v1/D19-5214
6. Zhang, J., Utiyama, M., Sumita, E., Neubig, G., Nakamura, S.: Guiding neural machine translation with retrieved translation pieces. In: Walker, M.A., Ji, H., Stent, A. (eds.) Proceedings of the 2018 Conference of the North American Chapter of the Association for Computational Linguistics: Human Language Technologies, NAACL-HLT 2018, New Orleans, Louisiana, USA, 1–6 June 2018, vol. 1 (Long Papers), pp. 1325–1335. Association for Computational Linguistics (2018). https://doi.org/10.18653/v1/n18-1120

7. Dempster, A.P.: Upper and lower probabilities induced by a multivalued mapping. In: Yager, R.R., Liu, L. (eds.) Classic Works of the Dempster-Shafer Theory of Belief Functions. Studies in Fuzziness and Soft Computing, vol. 219, pp. 57–72. Springer, Heidelberg (2008). https://doi.org/10.1007/978-3-540-44792-4_3

8. Szegedy, C., Vanhoucke, V., Ioffe, S., Shlens, J., Wojna, Z.: Rethinking the inception architecture for computer vision. In: 2016 IEEE Conference on Computer Vision and Pattern Recognition, CVPR 2016, Las Vegas, NV, USA, 27–30 June 2016, pp. 2818–2826. IEEE Computer Society (2016). https://doi.org/10.1109/CVPR.2016.308

9. Koehn, P., Knowles, R.: Six challenges for neural machine translation. In: Luong, T., Birch, A., Neubig, G., Finch, A.M. (eds.) Proceedings of the First Workshop on Neural Machine Translation, NMT@ACL 2017, Vancouver, Canada, 4 August 2017, pp. 28–39. Association for Computational Linguistics (2017). https://doi.org/10.18653/v1/w17-3204

10. Aharoni, R., Goldberg, Y.: Unsupervised domain clusters in pretrained language models. In: Jurafsky, D., Chai, J., Schluter, N., Tetreault, J.R. (eds.) Proceedings of the 58th Annual Meeting of the Association for Computational Linguistics, ACL 2020, Online, 5–10 July 2020, pp. 7747–7763. Association for Computational Linguistics (2020). https://doi.org/10.18653/v1/2020.acl-main.692

11. Ng, N., Yee, K., Baevski, A., Ott, M., Auli, M., Edunov, S.: Facebook fair's WMT19 news translation task submission. In: Bojar, O., et al. (eds.) Proceedings of the Fourth Conference on Machine Translation, WMT 2019, Florence, Italy, 1–2 August 2019, - Volume 2: Shared Task Papers, Day 1, pp. 314–319. Association for Computational Linguistics (2019). https://doi.org/10.18653/v1/w19-5333

12. Ott, M., et al.: fairseq: a fast, extensible toolkit for sequence modeling. In: Ammar, W., Louis, A., Mostafazadeh, N. (eds.) Proceedings of the 2019 Conference of the North American Chapter of the Association for Computational Linguistics: Human Language Technologies, NAACL-HLT 2019, Minneapolis, MN, USA, 2–7 June 2019, Demonstrations, pp. 48–53. Association for Computational Linguistics (2019). https://doi.org/10.18653/v1/n19-4009

13. Vaswani, A., et al.: Attention is all you need. In: Guyon, I., et al. (eds.) Advances in Neural Information Processing Systems 30: Annual Conference on Neural Information Processing Systems 2017, 4–9 December 2017, Long Beach, CA, USA, pp. 5998–6008 (2017). https://proceedings.neurips.cc/paper/2017/hash/3f5ee243547dee91fbd053c1c4a845aa-Abstract.html

14. Sennrich, R., Haddow, B., Birch, A.: Neural machine translation of rare words with subword units. In: Proceedings of the 54th Annual Meeting of the Association for Computational Linguistics, ACL 2016, 7–12 August 2016, Berlin, Germany, Volume 1: Long Papers. The Association for Computer Linguistics (2016). https://doi.org/10.18653/v1/p16-1162

15. Kingma, D.P., Ba, J.: Adam: a method for stochastic optimization. In: Bengio, Y., LeCun, Y. (eds.) 3rd International Conference on Learning Representations, ICLR 2015, San Diego, CA, USA, 7–9 May 2015, Conference Track Proceedings (2015). http://arxiv.org/abs/1412.6980

16. Johnson, J., Douze, M., Jégou, H.: Billion-scale similarity search with GPUs. IEEE Trans. Big Data **7**(3), 535–547 (2021). https://doi.org/10.1109/TBDATA.2019.2921572

A Multi-tasking and Multi-stage Chinese Minority Pre-trained Language Model

Bin Li[1], Yixuan Weng[2], Bin Sun[1], and Shutao Li[1]($\boxtimes$)

[1] College of Electrical and Information Engineering, Hunan University, Changsha, China
{libincn,sunbin611,shutao_li}@hnu.edu.cn
[2] National Laboratory of Pattern Recognition Institute of Automation, Chinese Academy Sciences, Beijing, China

Abstract. The existing multi-language generative model is considered as an important part of the multilingual field, which has received extensive attention in recent years. However, due to the scarcity of Chinese Minority corpus, developing a well-designed translation system is still a great challenge. To leverage the current corpus better, we design a pre-training method for the low resource domain, which can help the model better understand low resource text. The motivation is that the Chinese Minority languages have the characteristics of similarity and the adjacency of cultural transmission, and different multilingual translation pairs can provide the pre-trained model with sufficient semantic information. Therefore, we propose the Chinese Minority Pre-Trained (CMPT) language model with multi-tasking and multi-stage strategies to further leverage these low-resource corpora. Specifically, four pre-training tasks and two-stage strategies are adopted during pre-training for better results. Experiments show that our model outperforms the baseline method in Chinese Minority language translation. At the same time, we released the first generative pre-trained language model for the Chinese Minority to support the development of relevant research (All the experimental codes and the pre-trained language model are open-sourced on the website https://github.com/WENGSYX/CMPT).

Keywords: Multi-task · Multi-stage · Chinese minority · Generative pre-trained language model

1 Introduction

With the emergence of the pre-training language model, great progress has been made in the field of natural language processing [1]. The self-supervised method has achieved remarkable success in many tasks [2], which is designed to reconstruct the input text by using the AutoEncoder [3,4]. In the previous works, the generative sequence-to-sequence (seq2seq) model can be applied to a wide range

B. Li and Y. Weng—These authors contribute this work equally.
Supported by the National Key R&D Program of China (2018YFB1305200), the National Natural Science Fund of China (62171183).

of downstream tasks. Firstly, the text is destroyed by noise manipulation, and then the original text is reconstructed with the language model. The downstream task performance can be effectively improved by further fine-tuning [5].

For some low-resource languages, the self-supervised method is difficult to adapt to the downstream task directly because the corpus is relatively small. At the same time, the model will have a better understanding of high resource languages but ignore the learning between similar low resource languages [6].

The Chinese Minority languages have similarity and adjacency in cultural transmission [7]. This is because ethnic integration in East Asia has been going on continuously since ancient times [8]. The frequent iterations of the regime have promoted the social development of the Han nationality and the cultural exchanges among all ethnic groups. Chinese and minority languages have long been in contact, influenced, and integrated with each other [9].

Therefore, we propose the Chinese Minority Pre-Trained (CMPT) language model with multi-tasking and multi-stage strategies. The CMPT model improves the ability of cross-language understanding through pre-training, which is designed with denoising and contrastive learning between texts in different low-resourced languages. Specifically, we refer to the settings of the BART [10] to randomly mask the text and require the model to be restored. In order to improve the understanding ability of the encoder model, we refer to the setting of CPT [11] and add a single-layer masked language model (MLM) [12] decoder to the encoder output layer for joint training of generation and understanding. Due to the small number of minority languages, we learn close to the dense vector of language pairs with the same semantic meaning based on the cross-lingual contrastive learning between text pairs. This can pull the language pairs with the same semantic meaning to similar positions in the vector space and can help the model to better realize the migration and understanding of low-resource languages.

In order to further study the feasibility of a large-scale pre-training language model, we use DeepNorm [13] to implement a 256 layer into the CMPT model, which has 128 layers of the encoder and 128 layers of decoder, respectively. We believe that the model with depth can better extract the understanding ability between languages.

In conclusion, we have the following three contributions to this work:

1. We have proposed a CMPT model for Chinese Minority languages. Through the use of denoising tasks and contrastive learning, it has the ability to understand and generate meanwhile.
2. We have trained a 256-layer CMPT model and open-sourced it online, which greatly promotes the research of Chinese Minority language translation.
3. The CMPT model has achieved better performance in the shared task of CCMT2022[1] compared with the baseline method.

---

[1] http://mteval.cipsc.org.cn/.

2   Related Work

2.1   Pre-trained Language Model

In recent years, increasing pre-training methods have been used in the field of natural language processing [14, 15]. These methods can learn common knowledge from a large number of unlabeled texts. GPT uses a one-way decoder to perform generation tasks. Bert [4] introduces a mask language modeling (MLM) task, which can significantly improve the performance of the pre-trained language model through pre-training to learn the interaction between context tokens with longer training time and larger model parameter size. In order to realize the conversion of seq2seq, the BART [10] and the T5 [16] use the denoising task and mask restoration task for pre-training respectively. The BART has achieved SOTA in generation tasks like translation, while T5 has SOTA performance in understanding and summarization.

2.2   Multilingual Model

Large-scale multilingual pre-training can significantly improve the performance of cross-lingual migration tasks. The XLM-R [17] uses more than 2TB of multilingual data sets and is pre-trained in 100 languages [18]. This model can model multiple languages without sacrificing language performance through denoising pre-training. The mBART [19] has significantly improved in a variety of machine translation tasks. At the same time, it can also migrate to language pairs without bidirectional corresponding text.

The M2M [20] is the translation model that not only focuses on English but realizes the first real multi- to multi-lingual translation model by collecting supervised data of thousands of language pairs. The M2M model can achieve an improvement of more than 10 BLEU [21] score when focusing on non-English translation. In order to align the context representations between different languages, the VECO [22] adds a cross-attention module [23] to explicitly construct the interdependencies between languages. It can effectively avoid the generation of predicting masked words only conditioned on the context in its own language. In order to improve the efficiency of translation. Switch-GLAT [24] proposes a non-autoregressive translation method, which improves the translation performance by shortening the spatial distance between the replaced words and the original target language.

2.3   Chinese Minority Languages

The existing work for the Chinese Minority languages is relatively small, as the multilingual model is difficult to model indigenous languages and minority languages. Nevertheless, the CINO [25] has developed the first pre-trained language model for Chinese Minority languages, covering Chinese, Cantonese, and other six low-resourced languages. It is believed that for languages with scarce resources, multilingual pre-training can perform better than language pre-training. Also, the cost of data annotation for low-resource languages is reduced significantly. The CINO has the same model architecture as XLM-R [17, 26]. In order to adapt to minority languages, additional vocabulary expansion and vocabulary pruning have been carried out and the word embedding matrix is reduced to lower the size of the model. However, the CINO is based on language understanding, which does not have the ability to perform generation downstream tasks. Different from the previous work, our work focuses on the generative pre-trained language model to further advance the development of minority language translation.

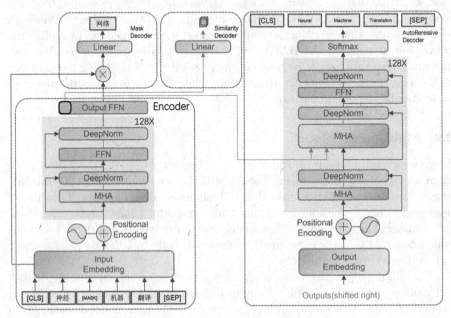

Fig. 1. Overview of the proposed Chinese Minority Pre-Trained (CMPT) language model.

3   Main Methods

3.1   Model Architecture

Recently, many works have combined language understanding and generation abilities [27–29] into the pre-trained language model. Inspired by the work [11], we incorporate both understanding and generation tasks into our Chinese Minority Pre-Trained (CMPT) language model. In order to better adapt the model to the downstream tasks of minority languages and make full use of the language pre-training tasks in low resource scenarios, we design different decoders into the CMPT with multi-task and multi-stage settings. As shown in Fig. 1, we have modified the Transformer [30] structure, which is mainly divided into four parts.

1. Bidirectional Encoder. We use a bidirectional self-attention encoder [30], which can leverage the semantic representation and text meaning.

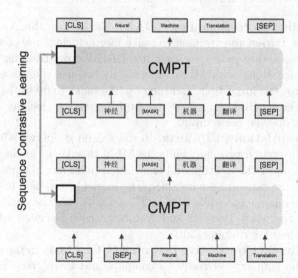

Fig. 2. The illustration of the cross-lingual contrastive learning, where the different translation pairs (Flipped Input-output) are required to learn the same semantics in the vector space between the *CLS*.

2. Mask Decoder. We adopt the single linear layer [31] to the output of the Bidirectional Encoder, where the input embedding is multiplied by the output. It is known as the MLM head to support the training of MLM pre-training task.

3. AutoReressive Decoder. We use the original transformer decoder structure, following the settings of BART [10,19] to design our model. The cross-attention is adopted to realize auto-regressive decoding.

4. Similarity Decoder. We input the *CLS* vector of the encoder into the single-layer similarity decoder to extract the semantic vector.

In the downstream tasks of the Chinese Minority language, the encoder can freely choose the decoder accordingly. For example, the comprehension task [32,33] uses the mask decoder, the generation [34] and translation task [35] uses the AutoRegressive Decoder, and the retrieval task [36,37] uses the similarity decoder. This pre-trained language model can meet more diversified requirements, and make efficient use of the parameters with suitable decoders.

3.2 Multi-tasking Multi-stage Pre-training

We designed four pre-training tasks with two-stage strategies to help the model learn language knowledge to make better use of the low resource corpus, which is shown as follows.

1. Mask Language Model (MLM) Task. We randomly mask the input text with a probability of 15%. We require the Mask Decoder to predict the masked token separately so that we can learn deeper semantic information. The input embedding is utilized to multiple with the output from the encoder for this MLM task.

2. Denoising Auto-Encoding (DAE) Task. For the AutoRegressive decoder, we use **two-stage** training to make more efficient use of the provided multilingual translation pairs. We first use DAE for pre-training for the first pre-training stage along with MLM. Specifically, we use the noise function to randomly destroy the input text, and then use the mask to fill in the corresponding position. The motivation is that the AutoRegressive Decoder can learn to reconstruct the original noise input.

3. Text Translation (TT) Task. In the second stage, we will change the DAE task to supervised training, while the MLM task keeps its original setting. Specifically, we input the multilingual translation pairs into the pre-trained language model as the same mini-batch [38]. The model is designed to generate the text of the other language while in this TT task. As for the choice of the loss function, both the Mask Decoder and AutoRegressive Decoder, we choose the Cross-Entropy loss for training [39].

4. Cross-lingual Contrastive Learning (CCL) task. In the second stage, we also add the similarity decoder to compare and learn the *CLS* output of mutual translation pairs, so as to shorten the vector space distance between texts with the same semantics. As shown in the Fig. 2, in this similarity decoder, in order to keep the same semantics between flipped translation sequence pairs, we use the sequence contrastive learning loss function, which is presented as follows.

$$L_{CL} = -\sum_{i=0}^{n} \left[\log \frac{\exp\left(f(x)^T f\left(x_i^+\right)\right)}{\exp\left(f(x)^T f\left(x_i^+\right)\right) + \sum_{j=1}^{m} \exp\left(f(x)^T f\left(x_j^-\right)\right)} \right] \quad (1)$$

where the x is the input sample of multilingual, while x_i^+ and x_i^- represent the positive and negative samples of translation pairs.

3.3   Model Parameter Details

Recent studies have shown that a deeper model can have better performance under the same parameter size, as the deeper model can deeply understand the original meaning of the language [40].

We first use the Xavier Norm [41] to initialize model parameters, where E is the number of layers of the encoder and D is the number of layers of the decoder.

$$\alpha^{Encoder} = 0.81(E^4 \cdot D)^{\frac{1}{16}}, \alpha^{Decoder} = (3D)^{\frac{1}{4}} \quad (2)$$

$$\beta^{Encoder} = 0.87(E^4 \cdot D)^{-\frac{1}{16}}, \beta^{Decoder} = (12D)^{-\frac{1}{4}} \quad (3)$$

Referring to DeepNet settings [13], we set the α and β values for the standard parameter normalization

$$std_{Encoder} = \beta^{Encoder} \times \sqrt{\frac{2}{\text{fan\_in} + \text{fan\_out}}} \quad (4)$$

$$std_{Decoder} = \beta^{Decoder} \times \sqrt{\frac{2}{\text{fan\_in} + \text{fan\_out}}} \qquad (5)$$

$$W_{Encoder} \sim N\left(0, std_{Encoder}\right), W_{Decoder} \sim N\left(0, std_{Decoder}\right) \qquad (6)$$

where the fan_in is the number of incoming network connections, while fan_out is the number of outgoing network connections from that layer.

Then, we use the DeepNorm [13] to implement deep model layers. Specifically, we add residual structure in layernorm for each layer.

$$\textbf{Layer}^{\text{Output}}_{\text{Encoder}} = LayerNorm(x \times \alpha^{Encoder} + f(x)) \qquad (7)$$

$$\textbf{Layer}^{\text{Output}}_{\text{Decoder}} = LayerNorm(x \times \alpha^{Decoder} + f(x)) \qquad (8)$$

where we first use the Encoder to encode sentences into a feature matrix $H \in \mathbb{R}^{x \times d \times t}$, which is then input into three different decoder layers.

For the mask decoder, we first dot product encoded hidden feature H with the weight of the input embedding layer $(CMPT^{Embedding})$, and then adopt the linear layer $(Linear^{Mask})$ to obtain the output vector

$$\textbf{Output}_{\textbf{Mask}} = Linear^{Mask}\left(H \cdot CMPT^{Embedding}\right) \qquad (9)$$

For the Similarity Decoder, we input the H^{CLS} vector into the linear layer $(Linear^{Sim})$ to obtain the semantic vector of the text.

$$\textbf{Output}_{\textbf{Similarity}} = Linear^{Sim}\left(H^{CLS}\right) \qquad (10)$$

We adopt the cross-attention mechanism to integrate H into decoder for the AutoRegressive Decoder. The attention function can be described as an output of a Query (Q) and a set of Key-Value (K-V) pairs mapping. The output is the weighting, and calculation between these QKV is presented as follows

$$\dot{H}^t_D = MultiHead\_SelfAtt(H^t_D) \qquad (11)$$

$$\ddot{H}^t_D = MultiHeadAtt(\dot{H}^t_D, H, H) \qquad (12)$$

$$H^{t+1}_D = LayerNorm(H^t_D \times \alpha^{Decoder} + \ddot{H}^t_D)) \qquad (13)$$

where t represents the current time, and the whole calculation is implemented as the recursive process for further auto-regression.

3.4   Model Setting Details

The CMPT is a Transformer-based [30] model that supports multiple languages. It has 256 hidden states, 8 attention heads, 128 encoder layers, and 128 decoder layers. The final model size of CMPT is 390 MB, which belongs to the base version for the pre-trained language model. In order to adapt to the minority languages, we adopt the CINO vocabulary [25], which has a number of 135359 in size.

In the pre-training phase, we set the maximum token length to 120 and deleted the excess text. We used a 15% mask rate and a maximum of 3-grams for span masking [42]. We have conducted 200000 steps (about one month) of pre-training in 8 GPUs of RTX6000 on the Pytorch[2] [43] and the hugging-face[3] [44] framework, with a batch size of 256. We implement distributed training with mixed precision based on the DeepSpeed [45]. As a result, we have fine-tuned the corpus officially provided by CCMT datasets, with a total of about 15,000,000 samples. We use an AdamW optimizer [46] with a maximum learning rate of 8e−5, followed by linear attenuation and warm-up optimizing schedules [47].

Table 1. Details of the Chinese Minority language corpus.

Language pair	Dataset	Number
Chinese	Monolingual	11,000,000 words
English Chinese	Train	9,037,417 sentences
	Dev	4003 sentences
Mongolian Chinese	Train	1,262,643 sentences
	Dev	1000 sentences
Tibetan Chinese	Train	1,157,959 sentences
	Dev	1000 sentences
Uyghur Chinese	Train	170,061 sentences
	Dev	1000 sentences

4   Experiments

We implement the experiments under the minority language corpus shown in Table 1. A variety of evaluation metrics are adopted, which can evaluate the generation quality of sentence level and word level meanwhile and show the detailed performance of the system more comprehensively. Specifically, we adopt "BLEU" [21], "ROUGE" [48], "METEOR" [49] and "CIDER" [50] as the evaluation metrics, which can assess the quality of translate, including fidelity and diversity.

In all experiments, we implement the Transformer [30] method as the baseline for fair comparisons since there is no other suitable method for the Chinese Minority language translation. This model is pre-trained in the same Chinese Minority language corpus, which is trained with equal limited training epochs. We repeated the experiment three times by changing different random seeds to ensure the fairness of the experiment. We use the learning rate of 1e−5 to fine-tune the translation of individual language pairs. Each experiment was conducted for 10 rounds. After each round, we conducted experiments in the dev set, and reported in the result table.

---

[2] https://pytorch.org.
[3] https://github.com/huggingface/transformers.

Table 2. Experiments for the CCMT 2022 shared task.

Language	Evaluation metrics	Ours	Baseline
Chinese ↓ English	BLEU_1	**0.531**	0.416
	BLEU_2	**0.378**	0.278
	BLEU_3	**0.277**	0.153
	BLEU_4	**0.207**	0.129
	METEOR	**0.288**	0.172
	Rouge_L	**0.468**	0.324
	CIDEr	**2.016**	1.564
English ↓ Chinese	BLEU_1	**0.143**	0.098
	BLEU_2	**0.031**	0.015
	BLEU_3	**0.011**	0.009
	BLEU_4	0.005	0.005
	METEOR	**0.129**	0.107
	Rouge_L	**0.177**	0.164
	CIDEr	**0.079**	0.067
Mongolian ↓ Chinese	BLEU_1	**0.155**	0.117
	BLEU_2	**0.052**	0.044
	BLEU_3	**0.029**	0.012
	BLEU_4	**0.016**	0.009
	METEOR	**0.136**	0.094
	Rouge_L	**0.149**	0.101
	CIDEr	**0.122**	0.114
Tibetan ↓ Chinese	BLEU_1	**0.363**	0.333
	BLEU_2	**0.253**	0.207
	BLEU_3	**0.202**	0.149
	BLEU_4	**0.168**	0.112
	METEOR	**0.419**	0.374
	Rouge_L	**0.380**	0.365
	CIDEr	**1.295**	0.774
Uyghur ↓ Chinese	BLEU_1	**0.217**	0.124
	BLEU_2	**0.053**	0.041
	BLEU_3	**0.028**	0.015
	BLEU_4	**0.017**	0.010
	METEOR	**0.148**	0.117
	Rouge_L	**0.249**	0.204
	CIDEr	**0.127**	0.108

Type	Source Language	Generation Language	Reference Language
Chinese ↓ English	通过相对集中诊疗和双向转诊，为罕见病患者提供较为高效的诊疗服务，延缓疾病的进展，减轻他们的痛苦。	The clinical services are provided to patients with rare diseases with more effective treatment through relative intensive diagnosis and bi-directional diagnosis, which can alleviate their pains and slow down the progression of diseases.	*Through relatively centralized diagnosis and treatment as well as two-way referral, we can provide more efficient services for patients with rare diseases to delay the progress of the disease and alleviate their pain.*
English ↓ Chinese	In 2008, Armisen, whose mother is Venezuelan and whose father is of German and Korean heritage, told New York Magazine's Intelligencer column that he wore honey colored makeup to portray Obama, who is biracial.	美国杂志《纽约杂志》的英文版《美国人》的英文版《美国人》是《纽约时报》的英文版	*阿米森的母亲是委内瑞拉人，父亲是德韩混血，2008年，他告诉《纽约杂志》的"情报"专栏，他使用蜂蜜色的化妆品来刻画奥巴马形象，因为奥巴马是混血儿*
Mongolian ↓ Chinese	ᠬᠢᠯᠢ ᠶᠢᠨ ᠬᠢᠨᠠᠯᠲᠠ ᠶᠢᠨ ᠲᠤᠰᠠᠯᠠᠭᠴᠢ ?	你听见了,也听见了,是照你向那地的妇人所应许的。	*你听说过她和某个当地男子走得很近的闲话吗?*
Tibetan ↓ Chinese	ང་ཚོའི་ཏང་གིས་རྟག་ཏུ་ཉིད་ནས་དང་ ཡོངས་ནས་དང་སྐུལ་བར་དུ་འགོ་ཁྲིད་ལས་ བྱེད་པའི་སློབ་སྦྱོང་དང་འཛིན་འ་མཆོ ད་ཆེན་སྟམ་དང་ཉིད་འཆི་ཡོད།	我们党从来都十分重视对全党特别是领导干部的学习,	*我们党历来重视抓全党特别是领导干部的学习,*
Uyghur ↓ Chinese	نىكسكۆرسىيە كۆرگىزمىنى 22 كزىنگە تەخمىنەن قىلىدىغانلار دۆلەت نىشپىر، قىتمىدىن نادىم ملك نوخشان نۇتكۆززۇلگمن مۆزبىدا يىگى نىچىدە كۆرگىزمىلەر تۆردىكى يارىتىلدى رىكورد	参观者共参观了22000多盏天文天台,参观了来自各国的大型艺术博物馆。	*平均每天有两万两千多人次的参观人数，创下了国博同类型展览的新纪录。*

Fig. 3. Case study of the proposed method.

4.1   Main Results

In the experiment of the shared task shown in Table 2, we can find that the CMPT has many to many translation abilities and supports translation tasks in different minority languages compared with the baseline method. For the same experimental setting, our method can achieve better performance than the baseline. Specifically, we can also find that CMPT has good translation performance, whether it is Chinese to English or ethnic minorities to Chinese. This further demonstrates the effectiveness of the proposed method. However, our method fails to obtain a high score for the English-Chinese translation, where the reason may be the limited size of the pre-training process.

4.2   Case Study

We randomly selected some translation results for comparison, which is shown in the Fig. 3. The further conclusion can be found that in the scenario of English to Chinese translation, the model generates repetition results, which may be because the model has a weak understanding of English due to insufficient training corpus. When using minority languages for translation, we can find that the model can generate relatively complete text. However, due to the insufficient understanding ability of the model, the semantics of the generated text may be biased.

5   Conclusion

In this work, we introduced a multilingual model CMPT that supports downstream generative tasks. It uses Chinese Minority languages for multi-task and multi-stage pre-training to comprehensively improve the ability of understanding and generation. We have conducted an evaluation of the translation task of the CCMT-2022, where the experimental results show that CMPT has achieved better performance both in understanding and generation compared with the baseline method. In the future, we believe that with more pre-training minority language corpus being used for the pre-training, the performance of the CMPT is expected to be further improved.

References

1. Han, X., et al.: Pre-trained models: past, present and future. AI Open **2**, 225–250 (2021)
2. Jing, L., Tian, Y.: Self-supervised visual feature learning with deep neural networks: a survey. IEEE Trans. Pattern Anal. Mach. Intell. **43**, 4037–4058 (2021)
3. Radford, A., Narasimhan, K.: Improving language understanding by generative pre-training (2018)
4. Devlin, J., Chang, M.-W., Lee, K., Toutanova, K.: BERT: pre-training of deep bidirectional transformers for language understanding. In: North American Chapter of the Association for Computational Linguistics (2018)
5. Li, B., Weng, Y., Xia, F., Deng, H.: Towards better Chinese-centric neural machine translation for low-resource languages. arXiv preprint arXiv:2204.04344 (2022)
6. Dabre, R., Chu, C., Kunchukuttan, A.: A survey of multilingual neural machine translation. ACM Comput. Surv. **53**, 1–38 (2019)
7. Zuo, X.: China's policy towards minority languages in a globalising age. TCI (Transnatl. Curric. Inq.) **4**(1), 80–91 (2007)
8. Zhou, H.-C., Long, J.R., Yaghi, O.M.: Introduction to metal-organic frameworks. Chem. Rev. **112**, 673–674 (2012)
9. Attané, I., Courbage, Y.: Transitional stages and identity boundaries: the case of ethnic minorities in china. Popul. Environ. **21**(3), 257–280 (2000)
10. Lewis, M., et al.: BART: denoising sequence-to-sequence pre-training for natural language generation, translation, and comprehension. In: Meeting of the Association for Computational Linguistics (2019)
11. Shao, Y., et al.: CPT: a pre-trained unbalanced transformer for both Chinese language understanding and generation. arXiv, Computation and Language (2021)
12. Taylor, W.L.: Cloze procedure: a new tool for measuring readability. J. Mass Commun. Q. **30**, 415–433 (1953)
13. Wang, H., Ma, S., Dong, L., Huang, S., Zhang, D., Wei, F.: DeepNet: scaling transformers to 1,000 layers (2022)

14. Clark, K., Luong, M.-T., Le, Q.V., Manning, C.D.: ELECTRA: pre-training text encoders as discriminators rather than generators. Learning (2020)

15. He, P., Gao, J., Chen, W.: DeBERTaV 3: improving DeBERTa using ELECTRA-style pre-training with gradient-disentangled embedding sharing. arxiv, Computation and Language (2021)

16. Raffel, C., et al.: Exploring the limits of transfer learning with a unified text-to-text transformer. arXiv e-prints (2019)

17. Conneau, A., et al.: Unsupervised cross-lingual representation learning at scale. In: Meeting of the Association for Computational Linguistics (2020)

18. Wenzek, G., et al.: CCNet: extracting high quality monolingual datasets from web crawl data. In: Language Resources and Evaluation (2019)

19. Liu, Y., et al.: Multilingual denoising pre-training for neural machine translation. Trans. Assoc. Comput. Linguist. **8**, 726–742 (2020)

20. Fan, A., et al.: Beyond English-centric multilingual machine translation. arxiv, Computation and Language (2020)

21. Papineni, K., Roukos, S., Ward, T., Zhu, W.-J.: BLEU: a method for automatic evaluation of machine translation. In: Proceedings of the 40th Annual Meeting of the Association for Computational Linguistics, Philadelphia, Pennsylvania, USA, pp. 311–318. Association for Computational Linguistics, July 2002

22. Luo, F., et al.: VECO: variable and flexible cross-lingual pre-training for language understanding and generation. In: Meeting of the Association for Computational Linguistics (2021)

23. Chaudhari, S., Polatkan, G., Ramanath, R., Mithal, V.: An attentive survey of attention models. arxiv, Learning (2019)

24. Song, Z., et al.: switch-GLAT: multilingual parallel machine translation via code-switch decoder. In: International Conference on Learning Representations (2021)

25. Yang, Z., et al.: CINO: a Chinese minority pre-trained language model (2022)

26. Lample, G., Conneau, A.: Cross-lingual language model pretraining. In: Advances in Neural Information Processing Systems (2019)

27. Dong, L., et al.: Unified language model pre-training for natural language understanding and generation. In: Advances in Neural Information Processing Systems (2019)

28. Bao, H., et al.: Unilmv2: pseudo-masked language models for unified language model pre-training. In: International Conference on Machine Learning (2020)

29. Du, Z., et al.: All NLP tasks are generation tasks: a general pretraining framework. arXiv, Computation and Language (2021)

30. Vaswani, A., et al.: Attention is all you need. In: Proceedings of the 31st International Conference on Neural Information Processing Systems, NIPS 2017, Red Hook, NY, USA, pp. 6000–6010. Curran Associates Inc. (2017)

31. Devlin, J., Chang, M.-W., Lee, K., Toutanova, K.: BERT: pre-training of deep bidirectional transformers for language understanding. In: Proceedings of the 2019 Conference of the North American Chapter of the Association for Computational Linguistics: Human Language Technologies, Volume 1 (Long and Short Papers), Minneapolis, Minnesota, pp. 4171–4186. Association for Computational Linguistics, June 2019

32. Qun, N., Li, X., Qiu, X., Huang, X.: End-to-end neural text classification for Tibetan. In: Sun, M., Wang, X., Chang, B., Xiong, D. (eds.) CCL/NLP-NABD -2017. LNCS (LNAI), vol. 10565, pp. 472–480. Springer, Cham (2017). https://doi.org/10.1007/978-3-319-69005-6_39

33. Xu, L., et al.: CLUE: a Chinese language understanding evaluation benchmark. In: Proceedings of the 28th International Conference on Computational Linguistics,

Barcelona, Spain (Online), pp. 4762–4772. International Committee on Computational Linguistics, December 2020

34. Hu, B., Chen, Q., Zhu, F.: LCSTS: a large scale Chinese short text summarization dataset. In: Empirical Methods in Natural Language Processing (2015)

35. Barrault, L., et al.: Findings of the 2020 Conference on Machine Translation (WMT20). In: Empirical Methods in Natural Language Processing (2020)

36. Bajaj, P., et al.: MS MARCO: a human generated machine reading comprehension dataset. arXiv, Computation and Language (2016)

37. Kwiatkowski, T., et al.: Natural questions: a benchmark for question answering research. Trans. Assoc. Comput. Linguist. **7**, 453–466 (2019)

38. Li, M., Zhang, T., Chen, Y., Smola, A.J.: Efficient mini-batch training for stochastic optimization. In: Knowledge Discovery and Data Mining (2014)

39. Chen, C., Zong, Q., Luo, Q., Qiu, B., Li, M.: Transformer-based unified neural network for quality estimation and transformer-based re-decoding model for machine translation. In: Li, J., Way, A. (eds.) CCMT 2020. CCIS, vol. 1328, pp. 66–75. Springer, Singapore (2020). https://doi.org/10.1007/978-981-33-6162-1_6

40. Tay, Y., et al.: Scale efficiently: insights from pre-training and fine-tuning transformers. arXiv, Computation and Language (2021)

41. Glorot, X., Bengio, Y.: Understanding the difficulty of training deep feedforward neural networks. In: International Conference on Artificial Intelligence and Statistics (2010)

42. Joshi, M., Chen, D., Liu, Y., Weld, D.S., Zettlemoyer, L., Levy, O.: SpanBERT: improving pre-training by representing and predicting spans. Trans. Assoc. Comput. Linguist. **8**, 64–77 (2020)

43. Paszke, A., et al.: PyTorch: an imperative style, high-performance deep learning library. In: Advances in Neural Information Processing Systems, vol. 32. Curran Associates Inc. (2019)

44. Wolf, T., et al.: Transformers: state-of-the-art natural language processing. In: Proceedings of the 2020 Conference on Empirical Methods in Natural Language Processing: System Demonstrations, pp. 38–45. Association for Computational Linguistics, October 2020

45. Rajbhandari, S., Rasley, J., Ruwase, O., He, Y.: Zero: memory optimizations toward training trillion parameter models. In: Proceedings of the International Conference for High Performance Computing, Networking, Storage and Analysis, SC 2020. IEEE Press (2020)

46. Loshchilov, I., Hutter, F.: Decoupled weight decay regularization. In: International Conference on Learning Representations (2018)

47. He, K., Zhang, X., Ren, S., Sun, J.: Deep residual learning for image recognition. In: 2016 IEEE Conference on Computer Vision and Pattern Recognition (CVPR), pp. 770–778 (2016)

48. Lin, C.-Y.: ROUGE: a package for automatic evaluation of summaries. In: Text Summarization Branches Out, Barcelona, Spain, pp. 74–81. Association for Computational Linguistics, July 2004

49. Denkowski, M., Lavie, A.: Meteor universal: language specific translation evaluation for any target language. In: Proceedings of the Ninth Workshop on Statistical Machine Translation, Baltimore, Maryland, USA, pp. 376–380. Association for Computational Linguistics June 2014

50. Vedantam, R., Lawrence Zitnick, C., Parikh, D.: CIDEr: consensus-based image description evaluation. In: 2015 IEEE Conference on Computer Vision and Pattern Recognition (CVPR), pp. 4566–4575 (2015)

An Improved Multi-task Approach to Pre-trained Model Based MT Quality Estimation

Binhuan Yuan[✉], Yueyang Li[✉], Kehai Chen[✉], Hao Lu, Muyun Yang, and Hailong Cao

Department of Computer Science and Technology, Harbin Institute of Technology, Harbin, China
yuanbinhuan@126.com, 20s003024@stu.hit.edu.cn,
{chenkehai,yangmuyun}@hit.edu.cn

Abstract. Machine translation (MT) quality estimation (QE) aims to automatically predict the quality of MT outputs without any references. State-of-the-art solutions are mostly fine-tuned with a pre-trained model in a multi-task framework (i.e., joint training sentence-level QE and word-level QE). In this paper, we propose an alternative multi-task framework in which post-editing results are utilized for sentence-level QE over an mBART-based encoder-decoder model. We show that the post-editing sub-task is much more in-formative and the mBART is superior to other pre-trained models. Experiments on WMT2021 English-German and English-Chinese QE datasets showed that the proposed method achieves 1.2%–2.1% improvements in the strong sentence-level QE baseline.

Keywords: Quality estimation · Multitask learning · mBART

1 Introduction

Machine translation (MT) quality estimation (QE) is used as an automatic evalua-tion for selecting the most suitable machine translation without golden reference. QE is usually implemented either in sentence-level or word-level. Sentence-level QE subtask takes HTER [3] Metric to represent the quality of MT, and the word-level QE task measures the translation quality by generating a quality tag for each word in the output of MT.

The sentence-level and word-level QE subtasks both rely on the triplets of *src* (source sentence), *mt* (machine translated sentence) and *pe* (post-edited sentence). Therefore, sentence-level task is usually training jointly with word-level task so as to improves model performance. It should be noted that, for sentence-level task, *pe* is only used for calculating the label HTER, it is not integrated into the training phase.

In contrast to existing practice, we propose to integrate pe into the sentence-level QE model, which is named as pe based multi-task learning QE. Following recent em-ployment of pre-trained model, we adopt a multi-task transla-

T. Xiao and J. Pino (Eds.): CCMT 2022, CCIS 1671, pp. 106–116, 2022.
https://doi.org/10.1007/978-981-19-7960-6_11

tion QE model based on mBART [4,5]. Evaluated on the WMT2021 English-German/English-Chinese QE dataset and CCMT2021 English-Chinese/Chinese-English QE datasets, the proposed method is revealed a substantial improvement in sentence-level QE compared with jointly training by word-level task. We also reveal that compared to other pre-trained models like BERT [1] and [2], mBART achieved better perfor-mance.

This paper is organized as follows. In Sect. 2, we introduce the related work of QE. The proposed multi-task QE method based on mBART is described in Sect. 3., we report the experiment and results in Sect. 4, and conclude our paper in Sect. 5.

2 Related Works

With the purpose of estimating machine translations without reference transla-tion, the early research on QE tasks adopted traditional feature extraction and feature selection methods to train the models. Commonly used features included the length of the translation, the matching degree of special symbols, punctu-ation, and capital letters, etc. Gaussian process [9], heuristic [12] and principal component analysis [16] were commonly used feature selection methods.

With the development of deep learning, QE tasks had gradually shifted into neu-ral network-based framework. The simple network of QE is based on con-text win-dow [6], and it could be improved by CNN and RNN [15]. In order to integrate large-scale parallel corpus into RNN model, the model could be implemented by Predic-tor-Estimator structure [7]. With the rise of transformer, transformer-based QE models was implemented for its abilities of using large-scale parallel corpus and learning lexical and syntactic information [8].

With the emergence of pre-trained model, researchers attempted to use pre-trained models (e.g., XLM [13] and XLM-R [14]) to implement machine transla-tion quality estimation, which obtained fairly good results compared with pre-vious re-search based on barely transformer. Those researches are both based on encoder framework, which consider QE as a regression task for matching HTER. However, As QE tasks and MT are highly related, QE models can also be implemented based on encoder-decoder framework. The QE model with encoder-decoder framework achieved the state-of-the-art performance in WMT 2017/2018 QE task [8] and mBART [4] based model achieved good results on DA (Direct Assessment) QE task [11]. It should be noted that previous methods usually neglected pe data in sentence-level QE task. In other words, information in *pe* data is unexploited. The only excep-tion is in word level QE, which relies on *pe* to derive the quality label for each word.

3 PE Based Multi-task Learning for Sentence Level QE

3.1 Multi-task Learning Framework for QE

Given that QE tasks is highly correlated with machine translation which is imple-mented by encoder-decoder architecture, we choose mBART [4] as our base model. mBART is based on multi-layers transformer architecture and utilizes the bidirec-tional modeling capability of the encoder while retaining the autoregressive feature. We feed the source text (src) into the encoder and the machine translation (MT) into the decoder, and the output of the decoder is used to implement the sentence level task and word level task, respectively.

The multi-task learning QE based on mBART is shown in Fig. 1. For sentence-level task, we take the last token which is a special token $<eos>$ to calculate the sentence-level loss, which we believe that the logit contains adequate information. We use sigmoid as the activation function. The loss function for sentence-level is as follows:

$$L_{sentence_level} = \mathrm{MSE}(\mathrm{HTER}, \mathrm{sigmoid}(FC(u))) \tag{1}$$

where u denotes the hidden representation for the special token $<eos>$. MSE represent Mean Square Error function, $L_{sentence_level}$ denotes the sentence-level loss, FC denotes a fully connected layer.

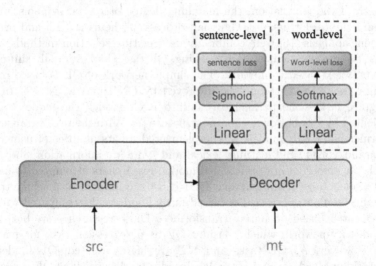

Fig. 1. Multi-task learning framework for MT QE

For word-level task (used as the baseline in this paper), we utilize each token's correlated logits to generate word-quality label. The loss function for word-level is as follows:

$$L_{word_level} = \sum_{i=1}^{k} (-I(\mathrm{label} = OK) \log (\mathrm{logit}_i[0]) - I(\mathrm{label} = BAD) \log (\mathrm{logit}_i[1])) \tag{2}$$

The final overall loss is the sum of sentence-level loss and word-level loss, $\aleph$ is a constant weight.

$$L = L_{sentence_level} + \alpha \times L_{word_level} \tag{3}$$

3.2 *PE* Based Multi-task Learning QE

Under the encoder-decoder structure of mBART, we design a translation task from *src* to *pe* as an auxiliary task for sentence-level QE. The model is shown in Fig. 2. For the translation part, we feed the right-shifted *pe* $x = [x_1, ..., x_{k+1}]$ into the decoder which share parameter with the sentence-level part.

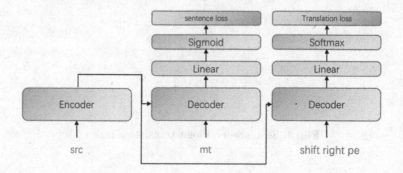

Fig. 2. Sentence-level joint translation task

The translation loss $L_{translation}$ is calculated by the cross-entropy loss function:

$$L_{\text{translation}} = \sum_{i=1}^{k} -\log\left(\text{logit}_i\left[x_{i+1}\right]\right) \tag{4}$$

where x_{i+1} denotes each token in the input sentence.

The final overall loss is the sum of sentence-level loss and translation loss, β is a constant weight.

$$L = L_{sentence_level} + \beta \times L_{translation} \tag{5}$$

Compared with word-level task, translation task can evaluate not only the trans-lation quality of each single word, but also the translation quality at the sentence-level by using the context information in the pe data. Meanwhile, compared with encoder-based QE structures, mBART can utilize pe data more directly and avoid additional label cost in word level quality annotation.

3.3 Multi-model Ensemble

Given that various models with different initialized parameters, we can utilize multi-ple models to construct our system. Following existing practices in this aspect, we further implemented three other different QE models, mBERT, XLM-RoBERTa-base and XLM-RoBERTa-large to obtain different information from the same data. We average the HTER obtained by these three models and our system to generate stronger performance.

mBERT and XLM-RoBERTa are both encoder-based multilingual pre-trained models. The framework of QE is shown in the Fig. 3. src and mt are concatenated as encoder input. The output of the encoder passes through the linear layer, which utiliz-es sigmoid as the activation function. For CCMT does not provide word level QE data, we didn't apply multi-task learning for encoder-based framework.

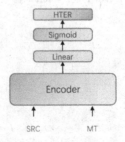

Fig. 3. Sentence-level joint translation task

4   Experiments

4.1   Dataset

To compare with recent public results, we use the QE data from WMT2021 Machine Translation Quality Estimation tasks for English-German, and CCMT2021 Machine Translation Quality Estimation tasks for English-Chinese. Each dataset contains both sentence-level and word-level tasks. The dataset of WMT2021 provided 7k samples for training in both directions, and CCMT2021 provided more than ten thousand samples, slightly more data than WMT2021. The dataset statistics are shown in Table 1.

Table 1. The statistics of quality estimation datasets.

Dataset	Train	Dev	Test
WMT2021 EN-DE	7000	1000	1000
WMT2021 EN-DE	7000	1000	1000
CCMT2021 EN-ZH	10070	1385	1412
CCMT2021 ZH-EN	14789	1445	1528

4.2   Model Training and Evaluation Metric

In the training process, AdamW is selected as the optimizer. We set the batch-size as 8 and the learning rate is set to 1e−5, and the warmup steps are 1000 steps. The train-ing adopts the early stop strategy, that is, if the model does not improve on the vali-dation set in 2000 steps, stop training. The proposed approach is trained over a single Nvidia 3090. In the sentence-level translation quality estimation task, three evalua-tion metrics are used: Spearman's Rank Correlation Coefficient (Spearman), Mean Absolute Error (MAE), and Root Mean Squared Error (RMSE). The Spearman corre-lation coefficient is used as the main metric, in which the higher value indicates better performance of the QE model. The mean absolute error and the root mean square error are also provided for reference, in which the lower value indicates better perfor-mance of the QE model.

4.3   Experimental Results and Analysis

We first compare mBART with other pre-trained models on the WMT2021 Dataset. We choose monolingual BERT, XLM-Roberta, and mBERT as base-lines. As shown in Table 2, the mBART model surpasses all the other pre-trained models and achieves the highest Pearson correlation in both DE-De and EN-ZH tasks.

Table 2. Experiment results with different pretrain models

Model		Pearson↑	MAE↓	RMSE↓
EN-DE	BERT	0.544	0.122	0.172
	bert-base-multilingual	0.544	0.123	0.176
	XLM-RoBERTa-base	0.505	0.125	0.175
	XLM-RoBERTa-large	0.548	**0.116**	0.176
	mBART	**0.554**	0.125	**0.166**
EN-ZH	BERT	0.27	0.234	0.312
	bert-base-multilingual	0.265	0.278	0.314
	XLM-RoBERTa-base	0.256	**0.232**	0.282
	XLM-RoBERTa-large	0.30	0.233	**0.270**
	mBART	**0.327**	0.253	0.304

The experiment results of our system on WMT2021 are shown in Table 3. It shows that the multi-task learning method can achieve better results compared with using mBART only. For sentence-level QE, jointly trained with translation task ob-tained better performance than the single word-level task. However, combining word-level task and translation task will lead to a performance decline. We also compare the proposed QE model with the best results of WMT2021. HW-TSC [9] utilizes the auxiliary data for training which is obtained by a mature translation system. IST-Unbabel [10] uses the ADAPT strategy and a more complicated feature extraction classifier to enhance its performance. As a result, there is still a gap between our method and the best results.

The experiment results of our system on CCMT2021 are shown in Table 4. The proposed approach outperforms all the other pre-trained models in the CCMT2021 dataset. Jointly training with translation task boost the performance of our mBART-based system, and the ensemble of multiple models can also make improvement in both directions.

Table 3. Experiment results with multitask on WMT2021

Model	Pearson↑	MAE↓	RMSE↓
WMT2021baseline	0.529	0.129	0.183
HW-TSC	**0.653**	**0.108**	**0.151**
IST-Unbabel	0.617	0.116	0.172
EN-DE mBART	0.554	0.125	0.166
mBART + word level	0.585	0.123	0.169
mBART + translation	0.606	0.119	0.167
mBART + translation + word	0.596	0.127	0.162
WMT2021 baseline	0.282	0.246	0.287
HW-TSC	**0.368**	0.248	0.297
IST-Unbabel	0.290	**0.220**	0.266
EN-ZH mBART	0.327	0.253	0.304
mBART + word level	0.335	0.235	0.280
mBART + translation	0.347	0.221	**0.265**
+ translation + word	0.338	0.230	0.272

4.4 Ablation Study

In this section, we will investigate the effect of translation task. We use *pe* (*post editing*) to correct the error of *mt* (*machine translation*) in different proportions, then the corrected mt is used as the input of decoder for the translation task. The result is shown in Table 4. We observe that with the increase of the correction ratio, the per-formance of the model improves significantly. This means that when introducing *pe* into sentence-level evaluation system, the proposed approach can obtain more useful information from *pe* data (Table 5).

Table 4. Experiment results on CCMT2021

Model		Pearson↑	MAE↓	RMSE↓
EN-ZH	mBART	0.348	0.085	0.125
	mBART + translation	0.375	0.089	0.118
	bert-base-multilingual	0.261	0.094	0.129
	XLM-RoBERTa-base	0.306	0.083	0.12
	XLM-RoBERTa-large	0.331	0.087	0.12
	Ensemble	**0.419**	**0.079**	**0.114**
ZH-EN	mBART	0.483	0.078	0.113
	mBART + translation	0.498	0.0745	0.116
	bert-base-multilingual	0.422	0.091	0.119
	XLM-RoBERTa-base	0.414	0.077	0.117
	XLM-RoBERTa-large	0.463	0.076	0.117
	Ensemble	**0.541**	**0.072**	**0.106**

Table 5. Effect of PE translation tasks

Model		Pearson↑	MAE↓	RMSE↓
EN-DE	Mt	0.570	0.123	0.168
	20%	0.585	0.120	0.176
	40%	0.593	0.131	0.190
	60%	0.594	0.119	0.169
	80%	0.597	0.121	0.169
	100%	**0.606**	**0.119**	**0.167**
EN-ZH	Mt	0.332	0.254	0.304
	20%	0.339	0.255	0.305
	40%	0.337	0.238	0.282
	60%	0.343	0.240	0.289
	80%	0.346	0.234	0.276
	100%	**0.347**	**0.221**	**0.265**

We also test the influence of weight on multi-task learning as shown in Fig. 4 and 5. Generally speaking, the performance of the translation multi-task method is better than the word-level multi-task method.

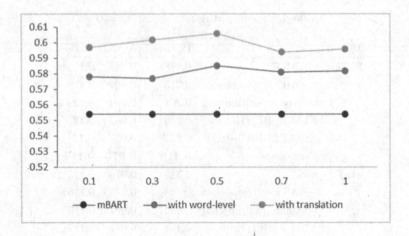

Fig. 4. Influence of joint training task weight on multi-task learning in EN-DE

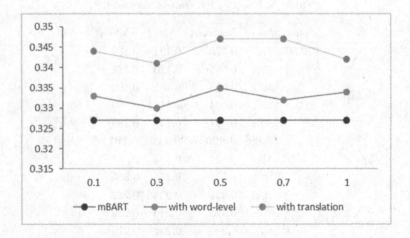

Fig. 5. Influence of joint training task weight on multi-task learning in EN-ZH

Moreover, we test different ways of input to train mBART like feed mt into the encoder and put src into the decoder or put src and mt into the encoder together, as shown in Table 6. Compared to other ways of input, our framework achieves signifi-cant improvements in EN-DE and EN-ZH tasks.

Table 6. Experiment results with different ways of input

Model		Pearson↑	MAE↓	RMSE↓
EN-DE	Encoder: src Decoder: mt	**0.554**	0.125	0.166
	Encoder: mt Decoder: src	0.438	0.137	0.193
	Encoder: src mt	0.417	0.146	0.205
EN-ZH	Encoder: src Decoder: mt	**0.327**	0.253	0.304
	Encoder: mt Decoder: src	0.241	0.261	0.281
	Encoder: src mt	0.201	0.272	0.295

5 Conclusion

In this paper, we describe our submission in the QE task, which consists of English- Chinese and Chinese-English tasks. Our system is implemented based on the mBART and multi-task QE learning strategies. We propose a sentence-level translation quality estimation model based on the mBART, which achieves better results than other cross-language pre-training models. We also present a training method to introduce translation task into multi-task QE learning which successfully integrates post-edited sentences into sentence-level QE task and greatly improve the system performance with a simple model architecture design.

Acknowledgement. This work is partially funded by the National Key Research and Development Pro-gram of China (No. 2020AAA0108000), and by the Key Project of National Natural Science Foundation China (No. U1908216).

References

1. Devlin, J., Chang, M.W., Lee, K., Toutanova, K.: Bert: pre-training of deep bidirectional transformers for language understanding. arXiv preprint arXiv:1810.04805 (2018)
2. Conneau, A., et al.: Unsupervised cross-lingual representation learning at scale. arXiv pre-print arXiv:1911.02116 (2019)
3. Specia, L., Farzindar, A.: Estimating machine translation post-editing effort with HTER: In: Proceedings of the Second Joint EM+/CNGL Workshop: Bringing MT to the User: Research on Integrating MT in the Translation Industry, pp. 33–43 (2010)
4. Liu, Y., Gu, J., Goyal, N., et al.: Multilingual denoising pre-training for neural machine translation. Trans. Assoc. Comput. Linguist. **8**, 726–742 (2020)
5. Tang, Y., Tran, C., Li, X., et al.: Multilingual translation with extensible multilingual pre-training and finetuning. arXiv preprint arXiv:2008.00401 (2020)
6. Kreutzer, J., Schamoni, S., Riezler, S.: QUality estimation from scratch (QUETCH): deep learning for word-level translation quality estimation. In: Proceedings of the Tenth Workshop on Statistical Machine Translation, pp. 316–322 (2015)

7. Kim, H., Lee, J.H.: A recurrent neural network approach for estimating the quality of ma-chine translation output. In: Proceedings of the 2016 Conference of the North American Chapter of the Association for Computational Linguistics: Human Language Techologies, StroudsBurg, PA, pp. 494–498. ACL (2016)

8. Fan, K., Wang, J., Li, B., et al.: "Bilingual Expert" can find translation errors. In: Proceedings of the AAAI Conference on Artificial Intelligence, vol. 33, no. 01, pp. 6367–6374 (2019)

9. Shah, K., Cohn, T., Specia, L.: A Bayesian non-linear method for feature selection in ma-chine translation quality estimation. Mach. Transl. **29**(2), 101–125 (2015)

10. Moura, J., Vera, M., van Stigt, D., et al.: IST-Unbabel participation in the WMT20 quality estimation shared task.: In: Proceedings of the Fifth Conference on Machine Translation, pp..1029–1036 (2020)

11. Zerva, C., van Stigt, D., Rei, R., et al.: IST-Unbabel 2021 submission for the quality estimation shared task. In: Proceedings of the Sixth Conference on Machine Translation, pp. 961–972 (2021)

12. González-Rubio, J., Navarro-Cerdán, J.R., Casacuberta, F.: Dimensionality reduction methods for machine translation quality estimation. Mach. Transl. **27**(3–4), 281–301 (2013)

13. Kepler, F., Trénous, J., Treviso, M., et al.: Unbabel's participation in the WMT19 translation quality estimation shared task. arXiv preprint arXiv:1907.10352 (2019)

14. Ranasinghe, T., Orasan, C., Mitkov, R.: TransQuest: translation quality estimation with cross-lingual transformers. arXiv preprint arXiv:2011.01536 (2020)

15. Martins, A.F.T., Astudillo, R., Hokamp, C., et al.: Unbabel's participation in the WMT16 word-level translation quality estimation shared task. In: Proceedings of the First Conference on Machine Translation: Volume 2, Shared Task Papers, pp. 806–811 (2016)

16. Mikolov, T., Chen, K., Corrado, G.S., et al.: Efficient estimation of word representations in vector space. Comput. Sci. (2013)

Optimizing Deep Transformers for Chinese-Thai Low-Resource Translation

Wenjie Hao[1(✉)] ⓘ, Hongfei Xu[1], Lingling Mu[1], and Hongying Zan[1,2]

[1] Zhengzhou University, Henan 450001, China
haowj9977@163.com, hfxunlp@foxmail.com, {iellmu,iehyzan}@zzu.edu.cn
[2] Peng Cheng Laboratory, Shenzhen 518000, China

Abstract. In this paper, we study the use of deep Transformer translation model for the CCMT 2022 Chinese↔Thai low-resource machine translation task. We first explore the experiment settings (including the number of BPE merge operations, dropout probability, embedding size, etc.) for the low-resource scenario with the 6-layer Transformer. Considering that increasing the number of layers also increases the regularization on new model parameters (dropout modules are also introduced when using more layers), we adopt the highest performance setting but increase the depth of the Transformer to 24 layers to obtain improved translation quality. Our work obtains the SOTA performance in the Chinese-to-Thai translation in the constrained evaluation.

Keywords: Low-resource NMT · Deep transformer · Chinese-Thai MT

1 Introduction

Neural machine translation (NMT) has achieved impressive performance with the support of large amounts of parallel data [1,27]. However, in low-resource scenario, its performance is far from expectation [10,12].

To improve the translation performance, previous work either study data augmentation approaches to leverage pseudo data [5,6,16,22,29] or benefit from models pre-trained on large-scale monolingual corpus [18,21].

Instead of introducing more data, in this paper, we explore the effects of different data processing and model settings for the CCMT 2022 Chinese↔Thai low-resource machine translation task inspired by Sennrich and Zhang [24].

Specifically, we adopt the Chinese↔Thai (Zh↔Th) machine translation data from CCMT 2022 of 200k training sentence pairs. We first apply strict rules for data cleaning, and employ the cutting-edge Transformer model [27]. We explore the influence of BPE merge operations on performance, and the effects of different model settings (embedding size, dropout probability). As previous work [2,8,13–15,17,28,30,31,33,36–38] shows that deep Transformers can bring about

T. Xiao and J. Pino (Eds.): CCMT 2022, CCIS 1671, pp. 117–126, 2022.
https://doi.org/10.1007/978-981-19-7960-6_12

improved translation performance, we adopt the setting of highest performance in ablation experiments for the Chinese↔Thai translation task but increase the number of layers to 24. We explore experiment settings with the 6-layer setting but adopt the best one to deeper models, because: 1) exploring the effects of these hyper-parameters with shallow models is more computation-friendly than with deep models; and 2) increasing the number of layers also introduces regularization, as adding new layers also brings dropout modules.

2   Background

2.1   Transformer

Vaswani et al. [27] propose the self-attention based Transformer model, evading the parallelization issue of RNN. Transformer has become the most popular model in NMT field. Transformer consists of one encoder and one decoder module, each of them is formed by several layers, and the multi-layer structure allows it to model complicated functions. The Transformer model also employs residual connection and layer normalization techniques for the purpose of ease optimization.

2.2   Low-Resource NMT

Despite that NMT has achieved impressive performance in high-resource cases [27], its performance drops heavily in low-resource scenarios, even underperforming phrase-based statistical machine translation (PBSMT) [10,12]. NMT normally requires large amounts of auxiliary data to achieve competitive results. Sennrich and Zhang [24] show that this is due to the lack of system adaptation for low-resource settings. They suggest that large vocabularies lead to low-frequency (sub)words, and the amount of data is not sufficient to learn high-quality high-dimensional representations for these low-frequency tokens. Reducing the vocabulary size (14k→2k symbols) can bring significant improvements (7.20→12.10 BLEU). In addition, they show that aggressive (word) dropout (0.1→0.3) can bring impressive performance (13.03→15.84 BLEU), and reducing batch size (4k→1k tokens) may also benefit. Optimized NMT systems can indeed outperform PBSMT.

2.3   Parameter Initialization for Deep Transformers

Xu et al. [36] suggest that the training issue of deep Transformers is because that the layer normalization may shrink the residual connections, leading to the gradient vanishing issue. They propose to address this by applying the Lipschitz constraint to parameter initialization. Experiments on WMT14 English-German and WMT15 Czech-English translation tasks show the effectiveness of their simple approach.

2.4 Deep Transformers for Low-Resource Tasks

Previous work shows that deep Transformers generally perform well with sufficient training data [13], and few attempts have been made on training deep Transformers from scratch on small datasets. Xu et al. [37] propose Data-dependent Transformer Fixed-update initialization scheme, called DT-Fixup, and experiment on the Text-to-SQL semantic parsing and the logical reading comprehension tasks. They show that deep Transformers can work better than their shallow counterparts on small datasets through proper initialization and optimization procedure. Their work inspires us to explore the use of deep Transformers for low-resource machine translation.

3 Our Work

3.1 Data Processing

The quality of the dataset affects the performance of NMT. Therefore, We first standardize the texts with the following pipeline:

1. removing sentences with encoding errors;
2. converting Traditional Chinese to Simplified Chinese through OpenCC;[1]
3. replacing full width characters with their corresponding half width characters;
4. converting all named and numeric character HTML references (e.g., >, >, &#x3e) to the corresponding Unicode characters.

For the training of NMT models, we segment Chinese sentences into words using jieba.[2]

We perform independent Byte Pair Encoding (BPE) [23] for Thai and Chinese corpus to address the unknown word issue with the SentencePiece toolkit [11].[3]

As the evaluation does not release the test set, we hold out the last 1000 sentence pairs of the training set for validation.

3.2 Exploration of Training Settings

We explore the influence of different training settings on the low-resource translation task in two aspects:

1. Vocabulary sizes;
2. Model hyper-parameters (embedding size and dropout probabilities).

For our experiment, we employ the Transformer translation model [27] for NMT, as it has achieved the state-of-the-art performance in MT evaluations [1] and conduct our experiment based on the Neutron toolkit [35] system. Neutron is an open source Transformer [27] implementation of the Transformer and its variants based on PyTorch.

---

[1] https://github.com/BYVoid/OpenCC.

[2] https://github.com/fxsjy/jieba.

[3] https://github.com/google/sentencepiece.

Table 1. Results (BLEU) on CCMT 2022 Th→Zh translation task with different vocabulary sizes.

Merge operations	6k	8k	16k	24k
Thai vocabulary size	5,996	7,997	16,000	23,999
Chinese vocabulary size	5,989	7,984	15,943	23,881
BLEU	27.07	25.70	**29.90**	28.87

Exploration of Vocabulary Sizes. Previous work shows that the effect of vocabulary size on translation quality is relatively small for high-resource settings [7]. While for low-resource settings, reduced vocabulary size (14k→2k) may benefit translation quality [24]. BPE [23] is a popular choice for open-vocabulary translation, which has one hyper-parameter, the number of merge operations, that determines the final vocabulary size. Following Sennrich and Zhang [24], we explore the influence of different vocabulary sizes for the Thai→Chinese translation task.

We train 4 NMT models in Thai→Chinese translation direction with different number of BPE merge operations, and the statistics of resulted vocabularies are shown in Table 1. Specifically, we perform independent BPE [23] for Thai and Chinese corpus with 4k/8k/16k/24k merge operations by SentencePiece [11].

For model settings, we adopted the Transformer with 6 encoder and decoder layers, 256 as the embedding dimension and 4 times of embedding dimension as the number of hidden units of the feed-forward layer, a dropout probability of 0.1. We used relative position [25] with a clipping distance k of 16. The number of warm-up steps was set to $8k$. We used a batch size of around $25k$ target tokens achieved by gradient accumulation, and trained the models for 128 epochs.

For evaluation, we decode with a beam size of 4 with average of the last 5 checkpoints saved in an interval of 1,500 training steps. We evaluate the translation quality by character BLEU with the SacreBLEU toolkit [20]. Results are shown in Table 1.

Table 1 shows that: 1) in general, the use of more merge operations (16k/24k) is better than fewer ones (6k/8k), and 2) the setting of 16k merge operations leads to the best performance for the Thai→Chinese translation task, achieving 29.90 BLEU points.

Exploration of Hyper-parameter Settings of Model. Hyper-parameters are often re-used across experiments. However, best practices may differ between high-resource and low-resource settings. While the trend in high-resource settings is using large and deep models, Nguyen and Chiang [19] use small models with fewer layers for small datasets, and Sennrich and Zhang [24] show that aggressive dropout is better for low-resource translation. In this paper, we also explore the effects of model sizes (embedding dimension and hidden dimension) and dropout probabilities on the performance.

Table 2. Results (BLEU) on CCMT 2022 Zh→Th translation task with different model settings.

Settings		A	B	C	D	E
Embbeding size	256	√				
	384		√	√		
	512				√	√
Dropout	0.1	√	√		√	
	0.3			√		√
BLEU		6.35	15.02	5.30	**24.42**	7.73

We train 5 NMT models in Chinese→Thai translation direction with different training settings as shown in Table 2. We set the number of BPE merge operations to 16k based on Table 1.

We experimented the Transformers with 6 encoder and decoder layers, 256/384/512 as the embedding dimension and 4 times of embedding dimension as the number of hidden units of the feed-forward layer, dropout probabilities of 0.1 or 0.3. We used relative position [25] with a clipping distance k was 16 and GeLU as the activation function. The number of warm-up steps was set to $8k$. We used a batch size of around $25k$ target tokens achieved by gradient accumulation, and trained the models for 128 epochs.

For evaluation, we decode with a beam size of 4, and evaluate the translation quality with the SacreBLEU toolkit [20] with the average of the last 5 checkpoints saved in an interval of 1,500 training steps. Results are shown in Table 2.

Table 2 shows that: 1) large embedding dimension is beneficial to translation performance, 2) aggressive dropout (0.3 in this paper) does not benefit the task, and 3) Setting D with 512 as the embedding dimension and 0.1 as the dropout probability is the best option, achieving a BLEU score of 24.42 in the Chinese→Thai translation task.

3.3 Deep Transformers for Low-Resource Machine Translation

To obtain good translation quality, we adopt the setting D, but use 24 encoder and decoder layers for better performance [2,8,13–15,17,28,30,31,33,36–38]. Parameters were initialized under the Lipschitz constraint [36] to ensure the convergence. We used the dynamical batch size strategy which dynamically determines proper and efficient batch sizes during training [34].

We use the best experiment setting explored with the 6-layer models for deeper models, because: 1) training shallow models are much faster than deep models, and 2) adding new layers also introduces regularization, as dropout modules are also introduced with these layers.

We train two models on the whole training set, which takes about 75 h to train one model on a nvidia RTX3090 GPU. We averaged the last 20 checkpoints saved with an interval of 1,500 training steps.

Table 3. Results on the CCMT 2022 Zh↔Th test set. The computation of BLEU scores for the test set are different from that for Tables 1 and 2.

	Th→Zh	Zh→Th
BLEU4	/	9.06
BLEU5	4.85	/

We decode the CCMT 2022 Zh↔Th test set consisting of 10k sentences for each direction with a beam size of 4. Results are shown in Table 3.

Table 3 shows that the CCMT 2022 Chinese-Thai low-resource translation task is still a quite challenging task and there is a quite large space for improvements. But to date, our study establishes the SOTA performance in the Chinese-to-Thai translation in the constrained evaluation.

4   Related Work

As data scarcity is the main problem of low-resource machine translation, making most of the existing data is a popular research direction to address this issue in previous work. There are two specific types: 1) data augmentation, and 2) using pre-trained language models.

Data augmentation is to add training data, normally through modifications of existing data or the generation of new pseudo data. In machine translation, typical data enhancement methods include back-translating external monolingual data [5,22], obtaining pseudo bilingual data by modifying original bilingual data, such as adding noise to training data [6,29] or by paraphrasing which takes into the diversity of natural language expression into account [16], and mining of bilingual sentence pairs from comparable corpus [32] (comparable corpus is a text that is not fully translated from the source language to the target language but contains with rich knowledge of bilingual contrast).

For the use of pre-trained language models in NMT, leveraging the target-side language model is the most straightforward way to use monolingual data [26]. Other work [18,21] directly uses word embeddings pre-trained on monolingual data to initialize the word embedding matrix of NMT models. More recently, some studies leverage pre-trained models to initialize the model parameters of the encoder of NMT [3,4,9].

Fore-mentioned studies require large amounts of auxiliary data. Low-resource NMT without auxiliary data has received comparably less attention [19,24]. In this work, we revisit this point with deep Transformers, and focus on techniques to adapt deep Transformers to make most of low-resource parallel training data, exploring the vocabulary sizes and model settings for NMT.

5   Conclusion

In this paper, we explore the influence of different settings for the use of deep Transformers on the CCMT 2022 Zh↔Th low-resource translation task.

We first test the effects of the number of BPE merge operations, embedding dimension and dropout probabilities with 6-layer models, then adapt the best setting to the 24-layer model, under the motivation that: 1) shallow models are fast to train, and 2) increasing the number of layers also introduces regularization for these added layers.

Acknowledgments. We thank anonymous reviewers for their insightful comments. We acknowledge the support of the National Social Science Fund of China (Grant No. 17ZDA138 and Grant No. 14BYY096).

References

1. Akhbardeh, F., et al.: Findings of the 2021 conference on machine translation (WMT21). In: Proceedings of the Sixth Conference on Machine Translation, pp. 1–88. Association for Computational Linguistics (2021). https://aclanthology.org/2021.wmt-1.1
2. Bapna, A., Chen, M., Firat, O., Cao, Y., Wu, Y.: Training deeper neural machine translation models with transparent attention. In: Proceedings of the 2018 Conference on Empirical Methods in Natural Language Processing, pp. 3028–3033. Association for Computational Linguistics (2018). https://aclweb.org/anthology/D18-1338
3. Clinchant, S., Jung, K.W., Nikoulina, V.: On the use of BERT for neural machine translation. In: Proceedings of the 3rd Workshop on Neural Generation and Translation, Hong Kong, pp. 108–117. Association for Computational Linguistics (2019). https://doi.org/10.18653/v1/D19-5611. https://aclanthology.org/D19-5611
4. Edunov, S., Baevski, A., Auli, M.: Pre-trained language model representations for language generation. In: Proceedings of the 2019 Conference of the North American Chapter of the Association for Computational Linguistics: Human Language Technologies, Minneapolis, Minnesota, vol. 1 (Long and Short Papers), pp. 4052–4059. Association for Computational Linguistics (2019). https://doi.org/10.18653/v1/N19-1409. https://aclanthology.org/N19-1409
5. Edunov, S., Ott, M., Auli, M., Grangier, D.: Understanding back-translation at scale. In: Proceedings of the 2018 Conference on Empirical Methods in Natural Language Processing, Brussels, Belgium, pp. 489–500. Association for Computational Linguistics (2018). https://doi.org/10.18653/v1/D18-1045. https://aclanthology.org/D18-1045
6. Fadaee, M., Bisazza, A., Monz, C.: Data augmentation for low-resource neural machine translation. In: Proceedings of the 55th Annual Meeting of the Association for Computational Linguistics, Vancouver, Canada (vol. 2: Short Papers), pp. 567–573. Association for Computational Linguistics (2017). https://doi.org/10.18653/v1/P17-2090. https://aclanthology.org/P17-2090
7. Haddow, B., et al.: The University of Edinburgh's submissions to the WMT18 news translation task. In: Proceedings of the Third Conference on Machine Translation: Shared Task Papers, Belgium, Brussels, pp. 399–409. Association for Computational Linguistics (2018). https://doi.org/10.18653/v1/W18-6412. https://aclanthology.org/W18-6412
8. Huang, X.S., Perez, F., Ba, J., Volkovs, M.: Improving transformer optimization through better initialization. In: III, H.D., Singh, A. (eds.) Proceedings of the 37th International Conference on Machine Learning. Proceedings of Machine Learning

Research, vol. 119, pp. 4475–4483. PMLR (2020). https://proceedings.mlr.press/v119/huang20f.html

9. Imamura, K., Sumita, E.: Recycling a pre-trained BERT encoder for neural machine translation. In: Proceedings of the 3rd Workshop on Neural Generation and Translation, Hong Kong, pp. 23–31. Association for Computational Linguistics (2019). https://doi.org/10.18653/v1/D19-5603. https://aclanthology.org/D19-5603

10. Koehn, P., Knowles, R.: Six challenges for neural machine translation. In: Proceedings of the First Workshop on Neural Machine Translation, Vancouver, pp. 28–39. Association for Computational Linguistics (2017). https://doi.org/10.18653/v1/W17-3204. https://aclanthology.org/W17-3204

11. Kudo, T., Richardson, J.: SentencePiece: a simple and language independent subword tokenizer and detokenizer for neural text processing. In: Proceedings of the 2018 Conference on Empirical Methods in Natural Language Processing: System Demonstrations, Brussels, Belgium, pp. 66–71. Association for Computational Linguistics (2018). https://doi.org/10.18653/v1/D18-2012. https://aclanthology.org/D18-2012

12. Lample, G., Ott, M., Conneau, A., Denoyer, L., Ranzato, M.: Phrase-based & neural unsupervised machine translation. In: Proceedings of the 2018 Conference on Empirical Methods in Natural Language Processing, Brussels, Belgium, pp. 5039–5049. Association for Computational Linguistics (2018). https://doi.org/10.18653/v1/D18-1549. https://aclanthology.org/D18-1549

13. Lan, Z., Chen, M., Goodman, S., Gimpel, K., Sharma, P., Soricut, R.: ALBERT: a lite BERT for self-supervised learning of language representations. CoRR abs/1909.11942 (2019). https://arxiv.org/abs/1909.11942

14. Li, B., et al.: Learning light-weight translation models from deep transformer. In: Proceedings of the AAAI Conference on Artificial Intelligence, vol. 35, no. 15, pp. 13217–13225 (2021). https://ojs.aaai.org/index.php/AAAI/article/view/17561

15. Li, B., et al.: Shallow-to-deep training for neural machine translation. In: Proceedings of the 2020 Conference on Empirical Methods in Natural Language Processing (EMNLP), pp. 995–1005. Association for Computational Linguistics (2020). https://doi.org/10.18653/v1/2020.emnlp-main.72. https://aclanthology.org/2020.emnlp-main.72

16. Mallinson, J., Sennrich, R., Lapata, M.: Paraphrasing revisited with neural machine translation. In: Proceedings of the 15th Conference of the European Chapter of the Association for Computational Linguistics, Valencia, Spain, vol. 1, Long Papers, pp. 881–893. Association for Computational Linguistics (2017). https://aclanthology.org/E17-1083

17. Mehta, S., Ghazvininejad, M., Iyer, S., Zettlemoyer, L., Hajishirzi, H.: Delight: deep and light-weight transformer. In: International Conference on Learning Representations (2021). https://openreview.net/forum?id=ujmgfuxSLrO

18. Neishi, M., Sakuma, J., Tohda, S., Ishiwatari, S., Yoshinaga, N., Toyoda, M.: A bag of useful tricks for practical neural machine translation: embedding layer initialization and large batch size. In: Proceedings of the 4th Workshop on Asian Translation (WAT 2017), Taipei, Taiwan, pp. 99–109. Asian Federation of Natural Language Processing (2017). https://aclanthology.org/W17-5708

19. Nguyen, T., Chiang, D.: Improving lexical choice in neural machine translation. In: Proceedings of the 2018 Conference of the North American Chapter of the Association for Computational Linguistics: Human Language Technologies, New Orleans, Louisiana, vol. 1 (Long Papers), pp. 334–343. Association for Computational Lin-

guistics (2018). https://doi.org/10.18653/v1/N18-1031. https://aclanthology.org/N18-1031

20. Post, M.: A call for clarity in reporting BLEU scores. In: Proceedings of the Third Conference on Machine Translation: Research Papers, Brussels, Belgium, pp. 186–191. Association for Computational Linguistics (2018). https://doi.org/10.18653/v1/W18-6319. https://aclanthology.org/W18-6319

21. Qi, Y., Sachan, D., Felix, M., Padmanabhan, S., Neubig, G.: When and why are pre-trained word embeddings useful for neural machine translation? In: Proceedings of the 2018 Conference of the North American Chapter of the Association for Computational Linguistics: Human Language Technologies, New Orleans, Louisiana, vol. 2 (Short Papers), pp. 529–535. Association for Computational Linguistics (2018). https://doi.org/10.18653/v1/N18-2084. https://aclanthology.org/N18-2084

22. Sennrich, R., Haddow, B., Birch, A.: Improving neural machine translation models with monolingual data. In: Proceedings of the 54th Annual Meeting of the Association for Computational Linguistics (vol. 1: Long Papers), Berlin, Germany, pp. 86–96. Association for Computational Linguistics (2016). https://doi.org/10.18653/v1/P16-1009. https://aclanthology.org/P16-1009

23. Sennrich, R., Haddow, B., Birch, A.: Neural machine translation of rare words with subword units. In: Proceedings of the 54th Annual Meeting of the Association for Computational Linguistics (vol. 1: Long Papers), Berlin, Germany, pp. 1715–1725. Association for Computational Linguistics (2016). https://doi.org/10.18653/v1/P16-1162. https://aclanthology.org/P16-1162

24. Sennrich, R., Zhang, B.: Revisiting low-resource neural machine translation: a case study. In: Proceedings of the 57th Annual Meeting of the Association for Computational Linguistics, Florence, Italy, pp. 211–221. Association for Computational Linguistics (2019). https://doi.org/10.18653/v1/P19-1021. https://aclanthology.org/P19-1021

25. Shaw, P., Uszkoreit, J., Vaswani, A.: Self-attention with relative position representations. In: Proceedings of the 2018 Conference of the North American Chapter of the Association for Computational Linguistics: Human Language Technologies, New Orleans, Louisiana, vol. 2 (Short Papers), pp. 464–468. Association for Computational Linguistics (2018). https://doi.org/10.18653/v1/N18-2074. https://aclanthology.org/N18-2074

26. Stahlberg, F., Cross, J., Stoyanov, V.: Simple fusion: return of the language model. In: Proceedings of the Third Conference on Machine Translation: Research Papers, Brussels, Belgium, pp. 204–211. Association for Computational Linguistics (2018). https://doi.org/10.18653/v1/W18-6321. https://aclanthology.org/W18-6321

27. Vaswani, A., et al.: Attention is all you need. In: Guyon, I., et al. (eds.) Advances in Neural Information Processing Systems, vol. 30. Curran Associates, Inc. (2017). https://proceedings.neurips.cc/paper/2017/file/3f5ee243547dee91fbd053c1c4a845aa-Paper.pdf

28. Wang, Q., et al.: Learning deep transformer models for machine translation. In: Proceedings of the 57th Conference of the Association for Computational Linguistics, Florence, Italy, pp. 1810–1822. Association for Computational Linguistics (2019). https://www.aclweb.org/anthology/P19-1176

29. Wang, X., Pham, H., Dai, Z., Neubig, G.: SwitchOut: an efficient data augmentation algorithm for neural machine translation. In: Proceedings of the 2018 Conference on Empirical Methods in Natural Language Processing, Brussels, Belgium, pp. 856–861. Association for Computational Linguistics (2018). https://doi.org/10.18653/v1/D18-1100. https://aclanthology.org/D18-1100

30. Wei, X., Yu, H., Hu, Y., Zhang, Y., Weng, R., Luo, W.: Multiscale collaborative deep models for neural machine translation. In: Proceedings of the 58th Annual Meeting of the Association for Computational Linguistics, pp. 414–426. Association for Computational Linguistics (2020). https://www.aclweb.org/anthology/2020.acl-main.40

31. Wu, L., et al.: Depth growing for neural machine translation. In: Proceedings of the 57th Annual Meeting of the Association for Computational Linguistics, Florence, Italy, pp. 5558–5563. Association for Computational Linguistics (2019). https://doi.org/10.18653/v1/P19-1558. https://www.aclweb.org/anthology/P19-1558

32. Wu, L., et al.: Machine translation with weakly paired documents. In: Proceedings of the 2019 Conference on Empirical Methods in Natural Language Processing and the 9th International Joint Conference on Natural Language Processing (EMNLP-IJCNLP), Hong Kong, China, pp. 4375–4384. Association for Computational Linguistics (2019). https://doi.org/10.18653/v1/D19-1446. https://aclanthology.org/D19-1446

33. Xiong, R., et al.: On layer normalization in the transformer architecture. In: III, H.D., Singh, A. (eds.) Proceedings of the 37th International Conference on Machine Learning. Proceedings of Machine Learning Research, vol. 119, pp. 10524–10533. PMLR (2020). https://proceedings.mlr.press/v119/xiong20b.html

34. Xu, H., van Genabith, J., Xiong, D., Liu, Q.: Dynamically adjusting transformer batch size by monitoring gradient direction change. In: Proceedings of the 58th Annual Meeting of the Association for Computational Linguistics, pp. 3519–3524. Association for Computational Linguistics (2020). https://doi.org/10.18653/v1/2020.acl-main.323. https://aclanthology.org/2020.acl-main.323

35. Xu, H., Liu, Q.: Neutron: an implementation of the transformer translation model and its variants. CoRR abs/1903.07402 (2019). https://arxiv.org/abs/1903.07402

36. Xu, H., Liu, Q., van Genabith, J., Xiong, D., Zhang, J.: Lipschitz constrained parameter initialization for deep transformers. In: Proceedings of the 58th Annual Meeting of the Association for Computational Linguistics, pp. 397–402. Association for Computational Linguistics (2020). https://doi.org/10.18653/v1/2020.acl-main.38. https://aclanthology.org/2020.acl-main.38

37. Xu, P., et al.: Optimizing deeper transformers on small datasets. In: Proceedings of the 59th Annual Meeting of the Association for Computational Linguistics and the 11th International Joint Conference on Natural Language Processing (vol. 1: Long Papers), pp. 2089–2102. Association for Computational Linguistics (2021). https://doi.org/10.18653/v1/2021.acl-long.163. https://aclanthology.org/2021.acl-long.163

38. Zhang, B., Titov, I., Sennrich, R.: Improving deep transformer with depth-scaled initialization and merged attention. In: Proceedings of the 2019 Conference on Empirical Methods in Natural Language Processing and the 9th International Joint Conference on Natural Language Processing (EMNLP-IJCNLP), Hong Kong, China, pp. 898–909. Association for Computational Linguistics (2019). https://doi.org/10.18653/v1/D19-1083. https://www.aclweb.org/anthology/D19-1083

CCMT 2022 Translation Quality Estimation Task

Chang Su[✉], Miaomiao Ma, Hao Yang, Shimin Tao, Jiaxin Guo,
Minghan Wang, Min Zhang, and Xiaosong Qiao

2012 Labs, Huawei Technologies Co., Ltd., Beijing, China
{suchang8,mamiaomiao,yanghao30,taoshimin,guojiaxin1,wangminghan,
zhangmin186,qiaoxiaosong}@huawei.com

Abstract. This paper presents the method used by Huawei Translation Services Center (HW-TSC) in the quality estimation (QE) task:
sentence-level post-editing effort estimation in the 18th China Conference on Machine Translation (CCMT) 2022. This method is based on
a predictor-estimator model. The predictor is an XLM-RoBERTa model
pre-trained on a large-scale parallel corpus and extracts features from
the source language text and machine-translated text. The estimator is
a fully connected layer that is used to regress the post-editing distance
scores using the extracted features. In the experiment, it is found that
pre-training the predictor with the semantic textual similarity (STS) task
in the parallel corpus and using augmented training data constructed by
different machine translation (MT) engines can improve the prediction
effect of the Human-targeted Translation Edit Rate (HTER) in both
Chinese-English and English-Chinese tasks.

Keywords: Translation quality estimation (QE) · Transformer ·
Pre-training

1 Introduction

The off-line technical estimation task of the 18th China Conference on Machine
Translation (CCMT) includes a sentence-level Chinese-English and English-
Chinese machine translation (MT) quality estimation (QE) task, which aims to
measure the MT quality by estimating the Human-targeted Translation Edit
Rate (HTER) of the translation without reference translations. This paper
describes in detail the data processing strategies, technical methods, and model
structure used by HW-TSC's Text Machine Translation Laboratory in this estimation task, as well as the performance of the used models in the Chinese-English
and English-Chinese MT QE tasks.

2 Estimation System

In this sentence-level QE task, HW-TSC uses the predictor-estimator structure
proposed in the early research [1]. As shown in Fig. 1, the language model XLM-
RoBERTaBase [2] (XLM-RB) is used as the predictor (L = 12, H = 768, A

T. Xiao and J. Pino (Eds.): CCMT 2022, CCIS 1671, pp. 127–134, 2022.
https://doi.org/10.1007/978-981-19-7960-6_13

= 12; Total Parameters = 288M) to extract source features from the source text and target features from the target text. After that, average pooling is applied to the extracted features of each sentence to obtain the source sentence features and target sentence features. The source sentence feature (SF), target sentence feature (TF), difference between the SF and TF (diff), and dot product of the source and target text features (prob) are concatenated to obtain a global feature. The global feature is sent to an estimator constructed by two fully connected layers (FFNs), which maps the feature to sample label space and performs regression prediction on the HTER score.

The final system submitted uses the ensemble model policy that uses the model with Dropout to average multiple predicted results, thereby improving the model robustness and significantly improving accuracy of the system in the test set. The ensemble models are:

1) Models that achieve the best perform in the development set during multiple training processes;
2) Best models selected from step 1) based on the development set, with random Dropout enabled.

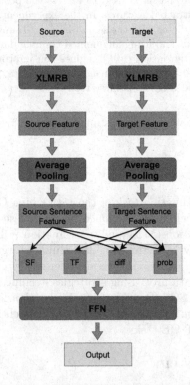

Fig. 1. Predictor-estimator based QE model for estimating sentence-level HTER score

3   Data

Training Data

1) In the English-Chinese task, the CCMT 2022 sentence-level translation QE task provides 3043 source sentences and 14,789 translations and corresponding editing results.
2) In the Chinese-English task, the CCMT 2022 sentence-level translation QE task provides 2503 source sentences and 10,070 translations and corresponding edited translations.
3) Google, Baidu, Youdao, and Huawei translation engines are used separately to translate the source sentences provided by the CCMT 2022 sentence-level translation QE task. The obtained translations generate additional training data together with the provided edited translations.
4) In addition to the data provided in the QE task, HW-TSC also uses the Chinese corpora provided in the English-Chinese, Chinese-English, Mongolian-Chinese, Uyghur-Chinese, and Tibetan-Chinese tasks of the CCMT 2022 bilingual translation task, as well as the English-Chinese and Chinese-English parallel corpora.

Development Data

1) In the English-Chinese task, the CCMT 2022 sentence-level translation QE task provides 2826 (1381 + 1445) source sentences, translations, and corresponding edited translations.
2) In the Chinese-English task, the CCMT 2022 sentence-level translation QE task provides 2528 (1143 + 1385) source sentences, translations, and corresponding edited translations.

Test Data

The off-line test set of the CCMT 2022 provides 10,000 parallel sentence pairs for the English-Chinese and Chinese-English sentence-level translation QE tasks separately.

4   Method

4.1   System Training

The model system used by HW-TSC is trained in three steps:

1) Chinese language model training. Referring to the previous research [3], in this paper, a masked language model (MLM) is trained on a large-scale Chinese corpus. This generates a model for extracting Chinese text features, which is used as a center language encoder (CLE) for the next-step training. From the word tokens of the Chinese sentences, one token is randomly selected and masked and then sent to the Transformer Encode. The obtained word feature vector is sent to a fully connected classification model, and the model predicts the masked word token, as shown in Fig. 2a.

2) Predictor pre-training. According to an early work [4], in this paper, the XLMRB model proposed in Sect. 1 is trained with the semantic textual similarity (STS) task on English-Chinese and Chinese-English parallel corpora. On the parallel corpora, the XLM-RB obtains feature vectors of the Chinese and English sentences separately, and the CLE model obtains the Chinese sentence feature vector. The mean squared error (MSE) loss function is used for separate supervised training of these vectors, making the sentence feature vectors obtained by the XLM-RB highly similar, as shown in Fig. 2b.

3) Translation QE model training. The XLM-RB trained in step 2 is used as the predictor to train the translation QE model on the translation QE training set.

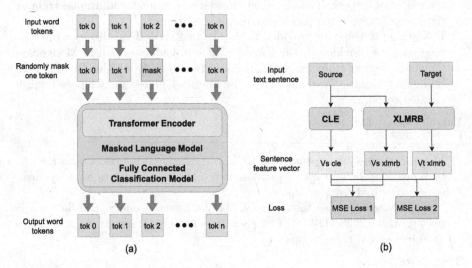

(a)   (b)

Fig. 2. (a): Masked language model, (b): Schematic diagram of the parallel corpus semantic textual similarity training task

4.2   System Test

As described in Sect. 1, the ensemble model policy is used in the final system submitted. In this policy, multiple models are used to separately predict the HTER scores of the sentences in the test set, and an average value of the HTER scores of each sentence is used as a score of the ensemble policy.

5   Experiment

5.1   System Environment

OS: Ubuntu 18.04.5 LTS

Deep learning framework: Pytorch 1.8.0
CPU: Intel(R) Xeon(R) Gold 6278C CPU @ 2.60GHz
Memory: 128 GB
GPU: Nvidia Tesla T4
GPU Memory: 16 GB

5.2   Experiment Settings

The system used by HW-TSC is an English-Chinese and Chinese-English multi-task system, and the same system trained is used to obtain the experiment results.

Training Process

Step-1 training 1 described in Sect. 4: In this paper, the sbert-chinese-general-v2 [5] model provided by Hugging Face is used as the pre-trained model to train the MLM on the corpus of 18 million Chinese sentences provided in the English-Chinese, Chinese-English, Mongolian-Chinese, Uyghur-Chinese, and Tibetan-Chinese tasks of the CCMT 2022 bilingual translation task. The pre-trained model sbert-chinese-general-v2 is obtained by training the BERT model of the bert-base-chinese [6] version provided by Hugging Face on SimCLUE, a dataset with millions of semantically similar texts.
Step-2 training described in Sect. 4: In this paper, the xlm-roberta-base [7] provided by Hugging Face is used as the pre-trained model for STS task training on the bilingual parallel corpus of 9 million of English-Chinese and Chinese-English sentences provided in the CCMT 2022 translation QE task under the sentence-transformers [8] framework.
Step-3 training described in Sect. 4: In this paper, the English-Chinese and Chinese-English training sets of the CCMT 2022 sentence-level translation QE task are used for training based on the system structure described in Sect. 2.

Training parameters used in the three steps are shown in Table 1.

Table 1. Training parameter settings.

Step	Batch size	Optimizer	Learning rate (lr)	lr scheduler
1	16	Adam[1]	$1.0e^{-4}$	–
2	8	Adam	$5.0e^{-5}$	–
3	8	Adam	$2.5e^{-5}$	Cosine Annealing Warm[2]

Note: 1) Adam: reference [9]. 2) Cosine Annealing Warm: reference [10].

Test Process

As described in this section, the model system used by HW-TSC is trained for 9 times. Top 2 models are selected based on the development set, and Dropout 0.1 is applied to the Top 1 model for three test tasks. A total of 6 results are obtained, and the average value of the 6 results is used as the result of the ensemble policy. Due to the limited amount of training data, to prevent overfitting, a model with a small Dropout value is used to predict the test set results, and then an average value is used. In this way, system robustness and accuracy can both be significantly improved. During the training, the maximum epoch is set to 10. In addition, early stopping of training is enabled: During the training, if the Pearson's correlation coefficient of the validation set is not among the Top 3 for 5 consecutive times, the training is halted immediately.

Comparison training is also performed in the experiment:

1) The XLM-RB model is used to train the model system directly following Step 3 by using the pre-trained model provided by Hugging Face without Step 1 and Step 2 and without using the augmented data produced by Google, Baidu, Youdao, and Huawei translation engines.
2) The Step-3 model training does not use the augmented data (AD) produced by Google, Baidu, Youdao, and Huawei translation engines.

5.3   Experiment Result

In this estimation task, the estimation metrics, mainly the Pearson's correlation coefficient, are automatically measured. Table 2 show the model system performance on the development set.

After comparison, the experiment results of the English-Chinese MT QE task show that:

1) The model pre-trained with the STS task can improve the Pearson's correlation efficient by 8.5% on the development set and by 0.5% on the test set.
2) The model pre-trained using the augmented training data generated by multiple translation engines can improve the Pearson's correlation efficient by 0.7% on the development set and by 0.1% on the test set.
3) The ensemble model policy that uses the model with Dropout to obtain the average value of multiple predicted results can improve the Pearson's correlation efficient by 7.3% on the development set and by 1% on the test set.

After comparison, the experiment results of the Chinese-English MT QE task show that:

1) The model pre-trained with the STS task can improve the Pearson's correlation efficient by 9% on the development set and by 2% on the test set.
2) The model pre-trained using the augmented training data generated by multiple translation engines can improve the Pearson's correlation efficient by 0.5% on the development set and by 1% on the test set.
3) The ensemble model policy that uses the model with Dropout to obtain the average value of multiple predicted results can improve the Pearson's correlation efficient by 5% on the development set and by 1.5% on the test set.

Table 2. Pearson's correlation between prediction of our different system and labels on development and test data.

Language	Model	Dev set	Test set
en-zh	w/o STS[1] & w/o AD	0.4561	0.3549
	w/o AD[2]	0.5413	0.3597
	Top 1[3]	0.5487	0.3607
	Ensemble[4]	0.6211	0.3704
zh-en	w/o STS & w/o AD	0.4663	0.4527
	w/o AD	0.5527	0.4741
	Top 1	0.5574	0.4850
	Ensemble	0.6008	0.5002

Note: 1) w/o STS: The model is trained directly following Step 3 without Step 1 and Step 2. 2) w/o AD: The Step-3 training does not use augmented data. 3) Top 1: The best single model with STS and AD. 4) Ensemble: The policy used by HW-TSC's system.

6   Conclusion

This paper presents HW-TSC's participation in the MT QE task in the 18th China Conference on Machine Translation. In the experiment, the pre-trained language model XLM-RoBERTa is used as the predictor to extract features from the source text and target text. The estimator concatenates the sentence features of the source text and target text after the minus and dot product operations, and performs regression fitting on the HTER scores through the fully connected layer. About the QE training data, the system used by HW-TSC uses the augmented data produced by Google, Baidu, Youdao, and Huawei MT engines. The experiment results show that in the MT QE task, pre-training the predictor with the STS task, using the augmented data produced by multiple translation engines, and adopting the ensemble model policy that uses a model with dropout to average the values of multiple predicted results can improve the accuracy of MT QE results on both the development set and test set. In the future experiment, the model structure of the estimator can be designed and tested in a more refined and effective manner. In addition, the future research and experiment will focus on how to better use the source text and target text for data augmentation on the limited QE data set, so as to generate QE data more similar to the real-world data, as proposed in an early work [11], to further enhance the QE result.

References

1. Kim, H., Lee, J.H., Na, S.H.: Predictor-estimator using multilevel task learning with stack propagation for neural quality estimation. In: Proceedings of the Second Conference on Machine Translation, pp. 562–568 (2017)

2. Conneau, A., et al.: Unsupervised cross-lingual representation learning at scale. arXiv preprint arXiv:1911.02116 (2019)

3. Devlin, J., Chang, M.W., Lee, K., Toutanova, K.: BERT: pre-training of deep bidirectional transformers for language understanding. arXiv preprint arXiv:1810.04805 (2018)

4. Reimers, N., Gurevych, I.: Sentence-BERT: sentence embeddings using siamese BERT-networks. arXiv preprint arXiv:1908.10084 (2019)

5. HuggingFace: sbert-chinese-general-v2 https://huggingface.co/dmetasoul/sbert-chinese-general-v2 (2022)

6. HuggingFace: bert-base-chinese https://huggingface.co/bert-base-chinese (2022)

7. NilsReimers: Sentencetransformers documentation https://www.sbert.net/ (2022)

8. HuggingFace: xlm-roberta-base https://huggingface.co/xlm-roberta-base (2022)

9. Kingma, D.P., Ba, J.: Adam: a method for stochastic optimization. arXiv preprint arXiv:1412.6980 (2014)

10. Loshchilov, I., Hutter, F.: SGDR: stochastic gradient descent with warm restarts. arXiv preprint arXiv:1608.03983 (2016)

11. Cui, Q., et al.: Directqe: direct pretraining for machine translation quality estimation. Proc. Conf. AAAI Artif. Intell. **35**, 12719–12727 (2021)

Effective Data Augmentation Methods for CCMT 2022

Jing Wang and Lina Yang(✉)

School of Computer and Electronic Information, Guangxi University, Nanning, China
lnyang@gxu.edu.cn

Abstract. The purpose of this paper is to introduce the specific situation in which Guangxi University participated in the 18th China Conference on Machine Translation (CCMT 2022) evaluation tasks. We submitted the results of two bilingual machine translation (MT) evaluation tasks in CCMT 2022. One is Chinese-English bilingual MT tasks from the news field, the other is Chinese-Thai bilingual MT tasks in low resource languages. Our system is based on Transformer model with several effective data augmentation strategies which are adopted to improve the quality of translation. Experiments show that data augmentation methods have a good impact on the baseline system and aim to enhance the robustness of the model.

Keywords: Machine translation · CCMT 2022 · Transformer · Data augmentation

1 Introduction

In the context of the rapid development of deep learning, neural machine translation (NMT) has attracted more and more attention from the academic community. We participated in four directions of machine translation evaluation tasks. And we built our translation systems based on Google's Transformer [11] model in all directions.

The reason why we selected the Transformer model is that it solved the problem of long-distance information loss. In addition, we applied BPE algorithm which Sennrich [9] proposed in 2016 to word-segmented texts to deal with the out-of-vocabulary (OOV) problem. Finally, we used several data augmentation strategies to generate pseudo data, enrich the diversity of data, and make up for the lack of training data. Data augmentation is defined by many authors as a solution to a data distribution mismatch problem [13]. In short, data augmentation has been used in low resource tasks due to the requirement of large amounts of training data.

The remaining part of the paper proceeds as follows. Chapter Two briefly describes the Transformer model. After that, Chapter Three is concerned with the data augmentation methodologies used for our model. Chapter Four then describes the experimental settings and discusses the results our model obtained. This paper ends with a conclusion and future work.

© The Author(s), under exclusive license to Springer Nature Singapore Pte Ltd. 2022
T. Xiao and J. Pino (Eds.): CCMT 2022, CCIS 1671, pp. 135–142, 2022.
https://doi.org/10.1007/978-981-19-7960-6_14

2   System Architecture

In CCMT 2022 translation evaluation tasks, we adopted our neural machine translation model based on the Transformer model. The Transformer model adapts the encoder-decoder architecture which is one of the most popular architectures. In recent years, the attention mechanism has been widely used to solve the insufficient dependency when modeling long sequences. Meanwhile, the attention mechanism is the most significant part of the Transformer model. And it also is an important reason why Transformer has achieved great success in many fields.

The decoder and encoder of Transformer have a similar structure consisting of n identical layers. Each layer contains two main modules: an attention mechanism module and a feed-forward neural network module. Scaled dot-product attention mechanism performs the following operations on the input query, key, and value as follows:

$$Attention(Q, K, V) = softmax(\frac{QK^T}{\sqrt{d_k}})V \tag{1}$$

where $\sqrt{d_k}$ is the dimension of the hidden layer state. Based on scaled dot-product attention, the calculation method of the multi-head attention mechanism can be expressed as:

$$MultiHead(Q, K, V) = Concat(head_1, ..., head_h)W^O \tag{2}$$

where $head_i = Attention(QW_i^Q, KW_i^K, VW_i^V)$. Multi-head attention enriches the representation of semantic information. When calculating the attention score, the input is divided into multiple parts on average, then each part is calculated as attention score independently. Finally, all the obtained attention scores are concatenated together as the output of the multi-head attention layer. After calculating the self-attention, the following feed-forward neural network is used to transform the input.

The residual connection [2] is also important in Transformer architecture. It can prevent the problem of vanishing gradients and increase the network depth further. The residual connection is employed around each of the two sub-layers, followed by layer normalization.

3   Methods

3.1   Data Augmentation

Data augmentation is an important machine learning method nowadays. It is based on the existing training sample data to generate more training data. Its purpose is to make the expanded training data as close to the real distributed data as possible and improve the translation quality further. In addition, data augmentation can force the model to learn more robust features and effectively improve the generalization ability of the model. Figure 1 shows the process of generating pseudo parallel corpus. In CCMT 2022, we use the data augmentation methods as follows.

Swap. Randomly select two words in the target sentence and exchange their order until words of $\alpha \cdot n$ sentence length are exchanged.

BPE-Dropout. BPE-Dropout [6] algorithm was proposed in 2020 by Provilkov et al. BPE-Dropout stochastically corrupts the segmentation procedure of BPE, leading to different subword segmentation with the same BPE vocabulary.

Synonym Replacement. Synonym Replacement is to replace a word with its synonym. And this word is randomly selected in the target sentence. We believe that synonym replacement can enrich the diversity of training data.

Word-Replacement. Use mgiza++[1] toolkit to obtain bi-directional alignment lexicon from the training data. $\alpha \cdot t$ source-target aligned words are selected at random and replaced by random entries in the bi-directional alignment lexicon.

Back Translation. Back Translation [8] is the process of translating the target language into the source language. On the one hand, it can augment the pseudo parallel pairs. On the other hand, it can improve the generalization ability of the model.

Fine Tuning. Fine tuning [1] is an effective method which can bring improvements to neural network. Our translation systems trained with data augmentation method were fine-tuned on the training set.

3.2 CE Task and EC Task

In Chinese-English machine translation tasks, our baseline system was developed in base Transformer model. Besides, we built two contrast systems which both use data augmentation strategies. One contrast system made the use of word-replacement operation. The other applied several data augmentation methods to enhance the performance of the model.

Specifically, we generated 1M synthetic data by the word-replacement operation. Word-Replacement makes use of statistical machine translation to generate a bilingual aligned lexicon. Sánchez-Cartagena et al. [7] used each of the multi-task learning data augmentation auxiliary tasks to stress the fact that the augmented data. In addition, we mixed several data augmentation methods, such as swap, insert, delete, and so on. We augmented 4M pseudo parallel data by using this method. The paper of [12] motivates this idea. The data and model settings of the CE task and EC task are consistent.

---

[1] https://github.com/moses-smt/mgiza.

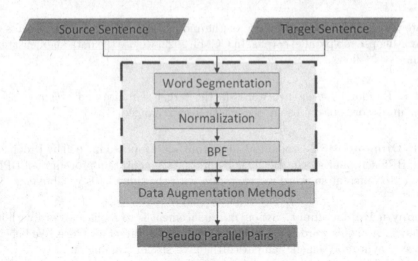

Fig. 1. Overall flow chart for data augmentation.

3.3   CThai Task and ThaiC Task

In Chinese-Thai low resource translation tasks, our systems applied data augmentation methods which included back translation and swap to improve the performance of translation. We used Tencent AI Lab Embedding Corpus for Chinese Words and Phrases[2] [10] to do synonym replacement. At the same with Chinese-English translation tasks, fine tuning was used in Chinese-Thai data augmentation systems.

For back translation, we applied only for the Thai-Chinese direction. And we conducted experiments to evaluate the impact of fine tuning technology on the model.

4   Experiments

4.1   System Settings

We use fairseq[3] [3] open-source framework to implement our translation systems. The toolkit fairseq was implemented in 2019. In bilingual Chinese-English directions, our Transformer model includes six layers for the encoder and six layers for the decoder, respectively. Each layer has the size of 512 hidden units. We also set the size of embedding layers to 512. The dimension of the feed-forward layer is 2048. And the multi-head self-attention mechanism has 8 heads. However, we set the encoder layer number and decoder layer number to 5 in the low resource translation tasks. The multi-head self-attention mechanism only has 4 heads. Table 1 shows the main parameters of our Transformer model. The parameter

---

[2] https://ai.tencent.com/ailab/nlp/zh/embedding.html.
[3] https://github.com/pytorch/fairseq.

patience stands for early cease training if valid performance doesn't improve for N consecutive validation runs.

Table 1. Model Settings

Parameter	Chinese-English	Chinese-Thai
Embedding Size	512	512
Encoder Layer	6	5
Decoder Layer	6	5
Dropout	0.3	0.3
Encoder Attention Heads	8	4
Decoder Attention Heads	8	4
Warm-up Steps	16000	8000
Patience	20	6

In the low resource translation tasks, the parallel corpus is limited so that we selected a slightly smaller Transformer model. Specifically, we apply layer normalization before each encoder block. The same goes for each decoder block. A major advantage of these settings is to prevent the model from over-fitting during training.

4.2   Data Pre-processing

As we all know, data pre-processing is an especially important part of machine translation. Data pre-processing is also the first step to solving practical problems by deep learning. It mainly includes duplicate removal, symbol normalization, word segmentation, and so on. Next, we will introduce our data pre-processing steps.

In the CE and EC task, the evaluation organizers provide about 9M Chinese-English parallel corpus and 11M Chinese monolingual corpus. We only use the NEU2017 corpus, the Datum2015, and the Datum2017 as the training set in Chinese-English MT tasks in our submitted systems. The test set consists of newstest2019.

In the CThai low resource translation task, the only bilingual parallel corpus is released. Therefore, we sample 195K randomly as the training set. The rest of the parallel data is divided into validation set and test set in a ratio of 2:3.

After splitting the training set, validation set, and test set, we begin to process the sentences. For English sentences, we tokenize the English word by the space first. Then, we need to learn the most suitable case form for English words due to the problems of different cases of the same word. For Thai sentences, we use pythainlp[4] to do word segmentation. It is a useful toolkit for us to split the Thai sentences. Finally, we use jieba[5] for Chinese sentences to tokenize the Chi-

---

[4] https://github.com/PyThaiNLP/pythainlp.
[5] https://github.com/fxsjy/jieba.

nese texts, whose advantages are fast and high accuracy compared with other Chinese word segmentation tools.

In all languages, we use Moses scripts[6] to normalize the texts from digits, punctuations and special symbols. Additionally, we use Subword-NMT[7] toolkit to learn and apply Sennrich's BPE from the tokenized texts. Lastly, those sentence pairs are removed which are less than 5 BPE tokens or more than 100 BPE tokens in the training set. We completed all our experiments on a single RTX3090.

4.3 Experimental Results

BLEU [4] is one of the most commonly used automatic evaluation methods for machine translation. We use sacrebleu[8] [5] to calculate the score of BLEU for our submitted results in CCMT2022.

In the CE translation evaluation task, we submit three translation systems, which include one baseline system and two contrast systems. Chinese and English do not share the alphabet, so we learn 16K BPE operations separately on Chinese and English texts by using Subword-NMT toolkit. Mixture DA is a data augmentation method that performs random swap, random insert, and random delete of words in sentences. Table 2 reports the performance of our CE translation systems. We can infer that data augmentation is effective due to the increment of 1.04 BLEU points in the validation set and 0.64 BLEU points in the test set. And we find that it is obvious that data augmentation methods increase the accuracy of the model.

Table 2. The BLEU scores of CE task

System	Valid set	Test set
Baseline	19.73	17.56
Mixture DA	19.67	16.66
Word-Replacement	20.77	18.20

In the EC translation evaluation task, we also submit three translation systems. It indicates the results of our submitted translation systems in Table 3. The methods of EC translation systems used are exactly the same as the CE task. We know clearly that word-replacement receives the best results among all EC translation systems from Table 3.

In the CThai translation evaluation task, we find that BPE-Dropout algorithm does not perform well on the low resource dataset through experiments. Then, we use synonym replacement method to generate Chinese-Thai pairs.

---

[6] https://github.com/moses-smt/mosesdecoder/tree/master/scripts.
[7] https://github.com/rsennrich/subword-nmt.
[8] https://github.com/mjpost/sacrebleu.

Table 3. The BLEU scores of EC task

System	Valid set	Test set
Baseline	14.49	23.20
Mixture DA	16.49	25.10
Word-Replacement	18.42	26.26

Table 4 reports the results of our translation systems. Synonym Replacement method obtains an obvious improvement. And it can perform better when it combines with fine tuning method.

Table 4. The BLEU scores of CThai task

System	Valid set	Test set
Baseline	11.63	11.97
Synonym Replacement	14.39	15.18
Synonym Replacement + Fine Tuning	15.12	15.64

In the ThaiC translation evaluation task, four translation systems are submitted. As shown in Table 5, we discover that reverse has a positive effect on the baseline system. In addition, it does not work for the model to only use back translation. When we add fine tuning to back translation method, the model obtains a better result. What's more, combining swap and fine tuning realizes the best performance in the ThaiC task.

Table 5. The BLEU scores of ThaiC task

System	Valid set	Test set
Baseline	12.13	16.27
Back translation	10.95	15.02
Back translation + Fine tuning	12.87	17.21
Swap + Fine tuning	14.00	18.28

5   Conclusion

In this paper, we described our translation systems in four translation evaluation tasks including Chinese to English, English to Chinese, Chinese to Thai, and Thai to Chinese. In all directions, our experiments proved that our translation systems have been improved on data augmentation methods. Our data augmentation strategies bring good performance to the baseline system in these translation evaluation tasks. In the future, we expect that we explore more data augmentation approaches, especially in some fields where parallel data is scarce. And we hope that our proposed data enhancement methods can be applied to different neural network models and datasets.

References

1. Chu, C., Dabre, R., Kurohashi, S.: An empirical comparison of domain adaptation methods for neural machine translation. In: Proceedings of the 55th Annual Meeting of the Association for Computational Linguistics, vol. 2 (Short Papers), pp. 385–391 (2017)
2. He, K., Zhang, X., Ren, S., Sun, J.: Deep residual learning for image recognition. In: Proceedings of the IEEE Conference on Computer Vision and Pattern Recognition, pp. 770–778 (2016)
3. Ott, M., et al.: fairseq: a fast, extensible toolkit for sequence modeling. arXiv preprint. arXiv:1904.01038 (2019)
4. Papineni, K., Roukos, S., Ward, T., Zhu, W.J.: Bleu: a method for automatic evaluation of machine translation. In: Proceedings of the 40th Annual Meeting of the Association for Computational Linguistics, pp. 311–318 (2002)
5. Post, M.: A call for clarity in reporting bleu scores. In: Proceedings of the 3rd Conference on Machine Translation: Research Papers, pp. 186–191 (2018)
6. Provilkov, I., Emelianenko, D., Voita, E.: Bpe-dropout: simple and effective subword regularization. In: Proceedings of the 58th Annual Meeting of the Association for Computational Linguistics, pp. 1882–1892 (2020)
7. Sánchez-Cartagena, V.M., Esplà-Gomis, M., Pérez-Ortiz, J.A., Sánchez-Martínez, F.: Rethinking data augmentation for low-resource neural machine translation: a multi-task learning approach. In: Proceedings of the 2021 Conference on Empirical Methods in Natural Language Processing, pp. 8502–8516 (2021)
8. Sennrich, R., Haddow, B., Birch, A.: Improving neural machine translation models with monolingual data. In: Proceedings of the 54th Annual Meeting of the Association for Computational Linguistics, vol. 1 (Long Papers), pp. 86–96 (2016)
9. Sennrich, R., Haddow, B., Birch, A.: Neural machine translation of rare words with subword units. In: Proceedings of the 54th Annual Meeting of the Association for Computational Linguistics, vol. 1 (Long Papers), pp. 1715–1725 (2016)
10. Song, Y., Shi, S., Li, J., Zhang, H.: Directional skip-gram: explicitly distinguishing left and right context for word embeddings. In: Proceedings of the 2018 Conference of the North American Chapter of the Association for Computational Linguistics: Human Language Technologies, vol. 2 (Short Papers), pp. 175–180 (2018)
11. Vaswani, A., et al.: Attention is all you need. In: Advances in Neural Information Processing Systems, vol. 30 (2017)
12. Wei, J., Zou, K.: Eda: easy data augmentation techniques for boosting performance on text classification tasks. arXiv preprint. arXiv:1901.11196 (2019)
13. Wei, X., Yu, H., Hu, Y., Weng, R., Xing, L., Luo, W.: Uncertainty-aware semantic augmentation for neural machine translation. In: Proceedings of the 2020 Conference on Empirical Methods in Natural Language Processing (EMNLP), pp. 2724–2735 (2020)

NJUNLP's Submission for CCMT 2022 Quality Estimation Task

Yu Zhang, Xiang Geng, Shujian Huang$^{(\boxtimes)}$, and Jiajun Chen

National Key Laboratory for Novel Software Technology,
Nanjing University, Nanjing, China
{zhangy,gx}@smail.nju.edu.cn, {huangsj,chenjj}@nju.edu.cn

Abstract. Quality Estimation is a task aiming to estimate the quality of translations without relying on any references. This paper describes our submission for CCMT 2022 quality estimation sentence-level task for English-to-Chinese (EN-ZH). We follow the DirectQE framework, whose target is bridging the gap between pre-training on parallel data and fine-tuning on QE data. We further combine DirectQE with the pre-trained language model XLM-RoBERTa (XLM-R) which achieves outstanding success in many NLP tasks in order to improve performance. With the purpose of better utilizing parallel data, several types of pseudo data are employed in our method as well. In addition, we also ensemble several models to promote the final results.

Keywords: Quality estimation · Pre-trained language model · DirectQE

1 Introduction

Machine translation quality estimation (QE) is the task of providing an estimate of how good or reliable the MT is without access to reference translations [15]. QE plays an important role in many real applications of machine translation. A representative example is machine translation post-editing (PE). Although the quality of machine translation for many language pairs has improved, most of the machine translations are still far from publishable quality. Therefore, a common practice for including machine translation in the workflow is to use machine translations as raw versions to be further post-edited by human translators [9]. However, post-editing low-quality machine translations spends more effort than translating from scratch [4] when QE can further improve post-editing workflows by offering more informative labels including, potentially, not only the words that are incorrect but also the types of errors that need correction [15].

Traditional QE methods make use of some hand-craft features, which are time-consuming and expensive to get [10]. Later, researchers try to generate automatic neural features by applying neural networks [1,14]. However, there are still serious problems as to the fact that QE data is scarce which limits the improvement of QE models. The Predictor-Estimator framework proposed by

T. Xiao and J. Pino (Eds.): CCMT 2022, CCIS 1671, pp. 143–150, 2022.
https://doi.org/10.1007/978-981-19-7960-6_15

Kim et al. [7] is devoted to addressing this problem, and under this framework, bilingual knowledge can be transferred from parallel data to QE tasks. The remaining drawback is that data distribution between parallel data and QE data differs. Cui et al. [2] propose the DirectQE method in order to bridge the gaps between pre-training on parallel data and fine-tuning on QE data. Nowadays, large-scale pre-trained language models have been widely applied in QE models [8], but DirectQE is not corporated with the pre-trained model which gives us insight into combining the two well-performing models.

This paper introduces our sentence-level quality estimation submission for CCMT 2022 in detail. We submit a model combining DirectQE with the pre-trained language model XLM-R for the first time. Therefore, on the one hand, the gaps between parallel data and QE data are bridged. On the other hand, the pre-trained models are well utilized in QE models. Furthermore, we try different pseudo data strategies from several aspects, including data generation and data tokenization which help us make full use of the parallel data consequently. Eventually, basic averaging ensemble and neural ensemble are used to get a better result.

2   Methods

2.1   Existing Methods

DirectQE. The DirectQE framework mainly contains two parts, the generator which is trained on parallel data to generate pseudo QE data, and the detector which can be pre-trained and fine-tuned with the pseudo data and real QE data, respectively, with the same object.

The generator of DirectQE is trained on the masked language model conditioned on source X. During the training procedure, for each parallel pair X, Y, DirectQE randomly masks 15% tokens in Y and tries to recover them. Then DirectQE predicts these masked tokens by sampling strategies according to the generated probability in the procedure of generating pseudo data. The annotating strategy is simple, it annotates the generated token as 'BAD' if it is different from the original one and the sentence-level score is the ratio of 'BAD' tokens.

The detector jointly predicts the word-level tags and sentence-level scores. It pre-trains on the pseudo QE data first and then fine-tunes on the real QE data with the same training object.

DirectQE obtained the state-of-art results when it was published.

QE BERT. QE BERT [8] uses the pre-trained model BERT (multilingual) [3] for translation quality estimation and contains two steps which are pretraining and fine-tuning separately. QE BERT further pre-trains BERT on parallel data on only the masked language model task and uses multi-task learning. In addition, the QE method based on pre-trained cross-lingual language model XLM [12] was proposed in [6].

2.2 Proposed Methods

Our proposed method contains two stages: generator and detector. The generator can be subdivided into two types, including a Transformer-based generator and an NMT-based generator. Figure 1 and Fig. 2 show the complete procedure of our methods with the Transformer-based generator and NMT-based generator separately.

Generator. The generator is trained to generate pseudo data with the use of parallel data. DirectQE adopts Transformer [16] as a generator. It functions as a word-level rewriter and is used to produce a pseudo translation with one-to-one correspondences according to the reference. In our method, we do not only adopt Transformer but also adopt a neural machine translation (NMT) as a generator, called Transformer-based generator and NMT-based generator separately. Furthermore, we try to use a Transformer-based generator to generate pseudo data at token-level and at bpe-level to eliminate the bias coming from the aspect of word tokenization.

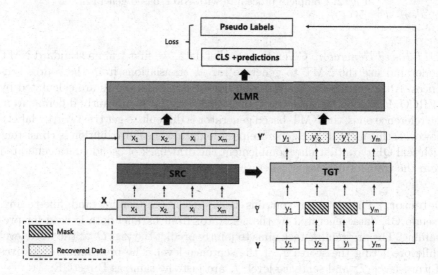

Fig. 1. Complete procedure with Transformer-based generator

Transformer-Based Generator. This part is similar to the generator in the original version of DirectQE. Given a parallel sentence pair, we randomly replace some tokens in reference with a special tag [MASK] and force the Transformer-based generator to recover the masked tokens. Pseudo data is annotated according to the comparison between recovered tokens and their standard tokens. Different from DirectQE, we sample the tokens according to the token generation probability to better determine the location where the errors in translations most likely occurred. Therefore, many recovered tokens may just be the same as the standard tokens causing that actual replacement ratio far below the mask ratio.

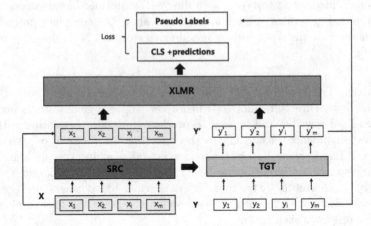

Fig. 2. Complete procedure with NMT-based generator

NMT-Based Generator. Given the parallel data, we first train a standard NMT model and use the NMT to generate target translations from the source sentences. After getting the translations, pseudo tags and scores are calculated by TERCOM [5] tool. Because the translations may be significantly different from the reference ones, the NMT-based generator is difficult to get trustworthy labels. However, this method can generate pseudo data whose distribution is consistent with real QE data that may complement the drawback of pseudo data generated from the transformer-based generator.

Detector. The detector contains two stages: pre-training and fine-tuning. Pseudo QE data generated by the generator from parallel data is used for pre-training. The pretraining task aims to jointly predict the tags O' at the word level while predicting the scores q' at the sentence level. The pretraining objectives of word-level $\mathcal{J}_w$ and sentence-level $\mathcal{J}_s$ are just the same as DirectQE:

$$\mathcal{J}_w\left(\mathbf{X}, \mathbf{Y}', o_j'\right) = \sum_{j=1}^{|O'|} \log P\left(o_j' \mid \mathbf{X}, \mathbf{Y}'; \theta\right) \tag{1}$$

$$\mathcal{J}_s\left(\mathbf{X}, \mathbf{Y}', q'\right) = \log P\left(q' \mid \mathbf{X}, \mathbf{Y}'; \theta\right) \tag{2}$$

The object of the fine-tuning procedure is a little bit different from pre-training for the reason that word-level labels are not provided in real QE data. Therefore, only sentence-level scores are predicted at the stage of fine-tuning.

In DirectQE, the detector encodes the source sentence with self-attention to obtain hidden representations and predicts word-level tags from the last encoder layer at the target side as well as sentence-level scores. Different from this, the detector in our method uses the XLM-R pre-trained language model as a basic framework, while the transformer is used in DirectQE.

We concatenate the source sentence with the pseudo target sentence as a joint input. For sentence-level scores, the standard method of XLM-R uses the token corresponding to the first special token [CLS] of the last layer, and we instead combine the average representations of all the layers with the last layer representation as a mixed feature to predict the scores.

3 Experiments

In this section, we will display the details of our experiments, including the dataset, hyper-parameters, the performance of single models, and so on.

3.1 Dataset

QE Dataset. All QE triplets (SRC, MT, HTER) that we use come from the CCMT 2022 QE task, and the language direction EN-ZH that we participate in consists of 14789 training data (TRAIN) and 2826 development data (DEV).

Parallel Dataset. Parallel data is transformed into pseudo data in the form of QE triplets to pre-train the XLM-R model. We use an additional 10,000,000 out of all 20,305,269 parallel sentences from the WMT 2020 QE task and actually do not make use of parallel data provided by the CCMT QE task.

3.2 Settings

Metrics. The main metric of the quality estimation sentence-level task is Pearson's Correlation Coefficient. Mean Absolute Error (MAE) and Root Mean Squared Error(RMSE) will be considered as metrics as well.

Hyper-parameters. For the transformer-based generator, we set the mask ratio to 45% and the average HTER score of the pseudo data is approximately 16% - 18%. Except for the above, other sets are the same as the original DirectQE model. For the NMT-based generator, an inverse sqrt learning rate scheduler is used to adjust the training learning rate and set dropout to 0.3. As to the part of the detector, the XLM-R-large is used, and all the parameters are updated.

Tokenize. We first use jieba to tokenize the Chinese dataset. In the step of the generator, we use BPE [13] to tokenize both the source and target sentences, while in the step of detector SentencePiece [11] is used to tokenize the sentences for XLM-R model. The step of BPE is set to 30,000, and we use all tokens after tokenization.

3.3   Single Model Results

The results of single models are shown in Table 1. Pure-XLMR refers to the model that makes no use of both generator and parallel data but only uses real QE data. All models that, with the help of parallel data, use 3,500,000 parallel data expect that Transformed-based (10 million) uses 10 million parallel data. Similarly, all models train the model on the token level, but Transformed-based (bpe level) trains on the bpe level.

Table 1. Single model results of the CCMT 2022.

Method	Pearson	MAE	RMSE
Pure-XLMR	0.5544	0.0917	0.1367
NMT-based	0.5624	0.0901	0.1349
Transformed-based	0.5969	0.0871	0.1320
Transformed-based (10 million)	0.6138	0.0854	0.1297
Transformed-based (bpe level)	0.5847	0.0891	0.1340

It is clear that the Pure-XLMR model without parallel knowledge does not get better performance compared to other models. Meanwhile, models combining DirectQE with pre-trained language model XLM-R perform best, and with more data and with token level can get better results.

3.4   Ensemble

We try two different ensemble methods at the sentence level. The averaging ensemble is the simplest ensemble method that averages all the results from model outputs. Neural ensemble refers to that we gather all the HTERs of both training datasets and development datasets from all of the models described above. Then we train a simple neural network model that learns to use these HTER values to predict the golden HTER values.

The ensemble results are shown in Table 2, and we can see that the neural ensemble result slightly outperforms the other one at the sentence level.

Table 2. Ensemble model results of the CCMT 2022.

Ensemble method	Pearson
Averaging	0.6219
Neural result	0.6294

3.5 Analysis

In this section, we will discuss the influence of the mask ratio in the pseudo data generation procedure. We set the mask ratio to 15%, 30%, 45%, 45%*2 and 45%*3. The 45%*2 means two 45% pseudo datasets are concatenated as one pseudo data to avoid the bad effects of the high mask ratio, meanwhile, 45%*3 is similar. The corresponding average HTERs of the pseudo data are about 5%, 10%, 16%, 27%, and 36% separately. The results are shown in Fig. 3.

As we can see, the best result corresponds to 16% average HTER. Coincidentally, the average HTER of the real QE data is approximately 16% as well. The average HTERs above that get the results of a slight decrease and the average HTERs below that decline more obviously.

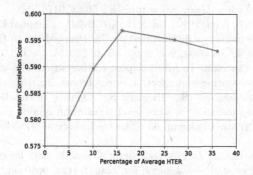

Fig. 3. QE performances according to different average HTERs

4 Conclusion

This paper describes our submissions for the CCMT 2022 Quality Estimation sentence-level task. Our systems are based on DirectQE architecture and built upon the Fairseq framework. To leverage the successful large-scale pretrained language model, we make a combination of the high-performing DirectQE method and XLM-R pre-trained model for the first time. We also take advantage of various forms of pseudo data to better make use of parallel data for further improvements at the same time. Experiments show that the proposed method is effective. Eventually, we use base and neural ensemble methods to get our final results.

References

1. Chen, Z., et al.: Improving machine translation quality estimation with neural network features. In: Proceedings of the Second Conference on Machine Translation, pp. 551–555 (2017)

2. Cui, Q., et al.: DirectQE: direct pretraining for machine translation quality estimation. In: Proceedings of the AAAI Conference on Artificial Intelligence, vol. 35, pp. 12719–12727 (2021)
3. Devlin, J., Chang, M.W., Lee, K., Toutanova, K.: BERT: pre-training of deep bidirectional transformers for language understanding. arXiv preprint arXiv:1810.04805 (2018)
4. Escartín, C.P., Béchara, H., Orăsan, C.: Questing for quality estimation a user study. Prague Bull. Math. Linguist. **108**(1), 343–354 (2017)
5. Golden, J.P.: Terrain contour matching (TERCOM): a cruise missile guidance aid. In: Image Processing for Missile Guidance, vol. 238, pp. 10–18. SPIE (1980)
6. Kepler, F., et al.: Unbabel's participation in the WMT19 translation quality estimation shared task. arXiv preprint arXiv:1907.10352 (2019)
7. Kim, H., Lee, J.H., Na, S.H.: Predictor-estimator using multilevel task learning with stack propagation for neural quality estimation. In: Proceedings of the Second Conference on Machine Translation, pp. 562–568 (2017)
8. Kim, H., Lim, J.H., Kim, H.K., Na, S.H.: QE BERT: bilingual BERT using multi-task learning for neural quality estimation. In: Proceedings of the Fourth Conference on Machine Translation, vol. 3, pp. 85–89 (2019)
9. Koponen, M.: Is machine translation post-editing worth the effort? A survey of research into post-editing and effort. J. Spec. Transl. **25**, 131–148 (2016)
10. Kreutzer, J., Schamoni, S., Riezler, S.: Quality estimation from scratch (QUETCH): deep learning for word-level translation quality estimation. In: Proceedings of the Tenth Workshop on Statistical Machine Translation, pp. 316–322 (2015)
11. Kudo, T., Richardson, J.: SentencePiece: a simple and language independent subword tokenizer and detokenizer for neural text processing. arXiv preprint arXiv:1808.06226 (2018)
12. Lample, G., Conneau, A.: Cross-lingual language model pretraining. arXiv preprint arXiv:1901.07291 (2019)
13. Sennrich, R., Haddow, B., Birch, A.: Neural machine translation of rare words with subword units. arXiv preprint arXiv:1508.07909 (2015)
14. Shah, K., Bougares, F., Barrault, L., Specia, L.: SHEF-LIUM-NN: sentence level quality estimation with neural network features. In: Proceedings of the First Conference on Machine Translation, vol. 2, Shared Task Papers, pp. 838–842 (2016)
15. Specia, L., Scarton, C., Paetzold, G.H.: Quality estimation for machine translation. Synth. Lect. Hum. Lang. Technol. **11**(1), 1–162 (2018)
16. Vaswani, A., et al.: Attention is all you need. Adv. Neural Inf. Process. Syst. **30** (2017)

ISTIC's Thai-to-Chinese Neural Machine Translation System for CCMT' 2022

Shuao Guo, Hangcheng Guo, Yanqing He[✉], and Tian Lan

Research Center of Information Theory and Methodology, Institute of Scientific and Technical Information of China, Beijing 100038, China
{guosa2021,guohc2020,heyq,lantian}@istic.ac.cn

Abstract. This paper introduces technical details of Thai-to-Chinese neural machine translation system of Institute of Scientific and Technical Information of China (ISTIC) for the 18th China Conference on Machine Translation (CCMT' 2022). ISTIC participated in a low resource evaluation task: Thai-to-Chinese MT task. The paper mainly illuminates its system framework based on Transformer, data preprocessing methods and some strategies adopted in this system. In addition, the paper evaluates the system performance under different methods.

Keywords: Neural machine translation · Self-attention mechanism · Context-aware system

1   Introduction

ISTIC participated in a low resource evaluation task: Thai-to-Chinese MT task. In this evaluation, our team adopted the Google Transformer architecture as the basis of our system. We collected data from three different sources to form the training set, which were the data released by the evaluation organization, the pseudo parallel corpus and the external data of self-built Thailand-Chinese dictionary and bilingual parallel corpus. The monolingual data released by the evaluation organizer of CCMT' 2021 was filtered to construct the pseudo parallel corpus through the back-translation method, the pseudo parallel corpus and the original given bilingual parallel corpus were used together as the training set of our neural machine translation system. Since the scale of given data was too small, the external data of self-built Thailand-Chinese dictionary and bilingual parallel corpus were introduced into training set. In terms of data pre-processing, we adopted general methods and specific methods for the given data, which mainly included filtering special characters, removing duplicate sentences, and bilingual tokenization. In the construction of the system model, we mainly used the context-aware system method, which took the surrounding sentences as the context and employs an additional neural network to encode the context. We adopted the method of model averaging and ensemble to get the final translation result and removed the spaces between the words of results and finally submitted XML format result to the evaluation organization.

T. Xiao and J. Pino (Eds.): CCMT 2022, CCIS 1671, pp. 151–160, 2022.
https://doi.org/10.1007/978-981-19-7960-6_16

The structure of this paper is as follows: the second part introduces our technical architecture of the machine translation system in this evaluation task; the third part explains the methods used in this evaluation task; the fourth part describes the core process, parameter settings, data pre-processing and experiments results.

2   System Architecture

Figure 1 shows the overall flow chart of our neural machine translation system in this evaluation which includes data pre-processing, data set partition, model training, model inference, and data post-processing.

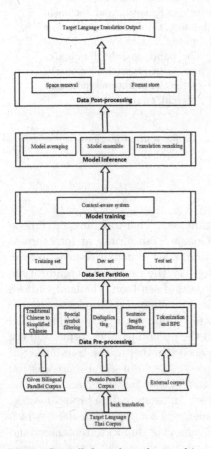

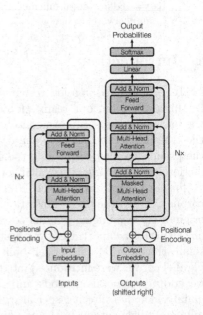

Fig. 1. Overall flow chart for machine translation tasks.

Fig. 2. Transformer model structure

2.1 Baseline System

The baseline system we adopted in this evaluation task is Google's Transformer, which has achieved significant results on machine translation since being proposed in 2017 [1]. Its whole network structure is absolutely built on attention mechanism instead of traditional CNN and RNN in deep learning, which has brought a series of advantages, such as consuming less training power, achieving algorithm parallelism, further alleviating long-distance dependence and most importantly, getting a better translation quality. Transformer is essentially an Encoder-Decoder structure, just like most seq2seq models. It consists of Encoder and Decoder (see Fig. 2). Both parts have n stacked identical layer blocks (n can be any number, our system set n to 6.). Every layer of encoder contains two sub-layers (see the left part of Fig. 2), which we call the self-attention sub-layer and the feed-forward sub-layer. The self-attention sub-layer calculates the output representation of a token by attending to all the neighbors in the same layer, computing the correlation score between this token and all the neighbors, and finally linearly combining all the representations of the neighbors and itself. Each layer of decoder includes three parts, masked self-attention mechanism, encoder-decoder attention sub-layer and feed-forward sub-layer [2]. Masked self-attention mechanism is responsible for summarizing the partial prediction history. Encoder-decoder attention sub-layer is used to determine the dynamic source-side contexts for current prediction. A residual connection [3] is employed around each sub-layers in both decoder and encoder, followed by layer normalization [4].

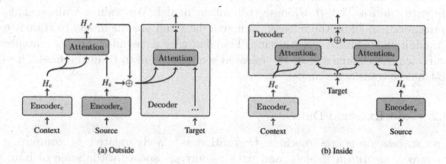

Fig. 3. An overview of two multi-encoder systems. In the Outside approach, Hs is the query and Hc is the key/value. In the Inside approach, Target is the query, Hs and Hc represent key/value.

2.2 Our System

Based on the transformer model, we build a context-aware system [5] leaving Transformer's decoder intact while incorporating context information on the encoder side [6]. This approach takes the surrounding sentences as the context and employ an additional neural network to encode the context, that is, there is a source-sentence encoder and a context encoder. Figure 3 shows two methods of integrating the context into NMT.

There are two methods for integrating the context into NMT. The method of outside integration (See Fig. 3(a)) is that the representations of the context and the current sentence are firstly transformed into a new representation by an attention network, then the attention output and the source sentence representation are fused by a gated sum. Alternatively, inside integration (See Fig. 3(b)) means decoder can attend to two encoders respectively and the gating mechanism inside the decoder is employed to obtain the fusion vector. There are two kinds of context that can be used to integrate into NMT. One is source context, another is target context. We often make train set and development set of source language as source context, and make train set and development set of target language as target context.

3   Methods

In this evaluation we try the following methods to improve translation performance.

3.1   Back Translation

Back Translation (BT) [6] is one of the most commonly used data augmentation method for machine translation tasks. In our Thai-to-Chinese task, we took three steps to train a Thai-to-Chinese translation model. We train a Chinese-Thai translation model on the released bilingual data and use the model to translate the additional Chinese sentences into Thai sentences as pseudo bilingual sentence pairs, which are mixed with the released sentence pairs to train the final Thai-to-Chinese translation model.

3.2   Add External Data

The success of neural machine translation is closely related to computing resources, algorithm models, and data resources, especially the scale of bilingual training data. In the Thai-to-Chinese task, the number of sentence pairs of parallel corpus available for training is as low as 200,000. Therefore, the introduction of external resources can effectively improve the performance of the machine translation system.

3.3   Model Averaging

Model averaging [7] refers to averaging the parameters of the same model at different training moments to obtain more robust model parameters, which helps to reduce the instability of model parameters and enhance the robustness of the model. After specifying the Max EPOCH parameter in the trainer and completing the training process, our team gets the best epoch checkpoint and the last EPOCH checkpoint, and averages the two checkpoints. The more stable and robust individual models obtained through the model averaging strategy will also be used for model averaging to jointly predict probability distributions.

3.4 Model Ensemble Strategy

Model ensemble [8] refers to that in the decoding process, multiple models simultaneously predict the probability distribution of the target word at the current moment, and finally make a weighted average of the probability distribution predicted by multiple models to jointly determine the final output after model ensemble.

4 Experiments

4.1 System Settings

The baseline MT system is based on Transformer trained only by the given bilingual parallel corpus. Outside integration and inside integration are also used in the experiments. Table 1 shows the parameters settings of the three systems. Since context-aware system [9] is fine-tuned on the basis of the baseline system, the value of initial state settings of baseline system is smaller than baseline system. Table 2 shows the Initial learning rate setting of three systems.

Table 1. Fundamental parameters settings of three systems.

Parameter	Value
GPU number (used for each model training)	1–3
Batch size	2048
Embedding size	1024
Hidden size	1024
Dimension of the feed-forward layer	4096
Self-attention layers (for both encoder and decoder)	6
Number of heads (multi-head self-attention mechanism)	16
Dropout probabilities	0.3
Merge operations (BPE)	32000
Maximum number of tokens	4096
Loss function	Label smoothed cross entropy
Adam betas	(0.9,0.997)
Maximum epoch number	50
Warm-up steps	4000
Initial learning rate (Baseline system)	0.0007
Context-aware system (inside integration)	0.0001
Context-aware system (outside integration)	0.0001

4.2 Data Preprocessing

In Thailand-Chinese task, the data used in the experiment includes bilingual parallel corpus released by evaluation organization; some external data, such as bilingual sentence pairs and dictionary; monolingual data and pseudo parallel corpus. Bilingual parallel corpus is 200000 sentence pairs. 13069 sentence pairs and 1400 word pairs are collected from Internet as a supplement for bilingual parallel corpus. Monolingual data is extracted by similarity calculation between Chinese development set and CCMT'2021 Chinese monolingual database index by Elasticsearch [10]. Pseudo parallel corpus is generated by back translation system, whose source language sentence is from Chinese monolingual data.

Preprocessing method we adopted includes a general method and a specific method for given data. Both methods are used to reduce the data noise and improve the data quality [11]. The main stages of preprocessing are shown below.

- Traditional Chinese to simplified Chinese
- Full-width characters to half-width characters
- Special characters filtering
- Duplicating
- Sentence length filtering
- Sentence length ratio filtering
- Tokenization

Among above, in the process of sentence length filtering, we get Chinese sentence length by calculating the number of 'character' and get Thailand sentence length by the number of 'token', based on which we remove sentence pairs whose source sentence length or target sentence length exceeds the range of [1, 200]. Sentence length ratio filtering excludes the sentence pairs whose ratio of source sentence length and target sentence length exceeds the range of [0.1, 10]. In the tokenization stage, Thailand tokenization is implemented by Python tools Thainlp [12] and Chinese tokenization is implemented using the lexical tool Urheen [13].

Table 2. Preprocessing results of training set data.

Type	Before preprocessing	After preprocessing
Bilingual parallel corpus	200000	191465
Dictionary	1400	1400
Bilingual sentence pairs	13069	6894
Pseudo parallel corpus	913432	901134
Chinese monolingual data	1000000	913432

All steps of preprocessing are done on bilingual parallel corpus. Duplicating, sentence length filtering, and sentence length ratio filtering, Chinese tokenization are carried out on Chinese monolingual data. Sentence length filtering and sentence length ratio filtering are implemented on the pseudo parallel corpus by back translation. Table 2 shows the data size comparison before and after preprocessing. 1000 sentence pairs are extracted respectively from the bilingual parallel corpus by evaluation organization as development set and test set. Finally 189465 sentence pairs are used as train set. All system below are trained on the development set and the test set. Their train set varies with different methods.

4.3   Experimental Results

thc-2022-istic-primary-a Model. Baseline system and other context-aware systems are all trained on the given bilingual parallel corpus. Table 3 shows the results of baseline system and context-aware system under two methods (inside integration and outside integration) and two context (source context and target context). These models are all trained 50 epoch. Table 4 shows the effect of context-aware system is better than baseline system and the effect of the context-aware system under outside integration with target context is better than other system. So context-aware system under outside integration with target context is chosen as thc-2022-istic-primary-a model. This model's integrated target context in decoder is train set of Chinese and development set of Chinese.

Table 3. Performance comparison in different system

System	BLEU (test)
Baseline system	42.71
Inside integration + source context	44.93
Outside integration + source context	44.31
Inside integration + target context	46.89
Outside integration + target context	47.37

Table 4. Performance comparison in different training set

Mixing proportion (given corpus/pseudo corpus)	BLEU (test)
1:0	42.71
1:0.25	38.24
1:0.5	34.97
1:1	26.13
1:2	23.37
1:3	20.85
1:4	18.21

We adopted back translation method to generate pseudo parallel corpus. Context-aware system under outside integration with target context is trained on the released bilingual parallel corpus by evaluation organization, where source language is Chinese, target language is Thailand. 900000 Chinese sentences are filtered from monolingual data and translated into pseudo Thailand sentences. We mix the pseudo parallel corpus into other corpus in different proportions as new training set to train models. Context-based System (outside integration+target context) is trained on the above training sets. From the results in Table 4 pseudo corpus does not bring performance improvement of translation.

thc-2022-istic-primary-b Model. We adopt a model averaging strategy in the decoding phase and different results above are combined in post-processing stage to obtain the final translation. They make a model averaging and ensemble on thc-2022-istic-primary-c model and finally get a model whose Bleu scoring is the highest and choose it as thc-2022-istic-primary-b model.

Table 5. Performance comparison of adding external corpus

Baseline training set	Dictionary	External sentences	BLEU (test)
189465	0	0	46.89
189465	1400	0	47.45
189465	1400	6894	47.62

thc-2022-istic-primary-c Model. We put Thai-to-Chinese dictionary and bilingual sentence pairs from Internet together with the released bilingual parallel corpus by evaluation organization as a new training set. Table 5 shows their performance comparison. From the results of Table 5, we can know external dictionary and bilingual sentence pair improve the translation effect. We choose this model as thc-2022-istic-primary-c model.

Table 6 shows the BLEU score [14] of three model submitted to evaluation organization.

Table 6. BLEU scoring test set (submitted models)

System	BLEU (test)
thc-2022-istic-primary-a model	47.37
thc-2022-istic-primary-b model	47.89
thc-2022-istic-primary-c model	47.62

4.4 Conclusion

This paper introduces the main and methods of ISTIC in CCMT' 2022. In summary, our model is constructed based on the Transformer architecture of the self-attention mechanism and a context-aware system. Although we tried the method of back-translation, it didn't work well. In terms of data preprocessing, several corpus filtering methods are explored. In the process of translation output, we adopt strategies such as model averaging and model ensemble. In the corpus filtering process, we use Elasticsearch to filter similar corpus. Experimental results show that these methods can effectively improve the translation quality. For machine translation tasks in low-resource languages, adding external dictionaries and parallel corpus can effectively improve translation performance. But in another view [15], it is worth exploring more to make more efficient use of small amounts of parallel training. Due to limited time, there are still many methods and techniques waiting us to exploit. Low-resource's neural machine translation is a very meaningful research problem. In the future, we will go into low-resource's neural machine translation and hope to make a contribution to it.

References

1. Vaswani, A., et al.: Attention is all you need. Adv. Neural. Inf. Process. Syst. **30**, 5998–6008 (2017)
2. Zhang, J.J., Zong, C.Q.: Neural machine translation: challenges, progress and future. Sci. China Technol. Sci. **63**(10), 2028–2050 (2020). https://doi.org/10.1007/s11431-020-1632-x
3. He, K., Zhang, X., Ren, S., Sun, J.: Deep residual learning for image recognition. In: Proceedings of the IEEE Conference on Computer Vision and Pattern Recognition, pp. 770–778 (2016)
4. Ba, J.L., Kiros, J.R., Hinton, G.E.: Layer normalization. arXiv preprint arXiv:1607.06450 (2016)
5. Voita, E., et al.: Context-aware neural machine translation learns anaphora resolution. In: Proceedings of the 56th Annual Meeting of the Association for Computational Linguistics, pp. 1264–1274. Association for Computational Linguistics (2018)
6. Sennrich, R., Haddow, B., Birch, A.: Improving neural machine translation models with monolingual data. In: Proceedings of the 54th Annual Meeting of the Association for Computational Linguistics, vol. 1, pp. 86–96, Berlin, Germany. Association for Computational Linguistics (2016)
7. Li, B., et al.: Does multi-encoder help? A case study on context-aware neural machine translation. In: Proceedings of the 58th Annual Meeting of the Association for Computational Linguistics, pp. 3512–3518. Association for Computational Linguistics (2020)
8. Claeskens, G., Hjort, N.L.: Model Selection and Model Averaging. Cambridge University Press, Cambridge (2008). https://doi.org/10.1017/CBO9780511790485
9. Lutellier, T., et al.: CoCoNuT: combining context-aware neural translation models using ensemble for program repair. In: Proceedings of the 29th ACM SIGSOFT International Symposium on Software Testing and Analysis, pp. 101–114. Association for Computing Machinery, New York (2020)

10. Elasticsearch Homepage: https://github.com/elastic/elasticsearch. Accessed 25 May 2022
11. Guo, H., et al.: ISTIC's neural machine translation system for CCMT' 2021. In: Su, J., Sennrich, R. (eds.) CCMT 2021. CCIS, vol. 1464, pp. 105–116. Springer, Singapore (2021). https://doi.org/10.1007/978-981-16-7512-6_9
12. PyThaiNLP Homepage: https://github.com/PyThaiNLP/pythainlp. Accessed 17 May 2022
13. Urheen: https://www.nlpr.ia.ac.cn/cip/software.html. Accessed 15 May 2022
14. Papineni, K., Roukos, S., Ward, T., Zhu, W.J.: BLEU: a method for automatic evaluation of machine translation. In: Proceedings of the 40th Annual Meeting of the Association for Computational Linguistics, pp. 311–318 (2002)
15. Sennrich, R., Zhang, B.: Revisiting low-resource neural machine translation: a case study. In: Proceedings of the 57th Annual Meeting of the Association for Computational Linguistics, pp. 211–221, Florence, Italy. Association for Computational Linguistics (2019)

Author Index

Printed in the United States
by Baker & Taylor Publisher Services